STUDIES IN AMERICAN POPULAR
HISTORY AND CULTURE

Edited by
JEROME NADELHAFT

A ROUTLEDGE SERIES

STUDIES IN AMERICAN POPULAR HISTORY AND CULTURE

JEROME NADELHAFT, *General Editor*

EARLY AMERICAN WOMEN DRAMATISTS: 1775–1860
Zoe Detsi-Diamanti

THE LYRICS OF CIVILITY
Kenneth G.Bielen

WRITING THE PUBLIC IN CYBERSPACE
Redefining Inclusion on the Net
Ann Travers

HOLLYWOOD'S FRONTIER CAPTIVES
Cultural Anxiety and the Captivity Plot in American Film
Barbara A.Mortimer

PUBLIC LIVES, PRIVATE VIRTUES
Images of American Revolutionary War Heroes, 1782–1832
Christopher Harris

TALES OF LIBERATION, STRATEGIES OF CONTAINMENT
Divorce and the Representation of Womanhood in American Fiction, 1880–1920
Debra Ann MacComb

READING COMICS
Language, Culture, and the Concept of the Superhero in Comic Books
Mila Bongco

THE CLUBWOMEN'S DAUGHTERS
Collectivist Impulses in Progressive-Era Girls' Fiction
Gwen Athene Tarbox

THE FACTORY GIRLS AND THE SEAMSTRESS
Imagining Gender and Class in Nineteenth Century American Fiction
Amal Amireh

WRITING JAZZ
Race, Nationalism, and Modern Culture in the 1920s
Nicholas M.Evans

AUTOMOBILITY
Social Changes in the American South, 1909–1939
Corey T.Lesseig

ACTORS AND ACTIVISTS
Politics, Performance, and Exchange among Social Worlds
David A.Schlossman

STUDIES IN THE LAND
The Northeast Corner
David C.Smith

FIRST Do No HARM
Empathy and the Writing of Medical Journal Articles
Mary E.Knatterud

PIETY AND POWER

Gender and Religious Culture in the American Colonies, 1630–1700
Leslie Lindenauer

RACE-ING MASCULINITY
Identity in Contemporary U.S. Men's Writing
John Christopher Cunningham

CRIME AND THE NATION
Prison Reform and Popular Fiction in Philadelphia, 1786–1800
Peter Okun

FOOD IN FILM
A Culinary Performance of Communication
Jane Ferry

HOLLYWOOD AND THE RISE OF PHYSICAL CULTURE
Heather Addison

HOMELESSNESS IN AMERICAN LITERATURE
Romanticism, Realism, and Testimony
John Allen

RETHINKING THE RED SCARE

The Lusk Committee and New York's Crusade against Radicalism, 1919–1923

Todd J.Pfannestiel

Routledge
Taylor & Francis Group
New York London

Published in 2003 by
Routledge
711 Third Avenue
New York, NY 10017

Published in Great Britain by
Routledge
2 Park Square, Milton Park,
Abingdon, Oxfordshire, OX14 4RN

First issued in paperback 2014

Routledge is an imprint of the Taylor and Francis Group, an informa business

Copyright © 2003 by Routledge

All rights reserved. No part of this book may be reprinted or reproduced or utilized in any form or by any electronic, mechanical, or other means, now known or hereafter invented, including photocopying and recording, or in any information storage or retrieval system, without permission in writing from the publisher.

Library of Congress Cataloging-in-Publication Data

Pfannestiel, Todd J.
Rethinking the red scare: the Lusk Committee and New York's crusade against radicalism, 1919–1923/by Todd J.Pfannestiel.
p. cm.—(American popular history & culture)
Includes bibliographical references and index.
ISBN 978-0-415-94767-1 (alk. paper)
1. Radicalism—New York (State)—History—20th century. 2. Communism—New York (State)—History—20th centuy. 3. Governmental investigations—New York (State)—History—20th century. 4. New York (State). Legislature. Joint Legislative Committee to Investigate Seditious Activities. I. Title. II. Series: American popular history and culture (Routledge (Firm)).
HN79.N4R34 2003
974.7′042–dc21 2003011866
ISBN 978-0-203-49785-2 Master e-book ISBN

ISBN 978-0-203-57782-0 (Adobe eReader Format)

ISBN 978-0-415-94767-1 (hbk)
ISBN 978-1-138-86801-4 (pbk)

Contents

	ACKNOWLEDGMENTS	vii
	INTRODUCTION	ix
CHAPTER 1	The Underlying Causes of the Red Scare	1
CHAPTER 2	The Formation of the Lusk Committee	17
CHAPTER 3	The Origins and Operations of the Soviet Bureau	35
CHAPTER 4	Reactions from Businessmen and the Lusk Committee	53
CHAPTER 5	The Rand School vs. the Lusk Committee	77
CHAPTER 6	From the Courtroom to the Legislature	100
	CONCLUSION	127
APPENDIX 1	Firms and Individual Agents Attempting To Conduct Business via the Soviet Bureau	139
APPENDIX 2	Contracts Concluded by the Soviet Bureau	150
APPENDIX 3	Lecturers, Rand School of Social Science, 1905–1920	151
APPENDIX 4	Course Listing, Rand School of Social Science, 1919–1920	153
	NOTES	160
	BIBLIOGRAPHY	193
	INDEX	208

Acknowledgments

SINCERE THANKS ARE OFFERED TO THOSE INDIVIDUALS AND ORGANIZATIONS who made the production of this book possible. Specifically, I wish to acknowledge the help of Professors Leisa Meyer, Gilbert MacArthur, Melvin Urofsky, and series editor Jerome Nadelhaft, all of who read drafts of the work and offered insightful comments that certainly improved the quality of the final product.

The earliest stages of the project were aided tremendously by the helpful archivists and staffs of the New York State Archives and Records Administration, the New York State Library, and the Tamiment Institute at New York University. Among those who deserve to be singled out for special praise are William Evans, Richard Andress, James Folts, and Daniel Linke.

The staff of the New Canaan Historical Society in New Canaan, Connecticut, proved to be a godsend at a point when the project seemed to stall for the lack of a small, but significant, piece of information. In addition, the society placed me in touch with Mr. Robert Johnson, a local high school history teacher in New Canaan whose interest in my project, as well as some good fortune in rummaging through a storage closet, yielded a wealth of personal papers and records about which historians often dream.

Funding for this project came from a variety of agencies to whom I am equally grateful, including the Woodrow Wilson National Fellowship Foundation, the College of William and Mary, and the Phi Alpha Theta Honor Society in History.

I wish to thank Blackwell Publishing and the journal *Diplomatic History* for permission to reprint selections from my previously published article. Portions of chapters three and four originally appeared in "The Soviet Bureau: A Bolshevik Strategy to Secure U.S. Diplomatic

Recognition through Economic Trade," *Diplomatic History,* 27:2 (April 2003): 171–192.

I also thank my students and colleagues at Clarion University who have continued to support me as I learn how to balance teaching, research, and service during the earliest stages of my professional career. Thanks is owed to Professors Brian Dunn, Robert Frakes, Beverly Smaby, George Michael LaRue, Anne Day, and others who have come and gone, as well as Lana McClune and Estella Wilkinson, who have provided more encouragement than they can possibly imagine.

Finally, overwhelming gratitude is owed to the one person without whom this project would never have come to light, Professor Philip Funigiello—a true scholar, mentor, and professional role model in every way.

All of these people, in addition to many others who are in my thoughts, if not these pages, have helped to improve the quality of this work. Any errors are solely my own, and due to no fault on their part.

Introduction

BENJAMIN GLASSBERG'S DAY BEGAN LIKE ANY OTHER. AFTER DRESSING, eating an early breakfast, and perusing the daily newspaper for the latest information on world and national events, he scurried off to Commercial High School where he taught history and government to the wide-eyed youth of Brooklyn. However, when he entered the classroom that morning of January 14, 1919, Glassberg was unaware of the turmoil that he, as well as the state and nation, would soon experience.

"Why is Bolshevism attacked with such hatred in the American press?" asked Edgar Grimmel, a fifteen-year-old student of Glassberg's. "The American people are being misled," his teacher replied. "Government officials are suppressing true reports from American Red Cross observers regarding the Russian Bolsheviki." Glassberg went on to denounce specific news accounts, published in what he labeled "the capitalistic New York press," of Bolsheviks murdering women and children in Russia.

Another student, Reginald Bud, interjected, "Are Lenin and Trotzky really German agents?" "Of course not," Glassberg answered. "Neither could be German agents because it was their propaganda which brought about the German revolution and ended the war."

"What about the ongoing debate concerning the red flag laws?" asked George Mack, the oldest student in the class. "Is Algernon Lee, the socialist alderman, correct when he claims the red flag can be displayed above the American flag?" Mack's teacher pondered the question for a moment, then slowly replied "Yes…in a sense."[1]

Such pronouncements apparently had a significant impact upon Glassberg's pupils. One student, Martin Carrol, later admitted that the statements "changed my mind from the United States to Russia, and gave me the opinion that the Bolsheviki were a good thing." When Calvin Kemble, an English teacher at the same school, began criticizing the Russian government the next day, he discovered several students defending the movement. Upon ascertaining the source of their information, he encouraged twelve of the boys to meet with school administrators and sign a statement charging Glassberg with uttering seditious statements. Two days later, on January 17, 1919, the principal of Commercial High School suspended him indefinitely, pending a termination hearing by the Board of Education of New York City.[2]

At the ensuing hearing, Assistant Corporation Counsel Edward Mayer portrayed Glassberg as a radical member of the Socialist Party attempting to cloud the minds of the impressionable youth of New York City. Student after student took the stand and testified against their teacher. Grimmel admitted that Glassberg's controversial statements "gave me an impression that he did not like the United States government, and that he wasn't sort of altogether true to the government." Mack was more succinct in his assessment; "Glassberg is a Bolshevik," he concluded.[3]

Through his lawyer, noted socialist Gilbert E.Roe, the embattled history teacher pleaded not guilty to all charges. Roe attempted to dismiss the students' claims as retaliatory accusations against a renowned "tough teacher who gave low marks." In addition, prominent character witnesses testified on Glassberg's behalf. Colonel Raymond Robins, a former member of the American Red Cross mission to Russia who recently had spoken before a U.S. Senate investigative committee, corroborated many of Glassberg's comments regarding the conditions in Russia. Eventually the accused teacher took the stand to refute many of the charges; however, he refused to answer any questions regarding his affiliation with the Socialist Party. "I am not on trial for being a Socialist," he claimed.[4]

As winter gave way to spring, alarm grew among civic leaders and some educators who believed that Glassberg represented only the tip of the iceberg. Kemble warned that "American Bolshevism, sadly in need of recruits and unable to gain them among those of mature years, is trying to proselytize among the serious thinkers of high school age." For proof he provided "inflammatory pamphlets" taken from students at the school, allegedly published by the socialist Rand School of Social Science and distributed by Glassberg. Capitalizing on Kemble's revelations, newspaper editors throughout the city immediately clamored for a thorough investigation of the roots underlying radical and seditious thought in New York. "Radicalism is not a popular sport in America," one editor concluded. "Every time it has tried to get a foothold some hardheaded and harder fisted agency has stepped in to block it off."[5]

Across town, at a Lower East Side elementary school, a grade school teacher sought to fight Bolshevism in her own way. As the snow began to fall in early December, 1919, Cynthia Carter tried to warm her sixth graders with a writing assignment to invigorate their patriotic fires, a one-page essay on Americanism. Many students wrote of the importance "to not listen to people who talk anti-Americanism," "to not let people tell you that we are having the wrong kind of government," and "to uphold the flag in every way." Most referred to the "evil deeds" planned and plotted by "radicals," "anarchists," and "troublemakers" in their effort to spread Bolshevism throughout the country. Some students even suggested solutions, ranging from "drive these radicals out of our democratic country" and "crush Bolshevism with brains," to "turning those anti-American people over to the authorities to suffer." One particular student concluded, "if such anti-American people are in this beautiful, free country we ought to hang them."[6]

Of the fourteen essays, one captured the spirit of Americanism more than the others. Despite numerous grammatical and spelling errors (reprinted here, in their original form), twelve-year-old John clearly expressed his sentiments concerning radicals in America. "If I were older," he began, "I might be able to get the Bolsheviky and other harmfull organizeations out of our country or americanize them." He went on to criticize their "lunitic thoughts," as well as to stress the need "to hammer it into the head of the Bolsheviky that they are wrong or else deport them." He concluded his essay by pointing out that "Our country is free to those who mind their own business and do not spoil other people's freedom." Even his sixth grade teacher recognized McCarthy's potential, as she commented at the bottom of the essay, "Note his name in connection with his first line. National hereditary trait. He could do it all himself!"[7]

Similar stories regarding education and the impact of political hysteria upon it dot the American landscape in the years immediately following the First World War; however, most historians and political scientists pay scant attention to such episodes, sometimes dismissing them as anecdotes peripheral to the major events of 1919: the strikes, the bombings, and the infamous Palmer raids of January 1920.[8] But in New York, the Red Scare did not end with the Palmer raids; nor did it end in 1921 or 1922. The same government, business, and civic leaders responsible for fomenting the scare in early 1919 continued to nurture it well into 1923, a full three years after the infamous Palmer Raids.

Specifically, the Joint Legislative Committee to Investigate Radical Activities in New York State, often referred to as the Lusk Committee for its chairman, Senator Clayton R. Lusk, led the charge. From its spectacular attacks on the Soviet Bureau and the Rand School of Social Science, to its less notable investigations into radical publishing houses and meeting halls, the Lusk Committee searched for subversives in every nook and cranny of New York State between June, 1919, and January, 1920. Along the way, the committee utilized many of the physical methods examined by previous scholars: police raids, seizure of property, arrests, espionage, and at one point even employing a safecracker.

While the Lusk Committee's longevity is worthy of examination, of greater interest is its narrowing focus and changing methods after January, 1920. In its early stages, the Lusk Committee mirrored other efforts around the country to track down communists, socialists, and anarchists whom they believed represented a tangible threat to the nation's safety. But despite all of the ballyhoo about radical infiltration of the cities, neither the Lusk Committee nor any other investigators uncovered a single subversive conspiracy. The only measurable success came in the area of education, where authorities had dismissed a handful of allegedly radical teachers and intimidated several others. Therefore, as the Red Scare progressed, the Lusk Committee focused much of their effort on eliminating radicalism from schools in New York; what had been of secondary interest to other investigations and patriotic organizations became the Lusk Committee's primary objective. This change in focus also required a change in methods. As 1919 came to a close, the committee abandoned physical raids in favor of court proceedings, such as the one to close the Rand School. When this method failed, they then turned to legislative action, urging the State to pass laws to ensure the loyalty of schools as well as teachers.

This study examines the efforts of the Lusk Committee in order to better understand three key points. First, as the Red Scare unfolded, repression became more focused, with education becoming the principal target. Second, as the targets changed, the methods of repression shifted from sensationalized raids and arrests to more subtle forms of legal and legislative proceedings. Finally, the Red Scare did not end in January, 1920, but advanced in this slightly different form until 1923, at which time shifting public perceptions of civil liberties played a significant role in bringing the episode to a conclusion, but only after the work of the committee had left its mark on thousands of New Yorkers—some harmed visibly, while countless others suffered a form of self-repression lest they become open targets as well. The legacy of the Lusk Committee bears out these points, as subsequent investigations into radical threats in New York State often included educators among their chief concerns, most notably in the McNaboe and Rapp-Coudert inquiries in the 1930s and 1940s respectively. Likewise, the methods employed in recent bouts of public hysteria—most notably the propensity to invoke patriotism in an effort to quickly pass questionable laws in the wake of the September 11, 2001, terrorist attacks—bear an eerie resemblance to those tactics employed by the Lusk Committee.

Good history should also tell a great story. An examination of the Lusk Committee provides just such an opportunity. Although the story begins with Benjamin Glassberg answering questions before a school board preparing to determine his fate, he truly was, as critics feared, only the tip of the iceberg. From bomb scares to courtroom antics, from riots to political intrigue, from lost Russian gold to subversive teachers, the story of the Lusk Committee has it all. Most important, the story allows scholars a chance to reopen the book on the Red Scare and better understand it as part of the continuum of political repression in modern American history, as opposed to an aberration in the history of a country founded upon the principles of freedom and democracy.

RETHINKING THE RED SCARE

Chapter 1
The Underlying Causes of the Red Scare

THE STORY OF THE RED SCARE THAT FOMENTED MASS HYSTERIA throughout the country in 1919–1920 actually began with America's efforts to demobilize following the armistice that ended the World War I on November 11, 1918. Demobilization included undoing a federal machinery that was unmatched in size up to that point in the nation's history. From the time President Wilson signed the declaration of war against Germany on Good Friday, April 6, 1917, until the first American troops set sail for Europe the following August, the federal government passed a series of laws and created several agencies to handle the country's war needs.[1]

Among the first passed by Congress were the Liberty Loan Act and the Selective Service Act, designed to ensure adequate funds and men to fight a successful war effort.[2] The War Industries Board, managed by Bernard Baruch, coordinated the nation's growing industrial complex to ensure an adequate stock of military supplies.[3] To secure an ample labor force, the government created the National War Labor Board, through which they offered unions fair wages, hours, and recognition of their right to organize and bargain collectively in exchange for no-strike guarantees. As a result, union labor received far greater recognition during the war than at any previous time. Federal officials also encouraged programs rationing various consumer goods, specifically food and scrap metal. Under the guidance of Herbert Hoover, the Food Administration encouraged all Americans to fast from certain foods on pre-designated days, and plant "victory gardens" in yards, vacant lots, and even one on the White House lawn.[4] Through such agencies and legislation, the federal government met the physical needs of war: money, men, supplies, and food.

A successful war effort, however, demanded mental as well as physical preparation. Authorities hoped conservation programs would create a spirit of public participation and lead the people at home to associate denial, shortage, and inconvenience with the German enemy. Official statements equated war with a life or death struggle to make the world safe for democracy from the barbaric Hun. In addition to the spirit of sacrifice, the federal government sought to raise patriotic fervor among large numbers of apathetic or openly antagonistic citizens through a vast array of propaganda designed to encourage Americans to hate all things German. The Committee on Public Information, led by George Creel, encouraged "one hundred per cent Americanism" through local and national bond drives, motion pictures, speeches, plays, newspaper articles, parades, and other similar devices. Among hundreds of drawings produced for the committee by James Montgomery Flagg was the famous "Uncle Sam Wants You!" recruitment poster. "Hate the Hun" films, including *Outwitting the Hun* and *Claws of the Hun,* attracted the services of such legendary directors as D.W.Griffith. As Frank Cobb, the editor of the New York *World,* claimed, through Creel's committee the federal government "conscripted public opinion as they conscripted men and money and materials. Having conscripted it, they dealt with it as they dealt with other raw recruits; they mobilized it. They goose-stepped it. They taught it to stand at attention and salute."[5]

Under Creel's guidance, the propaganda movement gained momentum, although not without a price. While the committee succeeded in generating overwhelming enthusiasm and support for the war, it also fostered a growing intolerance towards any who opposed the effort. People came to view wartime objectors, conscientious and otherwise, with scorn and to favor official coercion to make them fight. The Postmaster General refused fourth class mailing privileges to periodicals, specifically those of the Emergency Peace Federation and the Socialist Party of America, which questioned government policies or displayed pacifistic leanings. Anyone who continued to openly question the war effort faced potential prosecution under the Espionage and Sedition Acts, aimed at imprisoning individuals who criticized the government, promoted disloyalty, or aided the enemy in any way. Under federal sponsorship, private citizens organized spying committees, such as the American Defense Society and the National Security League, which offered badges and membership cards to zealous patriots who proved themselves worthy. Eventually, the quest for "100 per cent Americanism" turned into a German bashing crusade. Public schools ceased teaching the German language. Restaurants began serving "victory cabbage" and "liberty dogs" rather than sauerkraut and frankfurters. Symphonies throughout the country ceased playing Bach and Wagner. Upstanding citizens stoned dachshunds and German Shepherds. At one performance of Barnum and Bailey's circus, fans cheered when a Russian bear attacked a German animal trainer.[6]

The extreme nature of war-inspired hatred directed at anyone suspected of impeding or criticizing the military effort worried some critics. Senator Robert LaFollette of Wisconsin, a vocal opponent of America's entry into the conflict, questioned the aims of Creel's campaign of "Americanism." Supreme Court Justice Oliver Wendell Holmes also took issue with some of the wartime measures designed to silence critics. Although the court repeatedly upheld the convictions of men and women under the Sedition Act, Holmes held that individuals and groups had as much right to publish anti-war literature as the government had the right "to publish the Constitution of the United States, now vainly invoked by them."[7]

As a result of such statements, patriotic societies continuously took aim at critics, particularly at Senator LaFollette. One federal judge suggested that he be placed before a firing squad. Dr. Nicholas Murray Butler, president of Columbia University, added that "You might just as well put poison in the food of every American boy that goes to his transport as permit this man [LaFollette] to talk as he does." Despite such worries, however, federal officials successfully secured the hearts and minds of all Americans, whether through propaganda or imprisonment. In doing so, along with harnessing the productive capacity of the nation's industries and farms, America prepared itself for the war to make the world safe for democracy. Like a well-oiled machine, the U.S. rode the crest of federal machinery and legislation to a rather easy victory over the Germans in little more than eighteen months.[8]

Defeating the Axis forces presented few difficulties once the U.S. had fully committed its resources to the effort; however, the transition from war to peace wreaked economic and mental havoc upon American society, eventually culminating in the Red Scare that gripped the nation in 1919– 1920. In fact, the war itself was something of a disappointment for many Americans. The great struggle to make the world safe for democracy appeared a failure when, even before the general armistice, Russian Bolshevik leaders Vladimir Lenin and Leon Trotsky overthrew Alexander Kerensky's quasi-democratic government and predicted Bolshevism's inevitable victory over capitalistic systems worldwide. Although predicting world rule and obtaining it were vastly different, patriotic American citizens, attempting to adjust to changing national perspectives, nevertheless viewed Bolshevism as a possible danger to the American way of life. The difficult circumstances many Americans faced in the months following the end of the war appeared to corroborate their fears.[9]

After the armistice, the American people desperately needed strong government leadership to help them make the transition from wartime to peace; but federal authorities withdrew almost completely from domestic affairs. Agencies created to meet the demands of the war immediately can celed contracts and closed their doors, oftentimes allowing no more than a month for current production levels to continue. Although many factories succeeded in rapidly reconverting to peacetime production levels,[10] the economic and psychological impact upon the nine million war industries workers and their families was at times devastating. Compounding the problem was the reintegration of four million soldiers into a society ill-prepared to ease their transition. Of the four million American soldiers overseas in November 1918, over 600,000 returned home within weeks of the armistice signing; most of the remainder were home within a year. However, the federal government provided little for them beyond passage home; when the war ended, the only goal in the minds of Washington officials was to be certain the last man leaving turn off the lights.[11]

Caught between the forces of reconversion and military demobilization, the public faced a year of rising unemployment and skyrocketing prices coupled with insignificant gains in income. As soldiers returned home by the thousands, unemployment steadily rose before finally leveling off in the fall of 1919. Returning home to a country that promised their heroes whatever they wanted, soldiers' demands were simple; they wanted jobs, but found few. The rising cost of living also presented problems, not only for veterans, but also the general public. By 1919, the purchasing power of the American dollar was less than half what it was in 1913. Reports from the Bureau of Labor Statistics indicated that food prices had risen 84 percent, clothing 115 percent, and housing 130 percent over the same period. For the average American family in 1919, their cost of living was 100 percent higher than it was when the war started. Combined with the fact that income levels rose at most by 10 per cent during the war, many Americans, middle and working classes alike, found themselves in the worst economic shape in over fifty years.[12]

Although lack of organization and an overwhelming sense of pride prevented middle class Americans from effectively protesting the poor conditions they faced, working class individuals found great voice, due to their wartime gains via the National War Labor Board. Thanks in part to the labor-friendly atmosphere fostered by President Wilson since 1913, union membership had risen from less than 500,000 at the turn of the century to over four million in 1919. Although workers and management maintained an uneasy truce during the war, both sides were eager for a fight at its conclusion—workers looking to build upon their newfound recognition, and management anxious to destroy the principle of collective bargaining forced upon them by the federal government. Despite the best efforts of a small number of progressive-minded employers and workers who recognized the need to cooperate in order for America to flourish, the thrust of the "association movement" was still five years away. Management, as historian John Milton Cooper, Jr. wrote, "was bent on rolling back labor's war time gains." As economic conditions worsened, organized labor saw no recourse but to take their cause to the picket lines. Major strikes, infrequent in prior years, now became commonplace; by the end of 1919, over 3,600 strikes involving four million workers had occurred, numbers that exceeded the totals for all previous labor actions in American history combined.[13]

The non-economic aspects of demobilization, specifically the intolerance generated by the Committee on Public Information, proved even more difficult for the American people to handle. Creel's propaganda machine was so effective that when the armistice was signed, government-nurtured hate and militant patriotism among many Americans bordered on hysteria. While military demobilization was easily achieved with the swipe of a pen, the citizens of the United States were psychologically unprepared for the peace that followed. With the "barbaric Hun" no longer a potential threat, Americans sought a new enemy to serve as a scapegoat for the challenges facing them; radicals of all kinds proved to be easy targets.

In the months following the armistice, as more Americans found that their nation had fundamentally changed, and that they would have to face the uncertainties of the future rather than return to the security of the past, their fear of radical subversion grew. To many citizens, labor appeared militant in their demands. African-Americans, women, and first- and second-generation immigrants, having enjoyed new freedoms as a result of the war effort, seemed determined not to return to their former subordinate positions. More disturbing still was the introduction of legislation regarding allegedly radical ideas, such as women's suffrage, civil rights for minority groups, government-enforced wage standards, and evolution. Because of the ease and simplicity of placing the blame for such problems on a single factor, extremely conservative and patriotic citizens felt that an evil force was at work in the country.

The Russian Revolution and its self-professed aim of destroying capitalist countries was proof enough for many that this evil force was Bolshevism's agents at work in the United States.[14]

Americans based their hatred and fear of Bolshevism on a strange mix of truth and fiction. The hatred originated with Russia's decision to sign a separate peace with Germany in March 1918, after Lenin came to power; the fear came one year later when the Bolsheviks formed the Third International to coordinate a worldwide proletariat revolution, and appeared headed toward success in Germany, Poland, and Italy. The misrepresentation and miscalculation of the Bolshevik threat contributed even more so to the hysteria that grew into a Red Scare in America. Many Americans believed incorrectly that the separate peace treaty proved that the Russian Revolution was German controlled; thus, most had little difficulty in transforming their government-inspired hatred of Huns into hatred of Bolsheviks. Furthermore, the significant increase in labor uprisings in the U.S. convinced many observers that the revolution had arrived on America's doorstep as well.

The formation of two communist parties in the U.S. in 1919 pushed many citizens to the limits of their tolerance for radical political movements. Prior to their formation, only two groups had succeeded in organizing radicals in America to some extent, the Socialist Party and the Industrial Workers of the World. Although the I.W.W. was more aggressive in their radical activities, the Socialist Party was larger in membership, better organized, and had greater success in gaining political office; by 1919, Socialists held office in many state legislatures.[15] Although tolerated until 1914, the party quickly became a target of zealous American patriots when the war began. Meeting in St. Louis in April 1917, leaders of the party issued a resolution condemning American intervention in the conflict and blaming American businessmen and manufacturers for attempting to obtain profits at the expense of soldiers' lives. Fearing that participation in the conflict served only "to multiply the horrors of the war," as well as "to increase the toll of death and destruction and to prolong the fiendish slaughter," party members branded America's declaration of war a crime. In an effort to forestall such evil, the Socialist Party pledged to fight conscription, loan drives, and censorship, or essentially the government programs created by the Selective Service Act, the Liberty Loan Act, and the subsequent Sedition and Espionage Acts. With regard to men, money, and supplies, the party concluded to "let those who kindled the fire, furnish the fuel." Most important, the Socialist Party promised "active public opposition to the war through demonstrations, mass petitions, and all other means" within their power. Not content to maintain their principles in silence, the Socialist Party provided an obvious target for the general public, even after the war ended.[16]

Given the Socialist Party's overwhelming opposition to the war effort, many citizens believed them to be working in concert with Germany to destroy the American way of life. Mobs began raiding socialist meeting halls. The postal service rescinded fourth class mailing privileges to many socialist newspapers and magazines. Even the courts intervened and began prosecuting leading members of the party for aiding the enemy in time of war. Most notably, a federal court convicted Congressman Victor L.Berger of Wisconsin, a prominent figure in the party since its inception, as well as the first Socialist elected to the U.S. House of Representatives, for violating the Espionage Act when he questioned the conduct and goals of the war.[17] Eugene Debs, founder of the Socialist Party, suffered a similar fate as a result of his bitter opposition to the war.[18]

The Industrial Workers of the World represented the only radical organization, other than the Socialist Party, to gain a national following in America in the years leading up to and during the war. Although Berger, Debs, and other leading socialists professed political change through the ballot box, the I.W.W. favored direct action tactics, at times violent, to express their opposition to the capitalist system. Led by William "Big Bill" Haywood, the Wobblies, as they were more popularly known, included a variety of radicals, anarchists, socialists, and fringe elements of the American labor movement, all of whom supported the general strike as the most effective tool to undermine capitalism in America.[19]

In the years preceding the war, the Wobblies enjoyed limited success, specifically in western mining camps and lumber mills, as well as in textile mills of Lawrence, Massachusetts. However, even limited success had its price. With victory achieved, workers found little reason to remain affiliated with the I.W.W.; at its height, the Wobblies could count no more than 60,000 permanent members among their ranks. Success also generated publicity, which in turn resulted in a more concerted effort among business owners to break the Wobblies. Within months, industrialists successfully pressured Congress to consider legislation designed to deport aliens who advocated sabotage, destruction of private property, or the overthrow of the government by force or violence, a category into which many card-carrying members of the I.W.W. fell.[20]

Much like the Socialist Party, I.W.W. opposition to America's participation in World War I led federal authorities to intensify their investigation and repression of the organization. Patriotism held no sway over Wobblies; for them it was a senseless concept. Throughout 1917 and 1918, the I.W.W. printed dozens of antiwar pamphlets and posters urging resistance to the draft with messages such as "Don't Be a Soldier, Be a Man." Even those Wobblies who registered in accordance with the law acknowledged their I.W.W. membership and maintained their vocal opposition to the war. Eventually a poem printed in the I.W.W. official organ, *Industrial World,* captured the anti-war sentiment held by many Wobblies:

I love my flag, I do, I do,
Which floats upon the breeze,
I also love my arms and legs,
And neck, and nose, and knees.
One little shell might spoil them all
Or give them such a twist,
They would be of no use to me;
I guess I won't enlist.
I love my country, yes, I do
I hope her folks do well.
Without our arms and legs and things,
I think we'd look like hell.
Young men with faces half shot off
Are unfit to be kissed,
I've read in books it spoils their looks,
I guess I won't enlist.[21]

For many Wobblies, the question of patriotism was moot so long as they lived and worked in a country that they believed exploited labor and suppressed any efforts to improve their condition. Put simply, according to the I.W.W. leadership, loyalty to flag meant little to a, man who had no blanket to cover himself. Reflecting after the war on the I.W.W. stance against the conflict, Carleton Parker answered the question of why Wobblies were not patriotic to the United States. Having left their wives and children to head west looking for a job, slept in a "lousy, sour bunk house," and eaten food "just as rotten as they could give you," workers had little sympathy for patriotic causes, Parker explained; and if the conditions were not deplorable enough, the repression was unforgivable. "If every person who represented law and order and the nation beat you up, railroaded you to jail, and the good Christian people cheered and told them to go to it," Parker concluded, "how the hell do you expect a man to be patriotic?"[22]

In the growing wartime hysteria of 1917–1918, however, most citizens neither considered heartfelt rationale nor accepted anything less than 100 percent Americanism, a term rigidly defined as complete loyalty to nation and state with adherence to white, Anglo-Saxon, Protestant ideals. Much like the Socialist Party, the Industrial Workers of the World became a target for repression and a scapegoat for the post-war troubles that followed. According to one vocal critic of the I.W.W., the Wobblies were "the waste material of creation and should be drained off into the sewer of oblivion there to rot in cold obstruction like any other excrement." Such hatred was deeply felt and widespread among Americans who demanded complete loyalty during the war and feared a perceived radical threat afterwards. Historian David Mitchell explained in his work, *1919 Red Mirage,* that many regarded the Wobblies, "in the deepest sense, subversive." To average citizens, the I.W.W. had replaced Native Americans as the greatest public enemy and "had to be exterminated."[23]

The tradition of radicalism introduced by the Socialist Party and the Industrial Workers of the World between 1901 and 1917 continued in the post-war years with the formation of two communist organizations in America. In part due to the radicalizing influence of the Bolshevik Revolution, the Socialist Party split in 1919. The Left Wing of the party called for an immediate revolution in America to parallel the one in Russia. They continuously harangued Right Wing Socialists for their conservative stance on the issue; while the latter supported the rise of communism, they continued to favor democratic and constitutional means to achieve the goal. Following bitter fighting throughout the spring, the more conservative elements succeeded in expelling Left Wing members from the Socialist Party at their national convention in Chicago in August, 1919. Undaunted by the move, the group moved to a different room within the convention hall and immediately formed the Communist Labor Party. Led by former New York State Assemblyman Benjamin Gitlow, newspaper reporter John Reed, and millionaire William B.Lloyd, this new party pledged allegiance to the principles of the Third International and called for "the overthrow of capitalist rule and the conquest of political power by the workers." According to the Communist Labor Party, the time for waiting was over.[24]

However, the divisions within the radical parties were not complete. Continued animosity within the Left Wing, specifically between the native-born and foreign-born elements, led the latter to create a third organization in September, simply named the Communist Party of America. Although the Communist Labor Party was revolutionary in their stance, the Communist Party mirrored Russian Bolshevism completely, as witnessed by their manifesto, which they copied nearly word for word from the Third International. In it, they called for an "immediate proletarian revolution" that would result in "the overthrow of capitalism and the establishment of the dictatorship of the proletariat." The closing words to the manifesto left little doubt as to goals of the Communist Party: "Long live the Communist International! Long live the World Revolution!" Eventually, the alien-dominated Communist Party included 60,000 members among its rank and file, compared to 10,000 who joined the Communist Labor Party and the 30,000 who remained in the shrinking Socialist Party.[25]

Despite the fragmentation of the radical movement in 1919, as well as its relative insignificance in sheer numbers, its impact on a nation searching for someone to blame for the post-war economic upheaval and social turmoil was readily apparent. By the end of 1919, over fifty communist publications in 25 different languages circulated throughout the country; at least half of these originated in New York City. Although readership of these newspapers is difficult to quantify, due in large part to the postal ban on such literature, they clearly found a receptive audience in urban areas, particularly among the immigrant working classes. Even more difficult to trace were the "parlor Bolsheviks," or American intellectuals and professionals who, for a number of reasons, sympathized with communism. Some were reformers who saw in communism possible answers to the plight of the working poor. Others supported the cause simply out of fascination or novelty, much like the preoccupation with fads that would come to dominate the 1920s. In either case, the numbers were likely small. Gitlow later estimated no more than one million communists and communist sympathizers lived in the U.S. in 1919, or approximately one per cent of the entire population.[26]

Nonetheless, these "parlor Bolsheviks" seemed dangerous to the general public, which overestimated the size and influence of the threat as they blamed most of the country's ills on Bolshevism. Traveling through the U.S. at the time, a British journalist captured the essence of the emerging national hysteria when he observed "No one will forget the feverish condition of the public mind; it was hag-ridden by the spectre of Bolshevism." Comparing the condition to a nightmare, he recalled the words of one person who feared the conformity that repression forced upon the nation. "'America,' as one I was with at the time said, 'is the land of liberty—liberty to keep in step.'"[27]

The difficult months of transition from war to peace and the presence of a concerted radical movement in the country set the stage for the hysteria that became the Red Scare; all that remained was for a catalyst to link the two and provide the spark. The popular press and public officials were more than willing to oblige. As early as December, 1918, the Hartford *Courant* declared that the red flag, symbolic of a political system antagonistic to Americanism, had been raised from coast to coast. At the same time, the *Wall Street Journal* commended New York City's Mayor John Hylan for outlawing public displays of any red flag within the city. Furthermore, Boston's *Christian Science Monitor* maintained that serious investigation into Bolshevik activities in the United States should occur.[28]

Events at the end of the year appeared to corroborate such concern. On the final day of December, 1918, when a series of bomb explosions in Philadelphia wrecked the homes of three Pennsylvania government officials, a police inspector declared it was part of a nationwide Bolshevik plot. The police immediately seized a leader of the Revolutionary Labor Party because of his past demonstrations and activities. Although the authorities released him three days later for lack of evidence, Captain J.C.Mills of the Philadelphia police department nevertheless warned that outbreaks could be expected at any time in any part of the nation. Taking Mills' warning to heart, New York City police stationed special guards at the City Hall and Court House, increased the number of regular patrolmen on duty, and gave detectives special assignments to watch every suspected anarchist.[29]

At the national level, legislators who had long believed that recent immigrants from southern and eastern Europe were destroying Americanism used this growing fear to the utmost. The chairman of the House Committee on Immigration maintained that the country could keep European Bolshevism from its shores only by restricting the admission of foreign-born. Franklin Giddings, professor of sociology and history at Columbia University agreed. Defining Bolshevism as a "massing turmoil of criminal elements of society which had been freed from Russian prisons in 1917," he warned that some agents had already entered the United States disguised as political refugees. If citizens hoped to keep American institutions secure, Giddings continued, they must "refuse admittance to other Reds."[30]

Finally, in late January 1919, the U.S. Senate began discussing the advisability of extending the authority of the Overman Committee, then investigating the connection between brewing interests and German propaganda, to include a study of Bolshevism in the United States. While the Senate considered the move, a witness appeared before the committee whose testimony provided the final spark to transform concern to hysteria; he not only convinced the senators of the need for a thorough investigation, but also alerted the American public to the threatening link between post-war turmoil and revolutionary radicalism. The witness, Archibald E. Stevenson of New York, had been an agent of the Bureau of Investigation for the Department of Justice and later served as director of the Bureau of Propaganda for the Military Intelligence Division of the U.S. Army General Staff. Unable to separate what he considered the greatest security threat in the nation's history from the former war enemy, Stevenson explained the connection between Bolshevism and Germany. Branding the Marxist movement a branch of Germany's revolutionary socialism, he maintained that the present radical menace in the nation was an outgrowth of the German-inspired pacifist movement of the war years.[31]

Despite being warned that inclusion of a man's name in the Overman Committee record "damned, disgraced, and humiliated" him, Stevenson insisted on listing the names of dangerous people he considered disloyal owing to their pacifistic leanings during the war and radical inclinations afterwards. His list of names included Jane Addams, founder of Chicago's Hull House; Morris Hillquit, a socialist New York City attorney; Oswald Garrison Villard, editor of the liberal magazine *The Nation;* Charles A. Beard, former professor at Columbia University; the Reverend John Haynes Holmes of New York City's Church of the Messiah; Roger Baldwin, one of the founders of the National Civil Liberties Bureau; and many other individuals. Stevenson considered Baldwin one of the more dangerous radical sympathizers because of his organization's wartime aid to conscientious objectors. Also proof of treason, in Stevenson's mind, was the N.C.L.B.'s defense of the Industrial Workers of the World in 1919 against charges of obstructing the war effort. In his distorted attack on the bureau, however, he failed to clarify that the basic principle underlying its activities was the protection of freedom of speech, press, and assembly, rights guaranteed in the United States constitution.[32]

Turning his attention to education, Stevenson declared that many universities were little more than hotbeds of sedition, full of pernicious teachers. Members of the Overman Committee agreed, stating that some institutions of higher learning were nothing more than "festering masses of pure atheism" and "the grossest kind of materialism." In addition, they felt that the teaching in some universities was destructive to both the United States government and civilization in general. Another organization whose pacifistic activities drew the ire of Stevenson was the American Friends Service Committee of Philadelphia, more commonly known as the Quakers. He emphasized that one of the reasons why all such organizations were dangerous was the presence of intelligentsia among them. According to Stevenson, intelligentsia included "those anarchists who confined their operations to brain storms rather than physical force," yet were equally as dangerous.[33]

Apparently Stevenson could not decide just how great a menace radicals and their organizations were. Early in his testimony, he declared that threat affected only the large urban and industrial centers in the country, and everyone knew that few "real" Americans lived in such vile places. But in his summary he claimed that sedition had crept into all phases of American life, including churches, universities, and even the federal government, especially the Bureau of Immigration headed by well-known pacifist Frederic Howe. The solution, according to Stevenson, was simple: keep a close watch on radicalism, particularly in religious and educational institutions, especially in urban areas like New York City, the most dangerous of all places in the United States. Another important aspect of the solution was limiting immigration to people of Anglo-Saxon, Protestant stock.[34]

Reaction to Stevenson's revelations was swift. Observing, "the Lord moves in strange ways," committee members declared their support for their most significant witness, as well as their reliance upon his expertise. Although the connection between God's movements and Stevenson's testimony was left rather vague, some link evidently existed in the senators' minds. Several days after his appearance, the Senate voted unanimously to extend the Overman's Committee's authority to include an extensive investigation of Bolshevism throughout the country. However, public opinion of Stevenson's antics was mixed. Editors of *The Nation* found his behavior similar to "any notoriety-seeking, swivel chair hero in Washington...." In compiling his list of names, they observed, Stevenson "listed every tenth intelligent person belonging to any two organizations containing the words international, intercollegiate, civil liberties, peace, reconciliation, and other terms of ill omen."[35]

When the committee sent a copy of Stevenson's list of dangerous radicals to Secretary of War Newton Baker he ignored it, commenting, "The War Department did not undertake to censor the opinions of people in the United States during peacetime." The list, he declared, "named distinguished individuals devoted to high interests of country and mankind." Jane Addams, he concluded, "lends dignity and greatness to any list in which her name appears."[36] Discouraged by Baker's comments, as well as by the Overman Committee's subsequent unwillingness to draft or recommend a peacetime sedition law, Stevenson returned to New York where he began agitating for a similar legislative investigation at the state level. What federal officials in Washington remained unwilling to do, perhaps state officials in Albany would undertake.

New York provided fertile ground for Stevenson's warnings. On January 11, 1919, Major Fred W.More, the chief army intelligence officer for the northeast division, informed his superiors in Washington that "New York is undoubtedly the storm center of the present radical movement in the country; we should keep fully posted as to the progress of the movement there." In the minds of New Yorkers, more so than in any other city or state throughout the nation, Bolshevism was a foreign ideology imported by radical immigrants which, if left unchecked, would grow more devastating than the flu epidemic that gripped the country the previous year. When 35,000 women in 800 textile factories threatened to strike for higher wages and better working conditions in late January, the president of the Dress and Waist Manufacturers Association warned New York City Mayor John Hylan of an impending crisis. In an open letter, the president charged the "seditious women" with "prominently displaying the red flag" and "supporting the Socialist candidate for mayor, Morris Hillquit." Despite the misleading nature of such accusations, they had the desired effect upon many New York citizens; even more came to believe that Bolshevik agents were indeed attempting to destroy American institutions.[37]

The Board of Education confirmed many New Yorkers' growing fears when they accused and dismissed high school teacher Benjamin Glassberg for advocating radical doctrines in the classroom. William Ettinger, the Superintendent of New York City Schools, warned teachers that he had no room in his school system for instructors whose personal convictions made it impossible for them to teach the ideals of the American government. To ensure that students, as well as teachers, promoted loyalty, a Latin teacher at DeWitt Clinton High School organized a spy network of seventy students to seek out subversives. Upon discovering two students discussing the Bolshevik Revolution, the teacher held a classroom trial at which he lectured them on citizenship. Eventually, the school administration denied each boy his diploma on the grounds that they had repudiated their loyalty to America.

As concern grew over the possible radical indoctrination of students in public schools, the New York City Board of Education devised a questionnaire to test all students' knowledge of socialism. Sample questions included "Who are the Russian Bolsheviks, and what are their chief aims?" and "Do you believe Bolshevism to be a danger threatening the people of New York?" In a perverse system of scoring, students received higher marks for incorrect answers. Upon reviewing the scores, administrators proudly boasted that the students of New York City knew nothing about radicalism. As other cases of questionable loyalty among teachers steadily surfaced, the New York *Times* pinpointed the nation's schools as the breeding grounds for revolution in America. "Parents protect their children from tobacco and alcohol," the newspaper noticed, "yet allow their exposure to the deadliest drug that has ever taken reason prisoner"—namely, Bolshevism. "The preparatory seminaries of American citizenship," the *Times* concluded, "are becoming the nurseries of its overthrow."[38]

When the Overman Committee publicly identified New York as the center of revolutionary plotting in the U.S., alarmed city and state officials decided to take action. On March 12, 1919, the police raided the Union of Russian Peasant Workers located on the Lower East Side and arrested 162 men and women. Labeling the organization "a front for alien subversive activity," Detective Sergeant James Gegan informed reporters than none of the people present at the union was an American citizen, and only a few spoke English. However, the facts belied such characterization. When the police arrived, instead of finding bombs and guns, they found a mechanics class studying the parts of an automobile, another class discussing Russian literature, and a group preparing for band rehearsal. Furthermore, of the 162 people detained, the district attorney charged only four with criminal anarchy. Undaunted by the results, Gegan quickly added that the remaining 158 eluded prosecution only through "devious schemes of a radical nature."[39]

The fact that many other nationalities created similar relief societies to provide companionship and education in order to help them adjust to life in America seemed irrelevant to Gegan, as well as to other New Yorkers who viewed the raid as proof of the immediate danger facing their state. A subsequent article in the popular magazine *The Forum* further fanned the flames of hysteria by perpetuating the unfounded association between relief societies and radical thought. In his examination of the "insidious doctrines propagated in New York's Lower East Side," reporter John Bruce Mitchell described the meeting halls as "dingy, dirty, and filled with the stifling fumes of soiled clothing and unwashed bodies." According to the article, most of the men attending the radical gatherings wore "greasy black suits and had long, shaggy hair, uncombed beards mottled with food, drippy foreign accents, bulging red faces, fishy smiles, and thick glasses." Furthermore, their attention strayed from the radical teachings just long enough for their "furtive black eyes" to ogle the "garishly dressed females" in their presence.[40]

Within a month, city authorities enacted red flag laws and hall boycotts designed to control the filthy radicals described by Mitchell. Public displays of a red flag resulted in a twenty-five dollar fine or ten days in jail. Hall owners refused to rent their facilities for use by radical organizations. Mayor Hylan and Police Chief Enright wholeheartedly endorsed both measures, primarily in response to growing public criticism that they were too soft on what many perceived was a growing un-American presence in the city. Despite opposition from labor and socialist groups, Hylan refused to back down. In late April, he banned all foreign language meetings among groups who criticized the government.[41]

By the end of the spring, all of the pieces necessary for a Red Scare were firmly in place. Economic and social upheaval following the First World War combined with a scapegoat in the form of radical political organizations to create a volatile scenario. Public officials and a popular press willing to connect the two provided the spark. An easily manipulated public searching for answers became a captive and hysterical audience. Specifically in New York State, a self-proclaimed "red hunter" by the name of Archibald Stevenson joined forces with a politically ambitious freshman Senator from Cortland by the name of Clayton Lusk to undertake an investigation into radicalism. With the help of the conservative New York *Times,* whose editors were eagerly willing to serve as a conduit for their findings, Stevenson and Lusk held New Yorkers spellbound for the ensuing four years. The time for talk had passed, and New York was ready to take center stage in Act One of the "Great Red Scare."

Chapter 2
The Formation of the Lusk Committee

ON MARCH 14, 1919, THE NEW YORK *TRIBUNE* REPORTED "THE colossus of all amusements is soon to descend on New York in all its pomp and grandeur." Although the article referred to the impending arrival of the Ringling Brothers and Barnum & Bailey's Circus, it ironically foretold of another side-show spectacle preparing to hold the state spellbound in the ensuing months. For on the facing page of the same edition, the *Tribune* printed the conclusions of the arch-conservative Union League Club's investigation into the causes and nature of Bolshevik agitation in New York.[1]

The "Committee on Bolshevism," appointed in January 1919 by the club's executive director, and former Republican presidential candidate, Charles Evans Hughes, consisted of Archibald Stevenson, fresh from his appearance before the Overman Committee; Theodore F.Saxny and Robert C.Morris, two local attorneys; industrialist William D.Murphy; and the Reverend Charles A.Eaton of the United Methodist Church. Also known as the "Committee of Five," the group conducted a two month inquiry into the nature of radicalism, amassing in the process volumes of literature concerning the state of revolutionary socialism in Europe, as well as a summary of the history of radicalism in America. Of particular interest to committee members was a series of articles published in the *Messenger,* a socialist newspaper distributed among African-Americans in New York City, concerning the formation of the National Association for the Promotion of Labor Unionism Among Negroes, headquartered in New York City. The final report, which Stevenson presented to the entire membership of the Union League Club on the evening of March 13, reviewed the evidence and drew two sweeping conclusions: first, an attempt was currently underway to arouse discontent among African-Americans by disseminating Bolshevik propaganda among them; and second, radical forces presently infiltrating organized labor would, if not halted, eventually gain control of the American Federation of Labor. Although both contentions were widely circulated among reactionary elements, and oftentimes justifiably dismissed due to needless exaggeration, Stevenson succeeded in whipping the club into a combined state of red hysteria and patriotic frenzy to a degree seldom seen among its members.[2]

At the conclusion of the meeting, the "Committee of Five" recommended, and the Union League Club unanimously supported, a resolution urging President Woodrow Wilson to call a special session of the U.S. Senate to investigate the radical threat facing the country. Simultaneously, in a petition whose wording created controversy in subsequent months, the club implored the New York State Legislature to conduct a similar inquiry:

> Resolved, that the Committee on the Study of Bolshevism be and it hereby is directed to present to the Senate and Assembly of the State of New York, the recommendation of the Union League Club that a joint legislative committee should be appointed with *all necessary powers* to investigate the tendencies, ramifications, and activities of the Bolshevist or revolutionary movement in this State, with a view to the enactment of such legislation as may be necessary to protect the Government of the State and to insure the maintenance of the constitutional rights of its citizens.[3]

J. Henry Walters, President pro tem of the State Senate, responded quickly to the request. On March 20, 1919, he introduced a resolution to undertake such an investigation. Walters's sentiments regarding the inquiry reflected the growing mix of hysteria and patriotism developing rapidly throughout the state and nation. For many observers, the pervasive, albeit unfounded, fear of Bolshevik agitation in America was offset only by the sense of patriotic duty that mandated strong action against the radicals. In defense of his position, Walters warned his colleagues, "the propaganda of Bolshevism is running rampant in New York State," encouraging anarchists, socialists, and Industrial Workers of the World who were "once mutual enemies [to] sit around a common table and agree upon a common cause." "I am so alarmed over the reports which have reached me," he declared, "I am convinced that it is the duty of this Legislature to use its offices to stamp out this propaganda." Even more so, in light of the recent adjournment of the U.S. Congress, it was necessary for the state legislature "to intervene and protect, in so far as it can, the American government, our institutions and American ideals."[4]

The President pro tem based his conclusions upon information derived from sources whose identities he claimed "not to be at liberty to disclose." According to Walters, previous investigations revealed "a concerted, well organized movement with vast ramifications and heavy financial support, designed to overthrow the State and National Government." Such financial support allegedly included a $500,000 draft—intercepted en route from Moscow—which was intended to support radical activities in New York City.[5]

Despite Walters's unwillingness to reveal the source of his intelligence, the basis for the information as well as the impetus for the passage of such a resolution was obvious: the Union League Club report. Throughout the resolution, the President pro tem referred to "public knowledge" and the facts ascertained by the Overman Committee as his reason for the move. However, following the session, he admitted that the "reports more recent, more startling, and more immediately concerned with this State," prompted him to sponsor the crusade. Even more telling was the wording of the resolution, which paralleled that of the Union League Club's statement:

> ...Whereas, it is the duty of the Legislature of the State of New York to learn the whole truth regarding these seditious activities and to pass, when such truth is ascertained, such legislation *as may be necessary to protect the Government of the State and to insure the maintenance of the rights of its citizens.*
>
> ...Now, therefore, be it resolved, That a joint committee of the Senate and Assembly be and is hereby created...*to investigate the scope, tendencies and ramifications of such seditious activities* ¼ [6]

The similarities between the resolutions passed by the Union League Club and State Senate were not lost on the press, as most newspaper accounts attributed the formation of the investigative committee to Charles Evans Hughes.[7]

Plans called for the committee to consist of four senators appointed by Walters and five assemblymen selected by Speaker of the Assembly Thaddeus Sweet, with Walters and Sweet serving as members ex officio. The nominal purpose of the investigation, according to the President pro tem, was for the committee to examine the extent of radicalism in the state, report its findings to the Senate, and draft legislation to combat the threat. Existing statutes, he emphasized, were insufficient to cope with the "red menace." Should the investigation reveal a situation that required immediate action, Walters had faith that Governor Alfred

Smith would call a special session of the legislature to handle the problem.[8]

To assist committee members in their endeavors, the resolution granted "extraordinary powers to compel the production of witnesses, books, and documents" and all other powers normally held by a legislative investigating committee. The resolution did not grant the committee permission to conduct raids, make arrests, or undertake any other administrative function; it was to be purely an investigative body. In addition, the measure carried with it a $50,000 appropriation, approved by the entire body without the usual requisite of sending the proposal to the Senate Finance Committee. Some senators suggested an even larger budget, including acting minority leader, Senator John J.Boylan, who argued, "the State should devote all its resources if necessary to pulling the props from under the revolutionary movement." Walters agreed, adding "I trust that we shall not stop at anything or with anybody in our effort to tear Bolshevism up with the roots and hurl it into the sea."[9]

Although it passed unanimously in the Senate on the evening of March 21, the joint resolution produced vocal opposition in the lower house, primarily from the Socialist and Democratic assemblymen representing districts in New York City. Following a five day delay due to previous agenda items, the Assembly began a day-long, exhaustive debate of the resolution on the morning of March 26. Those who opposed the resolution contended the investigation would produce no useful results. They stressed, instead, that the legislature should concentrate its efforts on ascertaining and alleviating the alleged causes of domestic radicalism: namely, inadequate housing, poor working conditions, and low wages. Republican proponents of the measure targeted their two Socialist colleagues, August Claessens of New York and Charles Solomon of Kings County, for the brunt of their attacks. At one point, a number of Republicans began labeling Claessens and Solomon as "Bolsheviks," based upon a variety of loosely-worded definitions bandied about throughout the chamber.

While neither Socialist accepted Assemblyman Fertig's definition that Bolshevism encompassed "force, violence, and destruction let loose for the overthrow of the capitalist government," both agreed that the movement represented "universal social unrest." Solomon, responding to Fertig's challenge that Socialists promoted the violent overthrow of organized government, stressed that he and Claessens exercised duly-constituted legal means to achieve their agenda. "There are two Bolshevists here in this house," he declared,

...Claessens and myself. If you want to stop the spread of what you have been pleased to call Bolshevism, study the causes of social discontent and you will find them in the high cost of living, unemployment, inadequate housing conditions, and the intensity of the struggle for existence generally. What have you done to meet these conditions? And yet you wonder that what you call Bolshevism is spreading through the State.[10]

Claessens went further in his analysis, arguing that the Bolshevik bogeymen whom the legislature feared were overwhelmingly different from Socialists who sought change through peaceful means. "The Bolsheviki,". he explained, "believe the efforts to effect reforms in government through education, the use of the ballot, and parliamentary methods are ineffective and dilatory; therefore they advocate force." While true Socialists recognized this difference, Claessens contended, others did not:

The difference between me and you members of the majority is that I know the Bolsheviki and you don't. They come to my meetings. They heckle me. They ridicule me for my trust in relief through the ballot, education and parliamentary procedure. And I have no reply to make to them, for my experience in this assembly forces upon me the futility of progress through parliamentary procedure in this state while standpatters remain in control.[11]

Claessens eventually carried his criticism to the streets. In an open letter to his constituents, he chastised the Republican majority in the legislature, whom he labeled a "colossal aggregation of asses," for "burying every moderate and conservative request the workers begged of them" while "stupidly capping the session by running through...a resolution appropriating $30,000 for the investigation of the spread of Bolshevism in this state." To the jeers of many of his Assembly colleagues, Solomon reiterated Claessens assessment regarding the reactionary nature of the body. "I know this resolution will pass," he concluded, "because there aren't enough men and women in this chamber who have the courage of their convictions."[12]

Claessens's and Solomon's efforts notwithstanding, passage of the measure was a foregone conclusion. Owing largely to the efforts of Assemblyman Charles D.Donohue, the Democrats' minority whip who managed to keep all but eight of his party in line, the measure passed later that evening with only ten dissenting votes. The vast majority of the Assembly (110 of 120) strongly agreed with Donohue's warning that "We must not wait until disaster comes to the people of this state through this insidious disease of Bolshevism." The single alteration in the resolution involved reducing the appropriation from $50,000 to $30,000 so as not to deplete the legislature's contingency fund.[13]

The immediate public response to the creation of the committee was mixed. In a lengthy editorial, the New York *Times* appeared pleased with the outcome of the session. If the city was indeed the center of Bolshevik activities, it concluded, such an investigation "cannot come too soon." Although the charges "wore a face of incredibility at first sight," the newspaper left little doubt as to its official position in support of measures to "expose and punish...rich, native boudoir Bolsheviki" who undertake "persistent efforts to poison the young with their fatal teachings." Throughout the state, various patriotic organizations capitalized on the announcement to reiterate their important role in the crusade against radicalism. "We have talked and talked; but the time for talking about this thing has passed," Richard M.Hurd, chairman of the executive committee of the American Guardian Society commented. "Irrespective of what the committee from Albany may do, we intend to prosecute the fight on Bolshevik sympathizers here to the last ditch." Dr. William T.Hornaday, director of the American Defense Society, agreed that the time for action was nigh. "At this very moment, the lying lure of Bolshevism is working day and night to plunge the whole civilized world into chaos and ruin," he said. Even religious groups used the opportunity to express their patriotic stance. The Reverend William L.Sullivan of the All Souls' Church issued a vehement condemnation of Bolshevism in both patriotic and moral terms. "It is time for the church," he concluded, "to lead in taking up the cudgels against this menace in our midst."[14]

Even a number of radical organizations and labor unions, presumably targets of the committee's investigation, welcomed formal scrutiny of their endeavors, if only to clear their names of any wrongdoing. Julius Gerber, executive director of the New York branch of the Socialist Party, openly admitted, "Certainly we're revolutionary. Certainly we favor an industrial democracy rather than the present brand. Why not?" Regarding the committee's efforts, he offered to open the party's books and allow the committee to explore the sources of its funding. Theresa Malkiel, representing the Rand School of Social Science, also agreed to provide the committee complete access to the school's papers.[15]

Others expressed a willingness to cooperate with the investigation, but questioned whether the committee could halt the spread of radicalism without addressing the very real problems that workers faced in America. Hugh Frayne, the head of the American Federation of Labor, and for nearly two years a representative on the country's War Labor Board, promised the federation's unconditional support for the committee's inquiry, and "all other anti-Bolshevik campaigns." "We are fully alive to the present menace," he commented; however "what is needed is not sudden, convulsive protests, but steady, unremitting, plodding, unspectacular, day-to-day work" against it. Mindful of the labor unrest underpinning the so-called radical threat, Frayne sought to focus the committee's attention on the terrible working conditions throughout the state and country. In his mind there was but one sure way to conquer the Bolshevist menace: "to starve them with plenty," he said. "We may talk as much as we please about agitators and Russian influence. Undoubtedly both exist [and] must be stringently guarded against." However, he warned, "we cannot guard against them so long as we permit exploitation to exist anywhere, so long as we leave life insecure and insufficient for a great share of our population."[16]

Algernon Lee, socialist alderman in New York City and director of the Rand School, shared Frayne's concern for the working class, and expressed hope that the committee would generate serious discussion on the issue. "If they would honestly try to find out and make public the cause of the growth of what they call Bolshevism," he commented, "it may be well worthwhile; the subject is even more important than most people realize." Lee even offered himself as a potential expert witness on the topic. "Nothing would please me more," he stated, "than to go before such a committee and give them an array of facts which I have at hand bearing directly on the subject and drawn from personal inquiry and observation." Lee knew, however, that the committee would never summon him for such testimony, and he remained openly skeptical of their intentions. "I am sure that such facts are just what they will not want," he observed. "Legislative committees are usually of two kinds—whitewashing committees and committees for the discovery of mares' nests," Lee concluded. "This one will be of the latter class. Dollars to doughnuts, they will have their conclusions ready to start with and will carefully dodge any facts that do not tally with their purpose."[17]

Bolstered by the support of many, and undaunted by the criticism of few, the committee quickly began to take shape at the end of March 1919. It consisted of four senators appointed by the President pro tem: John J. Boylan, Daniel J.Carroll, Clayton R.Lusk, and John B.Mullan. Thaddeus Sweet, Speaker of the Assembly added five of his colleagues: Frederick S. Burr, Edmund B.Jenks, Louis M.Martin, Peter P.McEligott, and William W.Pellett. In addition, Sweet tapped Lusk, a freshman senator from Cortland, as chairman of the committee, although he never clarified the reasons underlying the selection. Lusk, a 1902 graduate of Cornell University's School of Law, whose background was in business and foreign trade, had served only two months in the legislature and had no previous experience in the investigation of radical activities. His views, however, were sufficiently conservative for the position. He frequently expressed his nativist attitude toward radicals by referring to them as "alien enemies." Specifically, Lusk blamed America's social problems on "the virtually unrestricted immigration...of criminals, paupers, and the politically discontented" who were largely "shiftless... and without ideals of honesty and personal morality." To him, the social, political, and economic harm created by radicalism was quite clear. "Here in the United States," he concluded, "it threatens practically everything that by tradition, and as a result of the established American habit of moral thinking, we hold dear."[18]

Within two weeks of his appointment, Lusk arranged a series of conferences with State Attorney General Charles D.Newton to outline the strategy underlying the investigation. Given the $20,000 cut in the original appropriation, both decided to limit the staff to essential members, and to make use of the state's resources as much as possible. As a result, Newton agreed to serve as official counsel to the committee, with the assistance of his Deputy Attorney General Samuel Berger. Furthermore, the committee repeatedly requested and received help from local district attorneys and police departments throughout the state, as well as from the Department of Justice and the Bureau of Immigration in Washington, D.C. The only private individuals Lusk hired were a small staff of translators to examine foreign newspapers, periodicals, and documents, and Clarence L.Converse, formerly a private detective for a local express company.[19]

To complete his staff, Lusk sought an expert in radical activities, someone with specific knowledge that he and his fellow committee members lacked. Archibald Stevenson eagerly leapt at the opportunity and offered his services as special counsel free of charge. Despite his disappointment concerning the Overman Committee's unwillingness to take concrete steps to combat radicalism throughout the country, Stevenson remained hopeful that the Lusk Committee's investigation would bear fruit. By the spring of 1919, Stevenson had clearly established himself as the foremost "red hunter" in the U.S. Years later, historian Walter Nelles described him as a zealot in his pursuit of radicals. "To such minds as his," he concluded, "'un-Americanism' was the crime of crimes, and the definition of 'un-American' was comprehensive." Specifically, critics decried the ideas for which Woodrow Wilson stood before the war because they were not helpful in defeating Germany. In Stevenson's mind, they were "equally 'un-American' after the war because they were not helpful in the greater task of crushing Bolshevism," Nelles concluded.[20] However, Stevenson's zealous approach to the investigation stemmed in large part from a firm belief in its task. A contemporary criticism of the committee's work, written by members of the People's Freedom Union in 1920, considered Stevenson sincere in his beliefs. "Anyone who talks with him for five minutes will appreciate his sincerity," they wrote; "he sees himself as one of the saviors of American institutions, now threatened by the menace of a foreign philosophy." Given that Stevenson believed "with all his heart and soul" that Bolshevism represented a serious threat to the American way of life, the People's Freedom Union understood why he committed his time and effort to assisting the Lusk Committee. Right or wrong, their report concluded, Stevenson's opinions came to dominate the work of the committee, to the point "that it might as fittingly be called the Stevenson Committee."[21]

Little was heard of the Lusk Committee for the remainder of March and most of April, 1919. During these intervening weeks, they established a temporary headquarters in the Murray Hill Hotel in New York City, where Lusk continued to work with Newton, together developing a strategy to expose the Bolshevik infrastructure in the state. Along with Stevenson, they used much of the time to manipulate the press in an effort to heighten public hysteria in order to justify the committee's subsequent activities. One week prior to its first official hearing, Senate President pro tem Walters, an ex-officio committee member, announced his possession of evidence that proved radicals in America received hundreds of thousands of dollars from Russia to promote propaganda in the U.S. He concluded "that there is a thoroughly organized plan worked out by the Russian Bolsheviki to seize the reins of government in this country, and the head and brains of this movement is right here in the heart of New York." Rather than questioning how Walters came into possession of this evidence, in light of the fact that the committee had yet to meet, the press embellished Walter's comments into front page headlines. The New York *Tribune*, for example, wrote of information revealed by "authoritative sources" concerning "parlor radicals" in the city. Stevenson's infamous lists clearly were not far in the offing.[22]

When Stevenson officially joined the committee, the press seized upon his appearance with glee. This intense young man with his card indexes and penchant for the detective role presented a rare opportunity. What may have been a dull legislative investigation became good copy with his daily revelations of plots for armed uprisings and nests of anarchists. Despite the lack of concrete proof, Stevenson and the committee members spent the next seven months filling newspapers with stories of impending revolution, and the newspapers willingly obliged. In what was typically the cut-throat business of professional journalism, where success or failure depended upon scoops and circulation, leading newspapers in New York City were in general agreement regarding the importance of the Lusk Committee's inquiry. The publicity was not at all accidental. On June 3rd, Lusk and Stevenson invited editors from major newspapers throughout New York City to a luncheon to discuss their impending investigation into radicalism. Editors of the New York *Call* correctly assessed the well-planned news strategy developed by the committee. "If anyone thinks that the Lusk Committee did not understand the importance of yoking up the newspapers in their campaign against Bolshevism they are in sad error," they wrote. With the mainstream press solidly supporting the investigation, the committee prepared to commence its inquiry.[23]

Events surrounding May Day, an international holiday celebrating labor solidarity, prompted Lusk to move beyond the preliminary stages of his work and undertake concrete steps to uncover the extent of radical plots throughout the state. On April 28, Mayor Ole Hanson of Seattle received a small package at his office. Since he was out of town on a speaking tour, it remained unopened throughout the day. However, before Hanson's secretary left that evening, she noticed the box leaking a corrosive substance across the mayor's desk. The solution was acid; the package, a homemade bomb. Hanson was indignant upon hearing of the attempt on his life. "If they have the courage why don't they attack me like men," he asked, "instead of playing the part of cowardly assassins?"[24]

Since the bomb did no damage, and the target was the noted red baiter credited for defeating the radical menace during the Seattle General Strike of the previous winter, the event created little stir among the general public. Even the New York *Tribune* devoted less than two paragraphs on the eleventh page of a twenty-two page edition to the story. However, it received greater attention when a similar bomb exploded the next day at the home of U.S. Senator Thomas Hardwick in Atlanta, Georgia. Hardwick was not present when the package arrived, but his maid lost both of her hands in the explosion, and his wife suffered serious burns about her face and neck. Although perplexed by the coincidence of two bombs a country apart, the authorities still found little reason to link the two events, or to raise suspicion of a concerted Bolshevik plot.

While Hanson may have been an obvious target of radical agitators, Hardwick was not. As former chair of the Senate Immigration Committee, Hardwick proposed stronger laws to prevent questionable aliens from entering the U.S.; however, he never came close to transforming his agenda into an anti-radical crusade. Even the socialist periodical, *The Liberator,* labeled him "about as near radical as a senator could get." Hardwick, himself, refused to label the bomb threat as part of a larger plot, instead attributing it to "just plain cussedness."[25]

Further revelations the next day would change the minds of both Hanson and Hardwick, as well as a nation increasingly captivated by newspaper headlines concerning the bombings. While riding the subway home from his job as a parcels clerk in a New York City post office, Charles Kaplan read the New York *Evening World's* coverage of the latest events in Atlanta. In particular, photographs of the bomb packages caught his eye, and further descriptions in the article compelled him to exit the subway and return to work. Upon entering his office, Kaplan examined sixteen packages he had set aside three days earlier for insufficient postage. They matched the newspaper description of the Hanson and Hardwick packages perfectly—seven inches long and a scant three inches wide, the "infernal machines" included a wooden tube filled with explosives and triggered by an acid detonator. Each package had a Gimbel Brothers return address, and was marked "Novelty Sample." After contacting the police, postal inspectors immediately began searching throughout their other city offices, as well as nationwide, to identify similar boxes. The investigation uncovered a total of 36 bombs designed to explode in conjunction with the May Day labor celebrations.[26]

The list of potential bomb victims read as a "Who's Who" of leading industrialists and government officials who championed anti-radical causes to varying degrees. Businessmen targeted by the bombers included investment banker and steel magnate J.P.Morgan, as well as oil refinery tycoon John D.Rockefeller. Most prominent among government officials on the list was U.S. Attorney General A. Mitchell Palmer, who had recently reorganized the Department of Justice to include a new General Intelligence Division to investigate seditious and anarchistic activities throughout the country and to compile an index file of leading radical agitators. To head the new division, Palmer chose a recent graduate of the Georgetown University School of Law, J.Edgar Hoover.

Other government targets of the bomb plot included Secretary of Labor William B.Wilson, Ellis Island Immigration Commissioner Frederic C.Howe, General Immigration Commissioner Anthony J.Caminetti, Postmaster General Albert S.Burleson, who had the authority to exclude radical literature from the U.S. mail, and Senators William H.King, Ellis Smoot, and Lee S.Overman, all strong opponents of organized labor. Among the prominent jurists whom the bombers intended to harm were Associate Justice of the U.S. Supreme Court Oliver Wendell Holmes, Jr., and Judge Kenesaw Landis, who presided over the trial and sentencing of Socialist Congressman Victor Berger and William "Big Bill" Haywood, the founder of the Industrial Workers of the World. Even state and local officials were not immune from danger; the bombers had prepared packages for delivery to Mayor John F.Hylan of New York City, Mayor William W. Wood of Boston, Governor Harold Sproul of Pennsylvania, and New York City Police Commissioner Richard Enright.[27]

The immediate response to the bomb plot teetered precariously between vigilance and hysteria. Front-page headlines across the country announced that "Reds Planned May Day Murders" and warned a nervous public to "Beware Box If It Comes Through Mail—Do Not Open It—Call the Police Bomb Squad." As a result, many concerned citizens destroyed normal mail and packages by submerging them in buckets and bathtubs filled with water in an effort to defuse suspected explosives. In the ensuing week, several newspaper and magazine editors clamored for authorities to take concrete measures to crush what they perceived to be a serious and extensive radical threat. Repeated calls to "hang the dynamitards" and "deport the human vermin" came from every circle. The Philadelphia *Inquirer* warned that, unless the government took action, "we may as well invite Lenin and Trotsky to come here and set up business at once." Benevolent societies and churches also issued a call to arms. In the journal *United Presbyterian,* church leaders encouraged "every true lover of God and his country" to "hit with an axe whenever and wherever appears this evil head of anarchy."[28]

Such press commentary served only to fan the flames of hysteria that had grown throughout the winter and spring of 1919. For months preceding the May Day bomb scare, newspapers and magazines inundated the American public with descriptions and cartoons of whiskered, wild-eyed radicals, wearing tattered coats whose pockets overflowed with bombs and dynamite. To some extent, the emerging stereotype had a basis in propaganda, if not fact. The wording of an anarchist poster, distributed throughout Boston in January 1919 in response to the rising threats of deportation, warned "the senile fossils ruling the United States" that they would soon "see red." It concluded "The storm is within and very soon will leap and crash and annihilate you in blood and fire.... We will dynamite you!" Subsequent investigations of alleged bomb plots in Chicago and Pittsburgh in March and April further perpetuated the emerging mental image, associating radicalism with extreme violence, in many Americans' minds. Although neither investigation uncovered any groups, conspiracies, or even actual weapons of destruction, such mysterious tales more than prepared the general public to explode when real bombs materialized.[29]

Not all newspapers viewed the May Day bombs as signs of a greater radical conspiracy, however. Although more cautious analyses were few and far between, they were present. The Pittsburgh *Post* warned against the temptation to resort immediately to wholesale arrests, deportations, and lynchings. Other journalists attributed the bombs to a small handful of extreme anarchists, discounting the notion of a larger, organized conspiracy. To suggest the latter, wrote the editors of the Seattle *Post-Intelligencer*, was "to convict ourselves of a mild form of hysteria." Radical publications, such as *The Liberator*, viewed the plot as an effort by the authorities to frame anarchist and socialist groups in America. The police and government officials "are interested in 'getting' the leaders of radicalism," the newspaper concluded, "and feel the need of a stronger public opinion before they can act."[30]

Despite some newspapers' efforts to downplay the conspiracy theory, most public officials acted swiftly upon the widespread belief that organized radicals were behind the effort to disrupt the nation's political and economic system. The New York City Police Department raided all known meeting places of the I.W.W. on the evening they discovered the packages, and heightened their surveillance of other suspected radicals. Over the subsequent week, detectives reported "good clues [and] progress" in their effort to "run down" those responsible for the bombs. Mayor Hanson, in typical fashion, offered his advice and personal assistance. "I trust Washington will buck up and hang or incarcerate for life all the anarchists," he said. "If the government doesn't clean them up, I will."[31]

The bomb scare also forced the Lusk Committee to expedite its investigation. The day following the discovery of the explosives, Lusk announced his plans to subpoena all socialist, anarchist, Bolshevik, and I.W.W. organizations that maintained headquarters in New York City. "We expect to go into this whole business of violence which is being advocated by prominent agitators," he stated. "We are sure that society will be made safer because of the facts we expect to unearth." Specific targets of the committee included those anarchist groups affiliated with Alexander Berkman and Emma Goldman, the Socialist Sunday Schools operating on the Lower East Side of the city, and the Left-Wing Socialists headquartered at the Rand School of Social Science. Of greatest interest, Lusk declared, were questions regarding such groups' funding, their ties to Bolshevik Russia, and their advocacy of violence to bring about social reform in America. However, he promised, the committee had "no intention of attacking the Socialist Party" simply because it existed in opposition to the Republican and Democratic parties. "The investigation is aimed at Reds who are trying to 'put over' reforms by violence under the protection of a well recognized party," he observed. Despite such laudable goals, the committee quickly succumbed to the hysteria gripping the country. In the ensuing six months no group, not even the "well recognized" Socialist Party, would escape Lusk's net.[32]

Events taking place on May Day added to the growing public fear of radicalism, and led the Lusk Committee to quicken the pace of its preliminary inquiry. Typically, the United States remained oblivious to the labor demonstrations occurring annually on May 1st throughout Europe; however, May 1, 1919, proved different. Several cities around the country witnessed socialists, communists, anarchists, and others staging elaborate parades and mass meetings. The police intervened in many cases and, with the help of outraged citizens, employed force to bring a swift, and often-times bloody, conclusion to the events. In Boston, 1,500 members of the Lettish Workmen's Association sponsored a red flag parade despite lacking a city permit for the event. When ordered by the police to cease their activities, the group continued to march amidst defiant choruses of "To hell with the permit!" Angered by the demonstration, bystanders formed themselves into small bands of vigilantes, intent upon stopping the marchers and detaining other socialists walking the streets. At one point the chaos erupted into a full-scale attack on the Boston Socialist Party headquarters. Eventually, the police arrested over 100 people during the riot; all were socialists. The courts later convicted fourteen of the marchers for disturbing the peace, and sentenced each to a maximum of eighteen months in prison.[33]

A similar series of events also erupted in New York City on May Day. Early that morning, a group of World War I veterans raided the Russian People's House, a social club for ethnic Russian immigrants located on East Fifteenth Street. In addition to collecting all of the printed material and setting it ablaze in the street, the soldiers forced those people gathered at the house to sing the *Star Spangled Banner*. Dissatisfied with the results of their handiwork, the soldiers joined a larger mob of 400 citizens later that afternoon to disrupt a reception at the new offices of the socialist newspaper, The New York *Call*. After smashing several pieces of furniture, the crowd forced the 700 guests into the streets and mercilessly beat seventeen of them. Days later, one soldier defended the riots, claiming they were a direct response to the inflammatory editorials published in the *Call* and other radical publications. The *Call* saw the event in a different light, and referred to the raids as "orgies of brutality."[34]

Despite the serious nature of the uprisings in Boston and New York City, they paled in comparison to the melee awaiting Cleveland that day. The trouble began when a group of Victory Loan workers attempted to stop a red flag parade that local socialist labor organizer Charles Ruthenberg led down Superior Avenue. The mob injured twenty socialist marchers in the fight that ensued. In a similar effort to stop a red flag march in the Cleveland Public Square, ex-soldiers drove a tank into the crowd of protesters, and sent five radicals to the hospital in ambulances. Additional riots erupted in the business district on Euclid Avenue, where patrons threw shoes, glass bottles, and other merchandise at socialist demonstrators, and on Prospect Avenue, where citizens raided the Socialist Party headquarters and hurled the office equipment and furniture into the street. As in Boston and New York City, all of those arrested by the Cleveland police were either socialists or members of other radical organizations.[35]

Although a hysterical, general public triggered the May Day riots in most cities, the press quickly blamed wild-eyed, bomb-throwing radicals for the violence. Newspapers throughout the country touted the demonstrations as dress rehearsals for the impending revolution. Cries urging legislators to "curb the Bolshevik menace threatening our country" dotted newspaper editorials from coast to coast. A few urged restraint, and warned that "cracking heads is no argument" to the alleged radical threat. But, many more journalists demanded immediate action even at the possible expense of the Bill of Rights. The editor of the Salt Lake *Tribune* lamented, "Free speech has been carried to the point where it is an unrestrained menace." The Washington *Post* offered a cure for the nation's ills: "Silence the incendiary advocates of force.... Bring the law's hand down upon the violent and the inciter of violence; do it now!"[36]

The May Day riots had a distinct effect on the Lusk Committee. Although they had originally planned for preliminary investigations to continue well into June, at which time they would commence public hearings, the committee hastened their pace. Following an emergency meeting on May 6, Senator Lusk announced to the press that the committee possessed "very serious and startling evidence...appalling in more ways than one" of a "red plan to bring New York City to a standstill by means of a massive demonstration." Although he refused to discuss details of the plan or to reveal the evidence, Lusk was convinced of the serious nature of the threat. "Many who were originally skeptical of the need for such an investigation as ours," he stated, "have become convinced and are impressed with the importance of the task." The time for waiting had passed; the urgency of the situation required immediate action. Lusk eagerly unleashed the men to whom he referred as his "secret service force" and "chief inquisitor" to help his committee "sift the chaff from the wheat" among the growing mounds of evidence in their possession.[37]

Any further impetus the Lusk Committee needed to begin producing tangible results occurred on the evening of June 2, 1919, when a series of bombs exploded within the same hour in eight major cities across the country, resulting in two deaths and several injuries. In addition to devastating the mayor's home in Cleveland, similar devices destroyed the homes of businessmen in Paterson, New Jersey, and in Philadelphia; judges' homes in Boston, New York City, and Pittsburgh; and a state legislator's residence in Newtonville, Massachusetts. The most spectacular bombing occurred in Washington, D.C., where the culprit killed himself while planting explosives near the front of Attorney General Palmer's residence. The bomb detonated prematurely when the person placing it tripped on the stairs leading to the front door, but it succeeded in destroying the facade of Palmer's home and broke neighbors' windows up and down the length of RStreet. Palmer and his family were home at the time of the explosion, having just retired for the evening. They were visibly shaken, but otherwise unharmed.[38]

A subsequent investigation of the bomb intended for Palmer revealed an array of contradictory evidence. Yet, the conclusion of that inquiry, as well as of the bombs planted in other cities, left no doubt as to the master-minds behind the explosions. The police decided that all were part of an anarchist plan to disrupt the government and business infrastructure of the United States. Although only body fragments remained from the man who attempted to plant dynamite outside the Attorney General's house, detectives concluded from his "dark skin color" and hat that he was an Italian immigrant from Philadelphia. When further inspection revealed two left legs among the rubble, police announced that there must have been two bombers, operating in conspiracy with one another, an explanation that led some newspapers to joke that two left legs certainly explained why the bomber stumbled on the front steps. The most incriminating evidence, according to investigators, was the discovery of an anarchist pamphlet on the ground near Palmer's home. Written by "The Anarchist Fighters" and entitled *Plain Words*, it concluded: "There will have to be bloodshed; we will not dodge; there will have to be murder; we will kill; there will have to be destruction; we will destroy; we are ready to do anything and everything to suppress the capitalist class."[39]

As with the bomb scare of the preceding month, the police, the press, and the public blamed advocates of anarchism, socialism, communism, radicalism, and other contrary "-isms" for the event. Together with the Seattle General Strike of the previous winter and the May Day disturbances still fresh in people's minds, it took little effort to convince many Americans of the existence of a concerted plot to bring revolution to the shores of their country. In the ensuing weeks, the calls for limitations on free speech gave way to vociferous cries for violent repression of the radicals responsible for such uprisings. Newspaper editors throughout the country demanded, "these gadflies be swatted," and that there be "a few free treatments in the electric chair." By mid-June, the general public was, as historian Robert Murray has written, "genuinely alarmed" by the perceived threat.[40]

The government response to the growing public outcry was swift. Palmer, who had previously dragged his feet in the investigation of radicalism, requested and received a $500,000 congressional appropriation to unravel radical plots throughout the nation and to prosecute those responsible. His new assistant, J.Edgar Hoover, assumed the responsibility for compiling files and indexing information on known radical individuals and organizations. On Capitol Hill, Senator Thomas Walsh of Montana sponsored legislation proposing a peacetime sedition law to imprison any person who displayed a red flag, distributed anarchistic literature through the mail, or supported the overthrow of the U.S. government. To some degree, such steps represented posturing by public officials who saw the issue of radicalism as a potential gold mine for the upcoming elections in 1920. To a greater extent, however, they were a direct response to a public growing more hysterical over the thought of Bolsheviks bringing revolution to America.[41]

While Palmer and Congress laid the groundwork for steps they would undertake months later, the Lusk Committee in New York prepared to take immediate action against those financing the plot and those who fanned the flames. The time for planning and talking had passed. The method of allowing radicals to proselytize without interference, Lusk noted, "was given a fair trial" for months, "and the result of ignoring those revolutionary activities was not highly satisfactory; the time has come for decisive action."[42] In the wake of the second bomb scare in just over a month, Senator Lusk scheduled the committee's first public hearing for June 12th, a full month ahead of the original schedule. Their initial target: the Soviet Bureau. Although Bureau officials claimed to operate nothing more than a commercial mission designed to secure economic ties with American businesses, Lusk suspected otherwise. In the minds of Lusk and many others, the Soviet Bureau represented the financial arm of the impending revolution that threatened the country.

The Lusk Committee's decision to quicken the pace of their investigation and target the Soviet Bureau capped a tumultuous spring for New Yorkers. Two bomb scares and a series of May Day riots convinced many citizens that the cries of "red revolution" represented a serious danger. Although in hindsight the events were largely coincidental, and clearly did not signal an all-out attack on the American way of life, their timing contributed to such an interpretation. Facing post-war economic and social upheaval, the presence of new radical political parties and organizations, and politicians urging the public to connect the two phenomena, spectacular events such as bombings and riots became volatile catalysts. The formation of the Lusk Committee was a predictable response to the growing public outcry. New Yorkers wanted their political leaders to safeguard their lives from the radical menace. Although a few wary legislators questioned the Lusk Committee's agenda, the vast majority of New Yorkers clamored for talk to give way to action. The Red Scare had reached New York City, and the colossus of all amusements was set to begin.

Chapter 3
The Origins and Operations of the Soviet Bureau

LED BY LUDWIG C.A.K.MARTENS, WHO SERVED AS THE UNOFFICIAL Soviet ambassador to the United States, the Soviet Bureau represented one of the most concerted efforts by Lenin's Bolshevik regime to normalize relations between Russia and the U.S. during the period of non-recognition, from 1917 to 1933. Upon receiving his appointment on January 2,1919, Martens established the offices of the Bureau in the World Tower Building in New York City. The location was indicative of Martens' stated mission: to establish economic ties with American businesses, including signing contracts to purchase supplies for Bolshevik Russia. However, from the outset, federal government officials questioned the Soviet Bureau's motives, and as a result wavered on the question to grant Martens formal diplomatic recognition.

Hoping to receive recognition through normal channels, Martens contacted the U.S. State Department on March 19, 1919. His credentials, signed by Soviet Commissar for Foreign Affairs, Gregory Tchitcherin, authorized Martens to undertake four tasks in the name of the Russian Federative Socialist Soviet Republic: (1) to assume jurisdiction over all real estate and property held by the embassy and consulates of the former Provisional Government; (2) to solicit and answer claims regarding the material interests of Bolshevik Russia; (3) to prosecute all civil and criminal cases on behalf of the Soviet government; and (4) to defray all expenses, receive money, and issue receipts in the name of the government.[1] Accompanying his credentials, Martens dispatched a memorandum to the State Department detailing the intentions of his government and providing an analysis of his country's internal affairs.

To dispel the repeated press accounts of chaos, terror, and violence in Russia, Martens stressed "that the Soviet Government has given all such proofs of stability, permanence, popular support and constructive ability as ever have been required from any Government in the world as a basis for political recognition and commercial intercourse." Furthermore, acknowledging that Russia's economic prosperity was tied to the development of commercial relations with the U.S., Martens announced his country's readiness to purchase $200,000,000 in railroad supplies, agricultural machinery, electrical supplies, automobiles, shoes, clothing, medical supplies, and food, among many other products. The director of the Bureau also emphasized Russia's ability to export numerous goods to the U.S., including flax, hemp, hides, furs, lumber, grain, and a variety of minerals.[2]

Uncertainty regarding the Bolsheviks' ability to maintain political control in the wake of Russia's ongoing civil war and a legacy of mistrust towards Lenin's regime made the State Department reluctant to grant Martens official diplomatic recognition. Throughout the spring of 1919, officials in Washington walked a fine line of maintaining open channels, yet not according the Soviets the formal recognition they sought. Secretary of State Robert Lansing confirmed the American position in a highly classified "green cipher" cable to the U.S. embassy in Petrograd. He noted the department's desire "to keep in somewhat closer and informal touch with Bolshevik authorities using such channels as will avoid any official recognition," but added, "This Government is by no means prepared to recognize Bolshevik Government officially." As late as March 21, 1919, the New York *Times* cited reports from "well-informed quarters in Washington" questioning the likelihood of Martens' recognition at any time in the near future.[3]

Nonetheless, newspapers continued to speculate on the official status of the Soviet Bureau. On March 22, 1919, the State Department denied receiving any credentials from the alleged Soviet representative. One week later, however, the department acknowledged the receipt of "certain papers ...sent to the State Department by Martens," but refused to comment officially on his efforts.[4] This ambiguity on the part of the State Department stemmed from its decision to wait for President Wilson's review of the findings of William Bullitt's secret mission to Russia to investigate the country's post-revolutionary political and economic conditions. Undertaken in March 1919, this fact-finding mission on behalf of the American and British governments was an attempt to alleviate tensions between the Bolsheviks and the Allies in order to pave the way for future relations. Martens banked on the success of the mission, hoping that a favorable report to the President might ensure America's formal recognition of the Soviet government in Russia. Bullitt, however, dashed those hopes when he reported on widespread atrocities that were occurring under Lenin's heavy-handed rule.[5]

The eventual failure of Bullitt's mission, capped by Wilson's repudiation of the Soviets' diplomatic initiative, resulted in the State Department's first formal announcement on May 6, 1919, regarding the Soviet Bureau in particular. Having refused recognition of Martens or any other representative of the Bolshevik regime, the State Department urged Americans to exercise "extreme caution" when dealing with the Soviet Bureau. This stated policy of non-recognition of the Bolsheviks, already in place in varying degrees since 1917, remained America's official position until 1933.[6]

Undaunted by the statement, Martens proceeded throughout the spring of 1919 to select a staff of workers to perform the daily tasks of the bureau. Gregory Weinstein, the Director of the Department of General Office Services for the bureau, drafted a memorandum entitled, "A Rough Diagram of the Proposed Organization of the Bureau of Soviet Russia," in which he proposed the creation of six committees under the control of individual administrators answering to "Chief Executive Officer" Martens. Of utmost importance, according to Weinstein, was the functional autonomy of each department. "The entire personnel of all divisions," he concluded, "may be consolidated in one large room, but it is essential that there be no mixing of duties. All matters relating to a particular division should be referred to the person having intimate knowledge and training of the matter."[7] Martens agreed with Weinstein's proposal, and established the departments essential to the bureau's successful operation: diplomatic, commercial, railroad, financial, statistical, and general office. Throughout its brief tenure, the Soviet Bureau employed a permanent staff of thirty people, with an additional ten assistants serving on a temporary basis.

Martens, himself, served as director of the bureau and representative of the Russian Socialist Federal Soviet Republic. Born of German parents in Bakhmut (now Artemovsk), Russia, on January 1, 1875, Ludwig Christian Alexander Karlovich Martens studied at the Petersburg Technological Institute until 1896. After joining Lenin's League for the Liberation of the Working Class in 1895, he served a three-year prison sentence in Kresty Jail for publishing and distributing illegal literature and for organizing strikes among factory workers. Deported to Germany in 1899, he moved to England in 1906, where he maintained close ties with Bolshevik leaders in Switzerland during the pre-war years. In 1916, Martens traveled to the United States where he became a frequent contributor to *Novy Mir,* the New York City Russian Socialist newspaper edited by Leon Trotsky. Prior to being named director of the Soviet Bureau in 1919, Martens served both as vice president of Weinberg and Posner, an engineering firm that soon developed close commercial ties with the bureau, and as the American representative of the Demidoff Iron and Steel Works, the largest steel producer in Russia. In a foretelling description of Martens, Benjamin Gitlow, a leader in the Communist Labor Party, portrayed the director of the Soviet Bureau as "a quiet, mild-tempered man; he did not look like a Russian. Fair of complexion, with blonde hair and mustache, he looked more like a middle class businessman than what went for the accepted description of a Bolshevik." Well-traveled, intellectual, business-oriented, experienced in revolutionary activities, and enjoying the full confidence of the Soviet authorities, Martens was the logical choice for directing Russian interests in the United States.[8]

Martens selected Santeri Nuorteva to serve as director of the Soviet Bureau's diplomatic department. Born in 1881 in Wiborg, Finland, to a Swedish father and Ukranian mother, Nuorteva briefly attended school in Finland before interrupting his studies for seven years to travel throughout Europe and South America. Upon his return, Nuorteva graduated from the University of Helsingfors in 1903 and began teaching foreign languages in local high schools. Joining the Finnish Labor Movement that same year, he became increasingly active as a newspaper editor and night school instructor in the socialist movement. His active roles in the abortive Russian Revolution of 1905 and in the reconstruction of the Finnish Constitution, earned Nuorteva a measure of political prominence in the country, and repeated election to the Finnish Parliament. His articles criticizing the policies of the Russian Tsar and the German Kaiser eventually led to Nuorteva's imprisonment in 1908 and in 1911. To avoid future confinement, Nuorteva immigrated to the U.S. in 1912, where he wrote numerous articles and books, organized night classes to educate Finnish immigrants in the English language, and lectured to Finnish Socialist groups.[9]

In charge of the commercial department was Abraham A. Heller, a Russian native who immigrated to America in 1891, and joined the socialist movement one year later. After graduating from Harvard University and entering the jewelry business in Paris for a number of years, Heller founded the International Oxygen Company in New York City, where he served as general manager until his appointment to the Soviet Bureau.[10] Equally important to the success of the commercial department was its assistant director, Evans Clark. Born August 9, 1888, in Orange, New Jersey, Clark earned degrees in economics from both

Amherst College and Harvard University, and a master's degree in political science from Columbia University. Clark affiliated with the Socialist Party in Cambridge, Massachusetts, in 1911, while studying at Harvard, and served as first president of the Boston Chapter of the Intercollegiate Socialist Society. From Cambridge, Clark moved to Princeton University where he taught political science from 1914 to 1917. His political leanings eventually cost him his job at Princeton when, in 1917, the University Trustees refused to renew his contract because of his involvement in local strikes. Later that year, as chairman of the Collegiate League for Morris Hillquit, Clark supported Hillquit's New York City mayoral campaign. Prior to his appointment to the Soviet Bureau, Clark was the director of the Bureau of Research for the Socialist aldermen's delegation in New York.[11]

Professor George V. Lomonossoff, whom Martens appointed to the position of director of the railroad department of the Soviet Bureau, had formerly served the Russian Provisional Government's Ministry of Ways and Communication as its representative in America. Committed to the Bolshevik cause, Lomonossoff relinquished to Martens on May 21, 1919, all "right, title and interests in and to all locomotives, car and freight car parts, rails, and railroad equipment" as well as all "contracts..., claims ..., monies, office furniture, books, files, documents, papers and other personal property" previously held by the Ministry of Ways and Communication. A significant portion of the financial assets Martens claimed to hold in America on behalf of the Soviet government included those forfeited by Lomonossoff when he renounced his affiliation with the Provisional Government and joined the staff of the Soviet Bureau. Recognized internationally as an expert on railroad and financial matters, his new responsibilities included purchasing rail materials, arranging ground transportation for products obtained in the U.S., and controlling railroad communications.[12]

Issac Hourwich, a native Russian and graduate of Petrograd University, served the bureau as the director of the statistical department, a division designed to collect data on American and Russian businesses. After immigrating to the U.S. at the turn of the century, Hourwich received his doctorate from Columbia University and accepted a position as professor of economics at the University of Chicago. Widely known as an authority on immigration, Hourwich served as the chief statistician on immigrant labor at the U.S. Department of Labor immediately prior to his appointment to the Soviet Bureau.[13]

Gregory Weinstein, the Director of the General Office Department, also known as the "chancellor" or "chief clerk," was born in Vilna, Russia, on July 1, 1880. After graduating from the Teachers Institute, he began a career of revolutionary activities as a Socialist in 1900. The Russian authorities arrested Weinstein at Brest-Litovsk in December 1905, and banished him to Siberia for four years. He escaped to Paris in 1906 and subsequently moved to Switzerland where, in 1911, he earned masters degrees in law and social science at the University of Geneva. In 1913, he emigrated to the U.S. where he accepted a position as associate editor of *Novy Mir,* before joining Martens' mission. Gitlow, a friend and fellow party member, remembered Weinstein as "an able writer, well versed in the movement, a good lecturer and speaker and in addition a fairly capable politician."[14]

Of the major participants in the Soviet Bureau's activities, none drew greater interest or provoked more intrigue than did the director of the finance department, Dr. Julius Hammer. Born in Odessa on October 3, 1874, Hammer emigrated to America with his parents one year later, where he eventually studied medicine. After joining the Socialist Labor Party early in his life, he became increasingly active in organizing steel mill workers into trade unions. His efforts led him to become a founding member of the American Communist Party in 1919. Preoccupied with a flourishing pharmaceutical business, Allied Drug and Chemical Company, and his duties as a physician, Hammer seemed ill-suited to serve as an active director in the Soviet Bureau. Three qualities, however, endeared him to Martens: his socialist leanings, powerful commercial connections, and financial assets. Industrialist and philanthropist Armand Hammer, writing about his father years later, recalled "My father did have a close connection with Ludwig Martens and as an unofficial trade adviser to the unrecognized Russian diplomatic mission in New York."[15]

With his staff in place to conduct the operations of his still unofficial "embassy" in the U.S., Martens next turned to the task of obtaining the capital to finance his venture. Though he had previously announced the Soviet government's willingness to purchase $200,000,000 worth of American products, Martens lacked the nearly $1,000 weekly funds to pay the salaries of his employees and the bureau's costs of operation.[16] Despite this shortfall, the Lusk Committee insisted that Martens' organization was financing the dissemination of radical propaganda throughout the country. In reality, the Soviet Bureau procured the bulk of its funds from a variety of sources, four of which were most prominent: (1) via private courier, (2) from funds held by Professor

Lomonossoff during his days as American representative of the Russian Provisional Government, (3) from money provided by the American Commercial Association to Promote Trade with Russia, and (4) from Dr. Hammer, the director of the Soviet Bureau's finance department.

J.Edgar Hoover's investigation of radical activities in 1919–1920 provided some credibility for the first theory, the existence of an international network by which Martens received money and his instructions via private courier from the Bolshevik authorities. In his book, *Masters of Deceit: The Story of Communism in America and How to Fight It,* Hoover recalled an episode when customs officials began searching seamen aboard the *S.S. Stockholm* when it docked in New York City. When one sailor turned back and ran down the pier, officials detained him for further investigation. A package found concealed in his trousers revealed a collection of envelopes, one sealed inside another, with the smallest holding over 200 uncut diamonds worth nearly $50,000. In addition, the package contained a type-written letter addressed to "Comrade Martens." "The smuggling of diamonds," Hoover wrote, "was one of the early Bolshevik techniques of financing operations in the United States."[17]

Benjamin Gitlow, in his autobiography *I Confess: The Truth About American Communism,* related a similar story in which he served as Martens' messenger. On November 8, 1919, while Gitlow addressed a meeting of the Lettish Club in Manhattan celebrating the anniversary of the Russian Revolution, police and private detectives raided the meeting and searched for membership cards among all who were present. "I had some confidential papers and money in my possession which involved Ludwig Martens, the official Soviet representative to the United States," Gitlow later wrote. "I slipped the package out of my pocket and dropped it behind the radiator in front of which I was standing."[18] Martenscorroborated such stories in his testimony before the Senate Foreign Relations Committee in February, 1920. In answer to questions posed by Senator George H.Moses of New Hampshire, he admitted that several couriers journeyed directly from Moscow to deliver funds to the Soviet Bureau, although few reached their final destination. According to Martens, several were shot in Finland and most others were captured in Germany.[19]

A second theory regarding the funding of the bureau, substantiated by a series of telegrams transmitted among Assistant Secretary of State Frank Polk, U.S. Ambassador to Sweden Ira N.Morris, and New York attorney Thomas L.Chadbourne, suggested that Professor Lomonossoff provided much of the original funding for the Soviet Bureau. In a revealing letter written five days after Martens' appointment as director, Chadbourne, representing Lomonossoff, requested Polk's assistance in locating the whereabouts of a large sum of Russian funds to which Lomonossoff laid claim: "Dear Frank. You were kind enough to say that [if] I could inform you of the status of the $25,000 item of personal funds belonging to Mr. & Mrs. Lomonossoff you would set in motion the machinery necessary to obtain it here for them." Following a series of telegrams, during which he located the money in Stockholm in the hands of Michael Gruzenberg, a Bolshevik agitator recently deported from Norway, Polk cabled Morris with the request "to facilitate transfer of this money to Prof. Lomonossoff in this country," provided the Minister in Stockholm could "do so without being involved with Bolshevik authorities." Simultaneously, Polk wired Chadbourne to inform him that, "while it is somewhat out of the department's line of action, I shall be glad...to see if I can have Mr. Gruzenberg remit the money to Prof. Lomonossoff." Regardless of the questionable nature of the State Department's actions, Polk succeeded in obtaining the bank draft from a Stockholm subsidiary of National City Bank of New York, and forwarding it to Lomonossoff, most likely for use in firiancing the Soviet Bureau.[20]

The third theory regarding the financing of the Soviet Bureau centered on the actions of the American Commercial Association to Promote Trade with Russia. Founded in January 1919, the association consisted of over 100 firms, many of which eventually signed contracts to conduct business with the bureau in the hope of pressuring the State Department, the War Trade Board, and the Federal Reserve Board to remove the restrictions on export licensing and financial transactions with Bolshevik Russia. Such firms included the Morris Meatpacking Company of Chicago, LeHigh Machine Company, and Bobroff Foreign Trading Company. The president of the group, Emerson P.Jennings, noted in his annual *Report to the Association* that the financial support of the Soviet Bureau "was the work of a group of American businessmen anxious to trade with Russia, rather than a plot financed by 'Soviet gold.'"[21]

Although Lomonossoff, the American Commercial Association, and the Bolshevik authorities, via private couriers, clearly provided some measure of funding for Martens' mission, the greatest amount of support came from the personal finances of Julius Hammer. Sometimes listed as "Treasurer" as well as Financial Director of the Bureau, Hammer, who did not himself draw a salary for his efforts, often provided the funds to meet the necessary demands of the weekly payroll. In his autobiography, Benjamin Gitlow commented that the "generous financial assistance" of Hammer "made the establishment of the 'Embassy' possible." A subsequent accountant's report concerning the activities of the Bureau corroborated Gitlow's claim.[22] Regardless of the source, Martens finally obtained enough funding to begin operations in earnest on April 1, 1919.

With the organization and funding in place, the Soviet Bureau was open for business. Martens began arranging the commercial contacts the Bolsheviks desired. In the years immediately following the Russian Revolution, Lenin had professed a strong belief in the necessity of American products for his country's economic and social improvement. During an interview with Karl H. von Wiegand of the American Universal Service news agency, he repeatedly stressed the Bolsheviks' willingness to offer American capitalists "gold for machines, implements, etc., which may be of use to us in transport and production. And not only gold but raw materials as well." The Russian leader reiterated his position in a subsequent interview with New York *World* correspondent Lincoln Ayre: "Some American observers are apparently beginning to realize that it is wiser to do profitable business with Russia than to make war on her, and this is a good sign. We shall require American goods, locomotives, automobiles, etc., more than those of any other country."[23]

Several observers, including both advocates and opponents of the Bolshevik ascendancy, corroborated Lenin's assessment. Most found an outlet for their views in the form of speeches and pamphlets circulated to American businessmen. A representative of the Russian Government Purchasing Commission during the tenure of the Provisional Government, speaking to the Foreign Trade Association of the Cincinnati Chamber of Commerce in April, 1917, emphasized the impact of the war on rendering the European powers incapable of supplying Russia with much needed industrial products. Following the war, only the United States with its war-time accumulation of capital and skilled workers would be capable of supplying the resources necessary "for pushing their foreign trade with Russia" and "developing her natural resources and means of transportation." The key to a mutually advantageous relationship, he suggested, was a combination of both American products and capital investment. Such a combination would allow Russia to develop its industrial capacity, as well as establish a favorable balance of trade. "It will be beneficial to the United States," he concluded, "because there is hardly any better investment for capital than a young country" like Russia.[24] Karl Radek, in his preface to New

York *Daily News* correspondent Arthur Ransome's report on the conditions in Russia, further underscored the fact that American capital had "its greatest market in the future" in Russia.[25]

Martens' endeavors throughout the spring of 1919 mirrored such sentiments. First, in an effort to liquidate the $200,000,000 in financial resources with which the bureau intended to conduct widespread commercial trade with American businesses, he immediately laid claim to all assets and property held by the former Russian Provisional Government. In a letter to Boris Bakhmeteff, whom the State Department continued to recognize as the official Russian ambassador in the U.S., Martens demanded the forfeiture of all money, property, and files of the Russian Embassy in Washington, D.C. The director of the Soviet Bureau declared that Bakhmeteff's position "became vacant" and his rights and titles "legally terminated" following the overthrow of the Provisional Government in November 1917; therefore, the so-called ambassador was "an alleged agent without a principal." Accusing Bakhmeteff and his staff of using Russian funds "for purposes openly hostile to the Russian people," Martens cautioned the ambassador to disregard the bureau's request "at your own peril."[26] Subsequent letters to National City Bank and Guaranty Trust Company reiterated Martens' claim to all Russian assets in the U.S., as did notices to many warehouses and firms holding Russian property.[27]

In the second step of his continued effort to organize commercial relations with American businessmen, Martens instructed Heller to write a pamphlet detailing the bureau's intentions. Published in late April, the pamphlet traced the history of American-Russian trade since 1913, under-scoring its relative insignificance during the prewar years. With the Bolshevik rise to power, however, Heller concluded, "there is an excellent opportunity of diverting the stream of Russian trade to the American market." Alluding to the comments of Poliakoff and Radek, he emphasized that "the United States is in a particularly favorable situation to replace Germany and Great Britain in the markets of Russia; she has some of the goods required practically in stock, ready to be shipped; she has the factories, the men, the raw material."[28] Inanappeal to efficiency-oriented and profit-minded American industrialists, Heller stressed the organizational aspects of the bureau: departments, under the guidance of competent directors, to deal with every branch of industry; the use of modern business methods to establish standards of quality and value; and the desire to purchase goods produced under trade union conditions, regardless of inherently higher prices. Furthermore, he repeated the willingness of the Bolshevik government to pay for American products in hard currency, in order to keep trade independent of the depreciated value of the ruble. Finally, the commercial director alluded to the availability of Russian ships, as well as easily accessible ports on the Baltic and Black Seas, which lent themselves to the success of a large volume of trade.

Such appeals struck a responsive chord among many American firms. Even before the bureau organized a staff and officially began operations, numerous businessmen expressed an interest in dealing with the Bolshevik representatives. By late March 1919, Martens felt he could "claim big success" with regard to his commercial proposition. Nuorteva concurred. "There has been a wider response than we anticipated," he claimed; "We are swamped with requests for commercial connections."[29] In an interview following the circulation of Heller's pamphlet, Martens provided a more detailed description of the bureau's early success. Contracts, he claimed, had been placed with nearly one hundred firms in the U.S., including a larger number of clothing and shoe manufacturers. Furthermore, his discussions with several banks yielded arrangements for Russian credit in America. The key, Martens emphasized, was for businesses to obtain an export license to allow shipment to Petrograd. The director of the Soviet Bureau was shrewd; he realized that for the American government to grant export licenses, some level of diplomatic or trade recognition must be proffered.[30]

On no less than five separate occasions representatives of the Soviet Bureau announced their readiness to receive bids from American manufacturers as soon as export licenses to Petrograd or Riga were secured. While at first glance not surprising—the U.S. government required export licenses for all goods shipped overseas, regardless of the destination—the licensing stipulation invoked by the bureau indicated their desire to achieve diplomatic recognition as well as secure trade relations. Rather than the standard procedure of the purchasing country obtaining the license, the Soviet Bureau placed the onus on the American manufacturers. Martens hoped that such a demand would result in businessmen pressuring the U.S. government to ease trade restrictions against Bolshevik Russia and recognize Lenin's authority. One businessman corroborated the bureau's strategy in an interview with the New York *Tribune*. In his opinion "the export license stipulation" was made by Russia "with the idea of stirring up interest upon the part of American manufacturers" in the removal of restrictions against that country.[31]

The third step in the initial operations of the Soviet Bureau involved Martens' effort to arrange a conference of technically skilled workers who wished to return and offer their services to Russia. Acknowledging the devastation Russia suffered due to the questionable policies of the tsarist regime, involvement in the war, and the effects of the revolution, Martens argued "that the great need of Russia today is for men of technical ability, men who have gone through colleges and have studied physics and chemistry and engineering and allied arts, as well as for men who are able to apply these arts in the creation of industries."[32] On May 10, 1919, in an open letter to all Russian citizens living in the U.S., he announced a conference to be held in New York City in early July to discuss a range of issues relating to the question of technically skilled workers, in particular: (1) to determine how many were willing to return and offer their services to their homeland; and, (2) to develop an educational network in America designed to train a greater number of Russian citizens in a variety of technical skills. Martens held high hopes for the success of the conference, believing that "among Russian citizens in America there is felt a keen desire to render a service to Soviet Russia with the knowledge and skill which they have acquired in America."[33]

In his keynote address to the conference participants, Heller reinforced Martens' sentiments. Citing numerous reports which concluded that "Russian industry is badly crippled," the commercial director placed much of the blame on "a lack of competent men, technically trained men, who could make one thing do in place of another or who could transfer articles from one place where they are less important to another where they are more urgently needed." Such tasks, he concluded, "require just the kind of talent which you, Comrades, have." In a final appeal for workers adept in the areas of transportation, mining, agriculture, and manufacturing, Heller pleaded, "Whatever little help we can give on this side of the water should be given freely and without reserve."[34]

Martens' followed the conference with a bid to develop a vocational education program designed to train Russian citizens living in America and prepare them for their return to Soviet Russia. In an effort to utilize the advantages extended by the educational institutions in the U.S., he devised a plan to enroll a significant number of Russian students in American schools. Through specialized and intensive training, compressed into the shortest possible time, Martens envisioned the formation of a Russian labor force experienced in the most recent technological advances. The Bolshevik representative communicated his interests in a letter to Dr. E.E. Brown of New York University. Conceding, "the past economic history of Russia has not been of such a nature as to train a large number of competent persons," the director of the Soviet Bureau requested information and circulars regarding programs which might allow Russian citizens to "avail themselves of the excellent educational resources of America."[35]

Despite the bureau's efforts to organize its financial resources, to issue positive statements concerning the mutual advantages of American-Russian trade, and to arrange for a technically-skilled labor force, the success of such endeavors depended upon a positive response from the U.S. government with regard to a commercial relationship between the Bolshevik regime and American firms. The Wilson administration, however, refused to sanction economic ties with a government that lacked official diplomatic recognition. As early as February 1919, the Federal Reserve Board, acting at the request of the State Department, prohibited foreign exchange transactions between the two countries. Claiming knowledge of evidence "that large sums of money had been made available in the United States for use of Bolshevik agents," the Board joined forces with Great Britain and France in suspending such arrangements.[36] Nonetheless, as of late April, the Bolshevik authorities in Russia and the staff of the Soviet Bureau anticipated an imminent end to the Allied economic blockade and a resumption of normal trade relations. Although U.S. authorities had taken no concrete steps toward the normalization of relations, Heller noted "many indications that trade relations will be established in the near future." The plan, he announced, was "to be prepared for such an eventuality, so that as soon as the existing blockade is lifted, goods may be shipped without a single day's delay."[37]

Heller's hopes were furthered bolstered by reports that a number of government officials, including U.S. Senators Henry L.Myers of Montana, Harry S.New of Indiana, William N.Calder of New York, and John H. Bankhead of Alabama, as well as chairman of the House Foreign Affairs Committee, U.S. Congressman Stephen G.Porter of Pennsylvania, all supported an end to the economic blockade of Bolshevik Russia. The vice-president of the Apex Spark Plug Company of Evansville, Indiana, wrote of the efforts of one government official on behalf of the Soviet Bureau's quest for official trade recognition. "We have the assurance of representative Oscar R.Luhring...that everything possible will be done to permit the shipment of our goods," he wrote. "Luhring has promised to enlist the aid of other representatives and senators in Washington along this line; ...we are not going to rest until the proper thing is done." Senator Joseph France of Maryland went so far as to introduce a resolution on the Senate floor directing President Wilson to "assure the people of Russia of our friendship, sympathy, and desire to cooperate with them and to re-establish with them full and cordial relationships of friendly intercourse, trade and commerce."[38]

Such hope proved fruitless, as one week later the State Department once again warned American businessmen to avoid negotiating with the Bolsheviks. In an official statement, the department cautioned: "As the Government of the United States has never recognized the Bolshevist regime at Moscow, it is deemed proper to warn American business men that any concessions from the Bolshevist authorities probably could not be recognized as binding on future Russian Governments."[39]

Alarmed by the turn of events, Martens immediately began a concerted effort to gain the State Department's approval of trade, if not diplomatic, relations between the two countries. In a statement issued the same day as the department's "no concessions" announcement, Heller challenged the government's position on both theoretical and practical grounds. In light of the traditional U.S. policy of non-interference in the internal affairs of Russia, he found the State Department's warning to be "absolutely at variance" with traditional American diplomacy. Under prevailing international law, no government had a right to annul obligations entered into by previous governments; therefore, the department's statement on future financial obligations represented "a great change from the viewpoint heretofore taken by officials."[40]

On a practical level, in a hopeful plea to businessmen, Heller claimed that such a financial policy would be "very disastrous to the economic interests of the United States." The commercial director advised the average American exporter "not to gamble on some imaginary possible change in Russia in the near future, but to use the opportunity right now." In an effort to encourage manufacturers to pressure the government to change its policy, a strategy which became a hallmark of the Soviet Bureau's actions, he concluded: "There can be no reason in the world why the economic interests in the United States should demand a policy which would lose the present opportunity of getting a market for American products."[41]

Isaac Hourwich, director of the statistical department, subsequently documented the history of trade relations between the U.S. and countries not yet accorded diplomatic recognition, thereby disclosing a paradox in the American policy toward Bolshevik Russia. Although the U.S. government refused to recognize the Bolshevik rise to power in

November 1917, it "always maintained that its [own] existence as an international entity dates from the 4th of July, 1776, and not from the date of its first recognition by foreign governments." Traditionally, Hourwich stressed, commercial intercourse was independent of formal recognition, and most governments viewed a blockade of trade as a hostile act preceding a formal declaration of war.[42]

Hoping to alleviate the tension between Martens and the U.S. authorities, Commercial Director Heller and his assistant, Evans Clark, traveled to Washington, D.C., in early May 1919 to discuss trade relations with a number of businessmen, congressmen, and government officials, including Senators Joseph France and Hiram W.Johnson, Congressman Porter, President of the War Finance Corporation Eugene Meyer, Jr., Tariff Commissioner William Kent, Acting Secretary of State Frank Polk, and Supreme Court Justice Louis D.Brandeis. Upon their arrival, the Soviet Bureau representatives engaged in two days of meetings designed to strengthen trade relations between the U.S. and Bolshevik Russia. At an initial interview with James P.Mulvihill, a shoe manufacturer from Pittsburgh, Heller disclosed the Bolshevik view regarding current U.S. policies: "The only obstacle that exists to the reopening of trade with Russia is the unwillingness of political circles in Allied countries and in the United States frankly to accept the situation in Russia such as it is and try to make the best of it." American attempts to "support factions opposed to the Russian Soviet Government" not only prevented Russia from improving its economic and social conditions, but also "stood in the way of obvious economic interests of the United States." Such interests included nearly 1,500 firms, which already expressed "an eagerness to avail themselves of the opportunities which the Russian market presents." The offices of the Soviet Bureau continued to receive an average of one hundred offers each day, Heller estimated, regardless of the "veritable campaign of slander conducted against the Russian Soviet Republic…especially against its representatives in the United States." Despite such obstacles, the Bolshevik government remained prepared to resume trade as soon as the officials in Washington modified their views; thus, they continued to offer payment on previous Russian governments' financial obligations to other nations in an attempt to stabilize the country's international credit. Heller also reiterated the bureau's willingness to pay in gold for all initial purchases of American products.[43]

During a meeting with Representative Porter and Acting Secretary of State Polk later that afternoon, Clark and Heller challenged the official policy of the U.S. government, inquiring "whether trade relations could not be permitted even if there was no diplomatic recognition." Although Polk replied, "no such precedent exists," the department official offered little explanation for previous cases to the contrary.[44] The next day, in a private meeting with Porter, Mulvihill, Polk, and Polk's assistant, Basil Miles (neither Heller nor Clark were invited, although Mulvihill later provided a detailed report to the commercial director), the Acting Secretary of State expressed a keen interest in Heller's comments regarding the number of American businessmen wishing to deal with the Bolsheviks. Mulvihill admitted that Russia offered a promising market for his product and he "knew of his own knowledge that the Soviet Bureau office in New York was crowded with American manufacturers who were anxious to do business...." To support his claim, the shoe manufacturer presented Polk with a file containing letters from twenty U.S. firms, including Ford Motor Company, wishing to trade with the Bolsheviks. Polk also acknowledged "that the State Department had received a great number of requests from all parts of the country to permit trade with Russia." Still, "for the present, nothing could be done."[45]

Unofficially, however, the State Department expressed a notable interest in Martens' activities, suggested by the mere fact that a private meeting with the Assistant Secretary of State did take place. In a telling interview with Nuorteva and Grenville MacFarland, the legal counsel for William Randolph Hearst, Polk admitted that the Allied program to feed Russia would ultimately result in official relations with the Bolsheviks. "There can be no question of sending materials into Russia as an act of charity," he admitted, "nor could any imports on such a large scale as Russia requires exist without involving the necessity of some agreement with the government as to exports, credits, etc." With regard to the Soviet Bureau's endeavors, Nuorteva noted that Polk "spoke of our work without any pronounced hostility." Furthermore, the Assistant Secretary of State acknowledged that Martens' preparations for the possible resumption of trade between the two countries were not misdirected energy. Above all else, Polk stressed the necessity of keeping his views confidential. Speaking with MacFarland about the bureau's funding, Polk claimed "he knew full well" that Martens had established communications with and was receiving huge sums of money from Moscow, but "did not want to know it officially."[46]

The remainder of Heller and Clark's mission to Washington, D.C., proved to be a minor success. Although their meeting with Carl Alsberg, Chief of the Bureau of Chemistry in the Department of Agriculture, "was of no particular importance," the representatives of the Soviet

Bureau succeeded in influencing Clarence Wooley of the War Trade Board, in the process "changing some of his ideas on the Russian situation" and parting "on very friendly terms." A final interview with Justice Brandeis revealed the latter's sympathy with the Soviet Bureau's intentions. Expressly opposed to American intervention in Russian internal affairs, Brandeis suggested a possible solution to the problem of trade restrictions and the Allied blockade. Heller later commented: "He said our solution lies in getting as much publicity as we can, in getting the liberal opinion of America on our side."[47]

Acting upon the advice of Brandeis and other sympathetic individuals, Heller and Clark encouraged Martens to adopt a strategy of indirect pressure to achieve the desired goals of the Soviet Bureau. By persuading American businessmen to lobby on behalf of the bureau for an easing of trade restrictions, the Bolshevik officials avoided any hint of propaganda or interference in U.S. government affairs. Also, through a carefully constructed publicity campaign, the Soviet Bureau obtained free press coverage of the more positive aspects of the mission. Finally, in a memorandum to Heller, Clark suggested creating commercial associations designed to inter est businessmen in conducting trade with the Bolsheviks. "Our campaign for the opening of export trade," he concluded, "would be greatly enhanced by arranging directly or indirectly for meetings of manufacturers in several large centers of production, i.e., New York, Boston, Philadelphia, Pittsburgh, Chicago, etc." Such meetings would be organized by selecting one or two of the prominent business leaders in each community, holding personal conferences to convince them of the benefits inherent in trade with Russia, and then encouraging them to organize conventions to disseminate similar information. Clark, however, acknowledging the negative image associated with the bureau, stressed, "These meetings would best be arranged by the interested party on the spot without any public recognition of the original stimulus of this Bureau."[48]

Clearly by the spring of 1919, faced with political obstinacy in Washington, the representatives of the Soviet Bureau came to realize that their success or failure rested upon the willingness of profit-minded American businessmen to pressure the U.S. government to permit commercial intercourse with the Bolsheviks. Three months of intensive lobbying among political officials at various levels yielded few favorable results. However, while Martens' and Hellers' appeals for an improvement in trade relations fell upon deaf ears among government officials, they struck a responsive chord among businessmen throughout the country who eagerly, but secretively, approached the Soviet Bureau to learn more about import and export possibilities. The ensuing agreements arranged between American firms and Bolshevik Russia via the Soviet Bureau became an important, although seldom examined, chapter in U.S.-Russian trade.

The Lusk Committee, too, expressed an interest in Martens' commercial endeavors, but not in terms of international trade. By mid-June committee members were convinced that the Bureau was responsible for financing the imminent revolution in America, and that it was their responsibility to stop the flow of money to the parlor Bolsheviks in New York. The resultant battle between the Lusk Committee and the Soviet Bureau revealed not only the extent to which the public tolerated heavy-handed repression when faced with a radical threat, but also the impact that a growing Red Scare mentality had on U.S.-Russian trade, as businessmen who were eager to deal with the Bolsheviks barely a month earlier quickly distanced themselves from any contact with Martens' operation.

Chapter 4
Reactions from Businessmen and the Lusk Committee

AMONG AMERICAN BUSINESSMEN, A FASCINATION WITH THE VAST, untapped Russian market had existed long before the Bolsheviks came to power. A significant degree of economic investment in Russia emerged in the late nineteenth century as contemporary observers quickly and eagerly reported the opportunities available to American capitalists. In 1896, the secretary of the U.S. legation to Siberia described the region as a "rapidly developing country, not yet itself in train to manufacture," where many possibilities in industry and commerce offered themselves for American enterprise. Consul Thomas Smith concurred, noting in 1899 that the time had arrived for Americans to "take advantage of the unexampled opportunities offered in Russia for the investment of capital."[1]

Journalists, as well, recognized and reported the limitless prospects that the Russian market extended to U.S. financiers. One likened Russia to the now vanished American frontier, labeling Siberia "The New California." Sidney Brooks, staff writer for the contemporary journal *World's Work,* summarized in 1901 the new possibilities to be found in the Russian market: "In a few decades, Russia will be known and recognized as the most tempting field…for moneyed enterprise in the world, and American millionaires…will find in the long-derelict Empire of the Tsars yet more profitable scope for their energies."[2]

Congressman Ebenezer J. Hill of Connecticut, upon completing his travels through Siberia in 1902, sketched an even more promising picture for American investment. He emphasized that entrepreneurs need not wait a decade to exploit the situation, for the U.S. already had a viable market in Russia. "As a nation and as individuals," he concluded, Americans had "the confidence, respect, and regard of all Russians."[3]

The response of American capital to such consular and journalistic advertising culminated in concessions totaling millions of dollars by the outbreak of World War I. As early as 1900, American enterprises expressed an interest in irrigation projects in the Trans-Caspian region, extensive railway construction, and Siberian mining concessions in the wake of the discovery of the Klondike field in Alaska. Of the initial negotiations in 1900, the New York business report *Bradstreet's* announced the establishment of a syndicate willing to spend 150,000,000 rubles on the reclamation and irrigation of the "Hunger Steppe" in Turkestan. Additional reports disclosed a consortium of U.S. businessmen from Philadelphia and Richmond interested in obtaining the right to build a rail line from St. Petersburg to Odessa at an estimated cost of $90,000,000.[4]

The contracts concluded between U.S. investors and the Tsarist government consisted of two types of ventures: portfolio investment, which included the purchase of tsarist bonds by trusts and insurance companies; and direct investment, the more common method of undertaking manufacturing enterprises on foreign soil. National City Bank, under the control of Rockefeller and Stillman interests, as well as the Guaranty Trust Company and Equitable Life Assurance Society, both under the auspices of J.R Morgan, engaged in many forms of portfolio investment in pre-revolutionary Russia. Viewed as a means to offer extensive loans, such investments ranged from twenty to thirty million rubles. By 1905, New York Life's total business in Russia exceeded 120,000,000 rubles, while Equitable Life Assurance invested nearly 115,000,000 rubles.[5]

The simplest form of American investment in Russia at the turn of the century, however, was direct investment, often in the form of commercial enterprises. Although many U.S. firms operated through foreign agents, some established branch locations in the larger cities of Russia. By 1904, Parke-Davis Pharmaceutical Co. of Detroit maintained an office in St. Petersburg; Werner and Pfleiderer Machine Tools Co. of Philadelphia, in Moscow; and S.S.White Dental Manufacturing Co., also in Moscow.[6] Eventually numerous firms, including Singer Sewing Co., International Harvester, and the International Bell Telephone Co. (the latter received a twenty year monopoly to install the Bell Telephone System in St. Petersburg, Moscow, Odessa, Warsaw, and Riga) participated in the widespread attempts to exploit such markets.

The overwhelming desire of American businessmen to tap into the vast markets of Russia, clearly evident in the decades preceding the revolution, also persisted in the years following the 1917 uprising. Similar to the journalistic accounts of the late nineteenth century, many American observers emphasized the possible benefits of trading with the Bolsheviks. Frank J.Taylor of United Press of America, in a cable to Secretary of State Robert Lansing, concluded: "The Soviet Government is ready to give outside capitalists wonderful concessions. Capitalists could make much money in Russia provided the Soviet Government remained in power and was honest."[7] Othersstressed the importance of maintaining good relations with the Bolsheviks in order to prevent the Germans from attaining the raw materials and markets of Russia. U.S. Ambassador to Russia, David Francis, in a report to Lansing in February 1918, recommended immediate authorization for the American commercial attaché in Russia to "enter contracts" and "control Russia's surplus products" in a concerted effort to "entirely exclude German commerce for the balance of the war."[8]

Other Allied powers also recognized the threat Germany posed, and therefore attempted to gain access to the Soviet Russian markets. In a confidential memorandum to Lansing, U.S. Ambassador to France William Mullins reported the willingness of the French government to assist the Bolshevik regime so long as Lenin "resists the German menace and defends Russia against German aggression."[9] A number of businessmen agreed with the assessments of Francis and Mullins, including a consortium of engineers who, in June 1918, informed Lansing that German attempts to possess the resources and markets of Russia "should be opposed in every way." In light of the most pressing needs of all Russians—boots, clothes, and agricultural implements—the engineers suggested the formation of a trade association designed to deal directly with the Bolsheviks. The group recommended: "An organization established to accomplish these ends, that is to sell articles at a moderate price, but not to give them away, and to maintain order would in our opinion rapidly gain popular support."[10]

The formation of the Soviet Bureau served the needs of most U.S. businessmen hoping to strengthen commercial relations with Soviet Russia. In Martens' mission, such firms found a direct tie to the Bolshevik regime, which translated into a means by which to access the vast Russian markets and reap enormous profits. Martens had no sooner opened his doors for business when a number of firms began inundating his office with requests for information.

Between January and June 1919, at which time the Lusk Commission raided the Soviet Bureau, nearly 1,000 firms offered their services and products to the Bolsheviks. Of that number, many contacted the bureau on their own initiative, without Martens' solicitation and regardless of the State Department's restrictions on trade with Soviet Russia. Interest in the endeavors of the Soviet Bureau began to reveal itself even prior to the organization of the Commercial Department. Writing Martens on March 21, 1919, Benson Stoufer of Cooper and Cooper Chemical Company expressed his firm's desire to begin contract negotiations "just as soon as you are in a position to begin active operations...." One week later, Robert Grant of the Grant Iron and Steel Company requested a luncheon meeting to "talk on the general iron and steel situation and the possibility of supplying Russia."[11]

Once Heller, who was himself a respected businessman through his work with the International Oxygen Company, received his appointment as commercial director, public awareness of the Soviet Bureau's activities heightened. In the month of April 1919, alone, the bureau issued letters of inquiry to over 5,000 firms and circulated press kits to nearly 200 trade papers throughout the nation. Such efforts elicited favorable responses, as Heller noted in his report of April 30, 1919. "There appears to be an increasing evidence on the part of manufacturers and dealers to do business with us," he announced, "and many are bending all efforts to procure export licenses."[12] A number of firms, referring to the bureau's desire to overcome U.S. trade restrictions, detailed their willingness to lobby the federal government to lift the unofficial economic blockade against Russia. The Graselli Chemical Company, American Aniline Products, and Arnold, Hoffman and Company, the last representing the Mathieson Alkali Works of Saltville, Virginia, all guaranteed the delivery of "prompt shipments in large quantities."[13] By mid-May, many U.S. firms readily accepted the onus of procuring the necessary export licenses. On May 15, W.S. Rupp of the Baugh Chemical Company informed Heller that his company was "now in a position to ship goods promptly, and would like very much to do business with Russia." Charles Steiner of the Marathon Tire and Rubber Company likewise acknowledged: "As far as export licenses are concerned for shipments to Petrograd, we assure you to secure these papers from our government."[14]

A few companies went further, to the extent of expressing overt sympathy with the Bolshevik cause along with their hope that the State Department would soon grant Martens official diplomatic recognition. In his initial letter to Heller on April 14, 1919, Sylvester M. Weimer of the Old Reliable Motor Truck Corporation closed: "I must thank you for the courtesy and while anticipating good business relations, may I not offer my felicitations, as I believe Mr. Martens Mission here will in due time receive proper official recognition and be accorded the same privileges as other accredited representatives." Benjamin Smith of the Carolina Junk and Hide Company concluded his inquiry in a similar vein: "Assuring you of my deepest sympathy for bleeding Russia as well as bleeding humanity everywhere, and hoping that there are brighter days in store for the human race in every land in the near future, I remain faithfully yours."[15]

Correspondence rapidly translated into interviews, with numerous firms sending representatives to New York City to meet with Martens, Heller, and Clark. The earliest conferences in mid-April included meetings with Ernest Kanseler of Ford Motor Company; J.F.Pierce of the meat-packing firm Armour and Company; and D.O.Frazer, export manager for a rival meatpacking interest, Swift and Company. Upon meeting with Heller, Frazer "considered the opportunity to get into Russian market favorable." Profuse in his proposals to aid the Soviet Bureau in any way, he "offered to consult the State Department on the possibility of shipments to Russia."[16] With regard to official trade restrictions, J.W.Abbott, representing several woolen mills in Pennsylvania and Virginia, commented in an interview with Dr. Samuel A.Stodel of the bureau, "he could get an export license for goods in his line to Soviet Russia. Was notified by telephone from Washington the day before." George E.Barrows of Bridgeport Rolling Mills lent credence to Abbott's assertion, stating "that in his opinion trade relations with Soviet Russia would be settled in a few weeks."[17]

The Sixth National Foreign Trade Convention, held in Chicago April 24–26, 1919, proved to be a rewarding contact between the Soviet Bureau and American businessmen. In detailed reports of their activities at the convention, Heller and Nuorteva concluded "that our presence in Chicago had produced a very good impression.... Our open, businesslike attitude was favorably commented upon." Upon establishing a temporary headquarters at the Hotel LaSalle, the two set out to accomplish dual tasks: Heller, to meet with a number of the over 1,000 manufacturers, exporters, and international bankers present at the convention; and Nuorteva, to answer press inquiries and dispel the erroneous rumors being spread by Russian counter-revolutionaries in attendance. According to Nuorteva, despite several negative propaganda campaigns, especially those conducted by the Russian-American Chamber of Commerce, "we had some success" in arranging contacts with many firms. In two days of conferences, Heller met representatives from over two dozen major U.S. enterprises, including International Harvester; Marshall Field and Company, the largest producer of cotton goods in the country; Sears, Roebuck and Company; and the meatpacking interests of Morris and Company, Cudahy Packing Company, and the United States Packing Company. In a subsequent interview with H.H.Merrick, president of the Mississippi Valley Association, Heller arranged for a conference with the prominent bankers and manufacturers of Chicago, to be held at a future date.[18]

Nuorteva experienced similar success in his endeavors, providing an endless stream of stories to many local newspapers, as well as placing an advertisement in the financial column of the Chicago *Daily Tribune* to announce the delegation's presence at the convention. Although the organizers of the convention denied Nuorteva an opportunity to address the body, both he and Heller "were swamped with visitors for two days," most of whom assured the Soviet Bureau officials "that they would try to do their best to overcome now existing obstacles to the resumption of trade." The success of the mission prompted the diplomatic director to recommend that the bureau establish a commercial branch in Chicago as soon as possible. Heller agreed, "It would therefore seem that the favorable impression thus far created by our activities should be kept up and, if possible, strengthened."[19]

In addition to personal interviews in their New York City offices, as well as appearances at major trade conventions, representatives of the Soviet Bureau contacted a number of American firms by speaking before trade associations and chambers of commerce throughout the country. A form letter sent to dozens of such groups included an overview of the bureau's operations and listed the items most desired by the Russian people. Expressing an interest "to become acquainted, through your organization, with the businessmen of your community," Heller requested meetings at which he could address an audience of manufacturers. Among the groups welcoming a representative of the bureau to speak before their assemblage were the chambers of commerce in Cincinnati, Baltimore, New York, and Utica, as well as the National Association of Hosiery and Underwear Manufacturers.[20]

The efforts of the Soviet Bureau through trade conventions, newspaper advertisements, correspondence, individual interviews, and group presentations resulted in an overwhelming response from American businessmen. One report, based upon investigations by the intelligence personnel of the Army and Treasury Departments, estimated that 941 companies expressed a desire to deal with the bureau. Similar accounts from the Directorate of Intelligence in Scotland Yard suggested that, regardless of the State Department's repudiation of Martens' mission, he had "a certain amount of success in attracting customers." A subsequent report from Scotland Yard provided greater detail in its assessment. "American firms put the question of profit foremost," it concluded, "for it appears that no less than 742 more or less important firms offered to do business with the Soviet Bureau." Recent estimates drew comparable conclusions regarding the volume of business conducted by the bureau. Georgi Arbatov, Director of the Institute of United States and Canadian Studies in Moscow concluded that "By the end of 1919, [Martens] had established contacts with about a thousand firms in thirty-two American states."[21]

Announcements from officials of the Soviet Bureau substantiated such estimates. From a survey of manufacturers conducted in late May 1919, Heller tabulated the following figures. As of May 24, a total of 853 firms communicated by letter with the Commercial Department. Of this number, 745 offered to sell their goods to Bolshevik Russia through the bureau: 647 stated no terms, 66 demanded cash, and 32 extended credit. Only 108 firms refused to deal with the bureau: 85 due to the lack of facilities to export to Russia, 23 for political reasons. In addition to the contacts via mail, 235 firms sent representatives to Martens' offices for personal conferences throughout the spring of 1919.[22] Louis Kantor, a reporter for the New York *Tribune,* visited Heller's office on May 7 to verify the bureau's volume of business. What he found amazed him. "Despite the State Department's warning...that it had not recognized L.C.A.K. Martens, and that American business men should be cautious in their dealings with the Russian Soviet Bureau which he heads, a visit to his offices ...found them fairly well filled with men said to be representatives of various American business concerns." By mid-November, Heller estimated that he "had talked business with about 2, 500 firms," all of whom were "firms with a capitalization of $1,000,000 or over." Such firms included "the big Chicago packers, Armour, Swift, Nelson Morris, and Cudahy," as well as the U.S. Steel Corporation, International Harvester, and M.C.D. Borden and Sons.[23]

Heller's comments triggered a firestorm of denials from businessmen who took exception to his assertion that their firms ignored State Department directives and attempted to deal with the Bolsheviks. So long as the negotiations were secret, hundreds of companies dealt with the Soviet Bureau. However, when their activities saw the light of day, amidst a radical hysteria gripping the nation, the denials were swift and vehement. In statements issued in the New York *Times,* G.F.Swift, Jr., and O.H.Swift of Swift and Company meatpackers emphatically denied any knowledge of Martens or the bureau. The former, in charge of his company's export department, stressed "I have never heard of this man before in my life. Most certainly I am sure that we have never had any dealings with him of any kind." One day later, Swift amended his story, and admitted having contact with representatives of the Soviet Bureau. He strongly declared, however, "We told them we would not, that we were not in the business of selling supplies to enemies of the United States." He further announced that neither he, nor any employee of his company, had ever attempted to influence government officials in Washington to formally recognize Soviet Russia. At the end of his interview with several newspaper reporters, Swift again reiterated, "We didn't want anything to do with them then and we don't want anything to do with them now."[24] Not surprisingly, he made no reference to Frazer's aforementioned April meeting with Heller, nor of the latter's proposal to deal with the Soviet Bureau and pressure the State Department to ease trade restrictions against the Bolsheviks.

Edward Morris of Morris and Company, conveniently forgetting his foreign sales manager's conference with Heller at the Sixth National Foreign Trade Convention in Chicago, issued a similar statement to the press: "We have never had anything to do with these people and we don't want anything to do with them. We would not sell them a dollar's worth of goods for cash or credit. We don't do business with our country's enemies." Likewise, Judge Elbert H.Gary of the United States Steel Corporation emphasized, "that there was no foundation for the statement that the Soviet representative here had any dealing" with his enterprise. Numerous other firms submitted similar denials, including Packard Motor Company, Westinghouse, Moline Plow Company, Pacific and Eastern Steamship Company, and Sheffield Farms-Slawson Decker Company.[25]

As expected, several officials in the federal government likewise publicly denounced any association whatsoever with the Soviet Bureau. Despite his previous meetings with Heller, Clark, and Nuorteva, Assistant Secretary of State Polk denied ever speaking with representatives of the bureau. In June 1919, Polk admitted only to meeting Nuorteva through a mutual friend some five months earlier, long before Martens opened his offices in New York, and even then "devoted most of the time to telling Nuorteva that the United States would never recognize any people or government that failed to respect the sanctity of diplomatic and consular offices."[26]

Although Martens destroyed several and transported the remainder of the Soviet Bureau's papers to Russia in January 1921, records seized by the Lusk Committee in June 1919 confirmed many of the bureau's contentions. As of June 12, 1919, 943 U.S. firms, representing one-half of the total number that had contacted the Soviet Bureau, expressed a desire to trade with the Bolsheviks via the bureau. Participants included major producers from New York City to San Francisco such as the Aluminum Goods Manufacturing Company, Armour and Company, Ford Motor Company, General Electric Company, General Motors Corporation, Goodyear Rubber Company, International Harvester, Proctor and Gamble Distribution Company, Sears, Roebuck and Company, Swift and Company, and U.S. Steel Products Company. Most of the firms manufactured machinery, chemicals, clothing, and processed foods, although the list contained some anomalies.[27]

Of the leading manufacturers conducting business with Russia, none provoked greater interest than did the Ford Motor Company. As early as 1916, company agent Gaston Plaintiff declared his firm's desire to gain access to the Russian market. Upon his return from a tour of the country, Plaintiff provided an enthusiastic appraisal of the situation. "In Russia," he wrote, "...once we get our factories started there, in automobiles alone we will do nearly as much as we are doing in America today." Plaintiff was amazed by the potential that the Russian market presented. "You cannot realize the thing," he informed his superiors; "It is so big it would stagger you." Should Ford wish to take advantage of the opportunity, Plaintiff estimated that the company could operate a minimum of six factories in Russia and return an enormous profit. He urged, however, that Ford must strike while the iron was hot. "I would like to get into that country now and organize a Russian company while they are enthusiastic about American businessmen," he concluded. "They want American manufacturers to come on inside now and get busy."[28] Officials of the Soviet Bureau likewise expressed a keen interest in the products manufactured by Ford. In a memorandum to Martens in April 1919, Nuorteva noted, "I believe it is very necessary for us in every respect to establish trade relations with Ford."[29]

During its brief tenure, the Soviet Bureau became one of the primary vehicles for Ford's efforts. Following an interview with Heller on April 12, 1919, Ernest Kanseler, a representative of the firm, stated "that the Ford Company considers their tractors suitable for Russian conditions, and that they are anxious to do business with Soviet Russia." Confident that the company would encounter little difficulty in obtaining export licenses, Kanseler stressed that the automobile manufacturer "is prepared to trade with [the Bolsheviks] on a regular basis." In a subsequent letter to Henry Ford, Martens requested a personal meeting, not only to facilitate commercial relations, but more so "to discuss...the social aspects of the regeneration of Russia" and detail how "Soviet Russia is inaugurating methods of industrial efficiency compatible with the interests of humanity and unhampered by the curse of greed and graft." Although Ford was unable to accommodate a personal interview, his general secretary, E.G. Liebold, arranged to meet with Heller and Nuorteva in Detroit in late April, following the Sixth National Foreign Trade Convention in Chicago. At the private conference, according to Martens, held "in the name of socialism," Liebold again emphasized his company's desire to "send tractors to Russian peasants...at the lowest possible price." Heller, Nuorteva, and Liebold concluded their discussion with an agreement to meet in New York City in early May.[30]

While the subsequent publicity regarding the Lusk Committee's raid of the Soviet Bureau limited Ford's dealings with Martens, the automobile giant nonetheless succeeded in finding other avenues through which to exploit the Russian markets. As early as March 1919, the company concluded a contract with Ivan Stacheeff and Company of Petrograd. In the ensuing two years, Ford sold 238 touring cars through the agent. Beginning in 1923, Ford conducted business with the Bolsheviks under the auspices of the Allied American Corporation of New York, a concern established by Julius Hammer and his sons. A brief interlude of direct negotiations with the Soviet government in the mid-1920s preceded Ford Motor Company's decision to sign a contract with the Supreme Council of National Economy of the U.S.S.R. on May 31, 1929 to construct a Model A plant in Russia. Ford simultaneously concluded a deal with the Amtorg Trading Corporation to guarantee the sale of 72,000 Ford vehicles over the next four years.[31]

Although Ford did not sign a contract with the Soviet Bureau, many other firms negotiated important deals with Martens, substantiating his November 1919, claim to have completed over $20,000,000 in contracts "mostly with the largest business houses in the United States."[32] Of the more illustrous agreements, Morris and Company promised delivery of fifty million pounds of food products for $10,000,000; LeHigh Machine Company, 1,000 printing presses for $4,500,000; Weinberg and Posner Engineering, machinery and tools worth $3,000,000; Fischmann and Company, clothing in the amount of $3,000,000; and Eline Berlow, a shipment of boots and shoes for $3,000,000.[33] By the end of 1919, the Soviet Bureau had signed contracts totaling $24,912,705. However, Martens completed payment on only one for which goods were shipped to Bolshevik Russia: $10,164 for a cargo of rubber shoes received via the Anthaus Trading Company of New York. An additional shipment of $10,000,000 in assorted merchandise from the National Storage Company arrived in Petrograd in September 1919; but, according to the director of the bureau, "Circumstances made it impossible for the company to perform the contract according to the original terms and was therefore abandoned."[34] Meager in his rate of success, Martens' efforts nonetheless foretold of impending improvements in trade relations between the two countries; by May 1920, Soviet contracts with U.S. firms reached total levels in excess of $300,000,000.[35]

According to many reports, numerous financial houses revealed a similar desire to extend their services to the Bolshevik representatives in America. Of greatest interest was the Guaranty Trust Company, under the control of J.P.Morgan. One confidential Scotland Yard report stated that the Soviet Bureau "received financial support...from the Guarantee Trust Company, although this firm has denied the allegation that it is financing Martens' organization."[36] Captain John B.Trevor of the Military Intelligence Department in New York substantiated the bureau's ties to Morgan's enterprise in a memorandum to the director of Military Intelligence. In his report, Trevor concluded that Guaranty Trust, under the direction of President Henry Sabin, "one of the most unscrupulous bankers in the city," was the "depository for persons financing Martens." Furthermore, Gaston, Williams, and Wigmore Company, export agents who conducted a large volume of business with Russia during the war, served as "fiscal agents for Martens." To support such claims, Trevor reported his discovery of a "most confidential luncheon" in early May 1919, at which twelve men were present, including Sabin and Nuorteva.[37]

Despite Trevor's claims of fiscal impropriety on the part of Guaranty Trust Company, the Lusk Committee uncovered little evidence to corroborate his story. While the Soviet Bureau maintained an account at Guaranty Trust, there was no indication of covert meetings with Sabin. In fact, the account remained open for only two weeks, April 15 through April 29, 1919, with a maximum balance of slightly less than $7,000. Tracing the financial assets of the bureau on behalf of the Lusk Committee, the accounting firm of Perley, Morse and Company noted the low levels of funds and unexplainable frequent shifting of accounts from one bank to another. From Martens' initial personal account at the Washington, D.C. branch of the Corn Exchange Bank, to Guaranty Trust Company, to concurrent arrangements at Public National Bank, Irving National Bank and the State Bank of New York, the bureau's accounts seldom exceeded one month in duration or $6,000 in resources.[38]

Rather than a willingness to embrace Martens and his mission, most American banking interests expressed some trepidation in dealing with the Soviet Bureau. As late as May 20, 1919, Associate Commercial

Director Evans Clark indicated that, while "manufacturers are eager to do business with Russia, ...bankers are hostile to us." Clearly, most efforts to establish positive relations between the large financial houses of New York and the Soviet Bureau emanated from the latter, not, as Trevor contended, from an "unscrupulous" desire on the part of individual bankers. Clark's subsequent advice to Heller reiterated the bureau's strategy. "There is a great need," he told the commercial director, "of reaching personally and making as good an effect as possible upon the biggest figures in American finance, i.e. J.P.Morgan and Co., National City Bank, First National Bank, Kidder Peabody, and others."[39] Hopeful of negotiating relations with major U.S. financiers similar to the beneficial ties realized with the large manufacturing interests, Martens anticipated a high degree of success in his endeavors. Enterprising politicians in New York however, who themselves anticipated a high degree of success in their careers, had other plans. The clash between Martens and the Lusk Committee in the ensuing six months threatened to dismantle not only the bureau's previous gains, but also the bureau itself.

A number of federal inquiries preceded the Lusk Committee's raid on the Soviet Bureau, most notably investigations by the War Trade Board and Department of Justice, as well as the aforementioned inquests by the Directorate of Military Intelligence and officials of the Treasury Department. Following a request by the War Trade Board to submit information regarding the bureau's activities, Evans Clark arranged for an interview with the assistant director of War Trade Intelligence, G.M.Bodman. Meeting with Bodman on April 25, 1919, Clark emphasized the bureau's desire to cooperate fully, as Martens' mission "had nothing to conceal" and was "glad to furnish information to those entitled to have it." He willingly provided information regarding the names and nationalities of the employees of the bureau, the general purpose and organization of the group, and the assets held in particular financial institutions. Upon conferring with Morris Hillquit, Commercial Director Heller subsequently submitted an Information Affidavit to the War Trade Board detailing the activities of the Soviet Bureau.[40] In a related series of interviews, Martens and his attorney, Charles Recht, met with R.W. Finch and Frederick E. Offley, representing the Department of Justice, on April 28 and May 16, 1919, resulting in Clark's trip to Washington, D.C., to meet with Thomas Scott, personal secretary to U.S. Attorney General A. Mitchell Palmer.[41]

The Lusk Committee's interest in the Soviet Bureau's activities grew in the spring of 1919, as they attempted to ascertain the sources of funds supporting the radical revolution threatening New York. Following the bomb scares of April and June, committee members sought to display their power by staging a spectacular raid that would strike at the heart of radicalism in New York City. Martens' bureau presented an alluring target. In his application for a search warrant on June 12, 1919, committee investigator Clarence Converse informed City Magistrate Alexander Brough that the Soviet Bureau had repeatedly attempted to distribute subversive literature throughout the country. "It was the intention of the said Bureau and the persons thereof to excite, through means of said literature, documents, books and papers in their possession, disorder, breach of the peace, and violent, generally revolutionary activity among the People of this State," he declared. Although his tone had been alarming, Converse's evidence consisted not of numerous "literature, documents, books and papers," but only of a three page typewritten article that he had found on the floor of the bureau offices during a visit the preceding day. The paper, entitled "Groans From Omsk," detailed the oppressive conditions under which workers labored in Omsk, Russia. In the only remotely seditious statement contained in the document, the article concluded: "Soviet as the form of government, Soviet as the form for emancipation of the workingmen; that is the watch-word of the workingmen from Omsk in the same way as that is the watch-word of all the revolutionary workingmen."[42]

Despite questions regarding the authorship of the document and the bureau's alleged possession of radical literature, Brough, a traffic court judge by profession, granted the search warrant. In the official wording of the warrant, which became a major issue in subsequent legal challenges, Brough instructed state officials to "make immediate search of the premises" and seize "all documents, circulars and papers printed or typewritten having to do with Socialist, Labor, Revolutionary or Bolshevik activities" as well as "all books, letters and papers pertaining to the activities of said Bureau." He also ordered that all papers obtained during the raid be promptly brought to his chambers. The warrant, to be executed by peace officers of the County of New York, made no mention of confiscating unrelated material or detaining employees of the Bureau. The mere issuance of a search warrant was evidence of the extraordinary power the Lusk Committee assumed. The normal instrument of a legislative investigating committee was the public or private hearing, supplemented with subpoenas to compel the presence of witnesses and the submission of documents. All of the material subsequently obtained by the Lusk Committee during its raid on the

Soviet Bureau could have been secured through normal means. However, the use of a search warrant and spectacular raid was more dramatic, and resulted in front-page press coverage.[43]

By 2:30 in the afternoon, Sergeant W.R.Brey of the New York State Troopers and Henry Grunewald of the Adams-Grunewald Private Detective Agency had assembled a force of twenty men at the Lusk Committee's headquarters in the Prince George Hotel. At 3:15 p.m., the troopers, private investigators, committee officials, and one British Secret Service agent[44] descended upon the Soviet Bureau, severed the telephone wires, detained Martens, Nuorteva, Heller, Weinstein, and Hourwich, and literally cleaned out the offices. Six troopers under Brey's command remained in the bureau overnight to complete the search and guard against the destruction of any papers or books. Contrary to Brough's orders, peace officers from the County of New York neither conducted nor participated in the raid. In fact, Captain William Bailey of the 23rd Precinct in New York City, in whose district the search occurred, later admitted he "had not been previously informed of the action" and could only assume "that the authorities had gotten together and the state forces invested with the proper prerogatives."[45]

In further violation of the warrant, the investigators seized a number of items unrelated to the search for documents of a revolutionary nature. Aside from the correspondence, pamphlets, speeches, and commercial files, which the warrant empowered the group to confiscate, the state officials also appropriated cash boxes, briefcases, entire file cabinets and desks, photographs of Martens' wife and children, a Soviet flag, and a velvet Russian cap. Martens later observed, "the premises resembled the scene of a pogrom."[46] The committee also violated the intent of the search warrant by maintaining possession of the materials for eight days before submitting them to Brough's chambers. Not until Martens brought suit to vacate the warrant did the magistrate take action to seize control of the documents, and even then the committee subsequently reacquired them by issuing a subpoena on Brough's office.[47]

Mindful of the heavy-handed tactics employed during the raid, Lusk denied any knowledge of the committee's use of search warrants. While freely admitting he issued subpoenas to force the appearance of Martens and his associates, Lusk told reporters "I understand the search warrant was issued by Magistrate Alexander Brough. Beyond that I know nothing about it. I suppose you ought to go to Attorney General Newton for the information you are seeking." When informed of Lusk's statement, Newton replied, "The raid was not conducted under any directions issued by me, nor did I take any steps to procure the search warrant that Magistrate Brough issued." The paper trail ultimately led to Archibald Stevenson who, while emphasizing he was unwilling to assume full responsibility for the search warrant, admitted "I have heard all about the raid and it seems to have been a rather neat job." Subsequent inquiry revealed that Deputy Attorney General Robert S.Conkling had obtained the warrant on behalf of the committee. As for the use of state troopers, Lusk preferred to consider them "process servers" who acted both as executors of the warrant as well as agents serving the subpoenas. Steadfast in his denial of any knowledge of the matter, Lusk concluded, reportedly with a smile, "It seems that by some strange coincidence some other proceeding affecting the Soviet Mission is under way at the very moment our committee wants the members of the mission as witnesses; such things happen once in a while."[48]

The most questionable aspect of the raid, however, was not the issuance of the search warrant, but the Lusk Committee's decision to detain Martens, Nuorteva, Heller, Weinstein, and Hourwich and transport them directly to city hall for interrogation. Although given the broad power to subpoena witnesses to appear and testify at public hearings, neither the joint legislative resolution nor Brough's warrant granted the committee the right to arrest alleged radicals. Upon the arrival of the Soviet Bureau officials under heavy police guard to city hall, Lusk subjected Martens and Nuorteva to nearly four hours of intense questioning. In another denial of due process, Attorney General Newton prohibited Charles Recht and Edwin Stanton, the attorneys secured by Evans Clark to represent Martens and his staff, from being present during the questioning.[49] When Martens attempted to deflect the committee's inquiry by claiming diplomatic immunity as the official representative of the Soviet government, Newton responded that the State Department had not granted recognition to the Soviets and then continued to question him about his citizenship and the bureau's activities.

The attitude of Martens and the Soviet government toward the raid was not as light or flippant as was Lusk's, Newton's, or Stevenson's. Nuorteva declared that "The raid was an outrage," and added:

Twenty detectives rushed into our offices and at their hands we received the roughest kind of treatment, short of physical violence. They refused to let us communicate with our lawyers, they cut our telephone wires, they barred all the doors and refused to let any of the attaches and workers leave the offices.[50]

Martens, stressing his policy of non-interference in U.S. government affairs, concluded, "There can be no legitimate reason for raiding our office and the most minute investigation will reveal no reason." Holding to his belief that the Soviet Bureau represented an official diplomatic mission, Martens labeled the raid "an unwarranted breach of the first principles of international hospitality." On June 17, speaking before a crowd gathered at Madison Square Garden, he protested "U.S. government interference with Russian internal affairs." The bureau director specifically blamed Stevenson and the Union League Club for fomenting the antiradical hysteria upon which the Lusk Committee had acted.[51]

Recht fueled the political hysteria further when he issued the bureau's official statement concerning the raid. Martens' attorney considered the action "unnecessary and mainly for the purpose of spectacularism." In judicial terms, he found the committee's actions to be "a most wanton piece of legal violence." Recht concluded that the search warrant was invalid, and that the men who enforced it committed misdemeanors and more serious offenses. He was particularly angered by the continued presence of state police within the Soviet Bureau's offices for a day following the raid; only when he lodged an official complaint did the attorney general remove the troopers.[52] Nuorteva agreed with Recht that the raid rested legally upon far from solid ground. He accurately predicted that it would be remembered only as "a characteristic episode of the reign of hysteria prevailing at the time."[53]

Martens and the Bolshevik government officially protested the committee's actions in a series of telegrams to Secretary of State Lansing. Immediately following the raid, the director of the Soviet Bureau cabled the State Department to "most emphatically protest against the indignity to which my office, and thereby the Government and the people whom I have the honor to represent, have been subjected...." On July 1, Tchitcherin issued a similar protest from Moscow, revealing his government's fear that Martens' arrest "may not be an isolated case, but forms part of a general persecution of Russian citizens loyal to their people's Government...." In a veiled threat to American officials, the Commissar for Foreign Affairs expressed his hope "not to be compelled reluctantly to take reprisals against American citizens to be found on Russian territory." In his reply, Acting Secretary of State W.B.Phillips denied Tchitcherin's allegations and warned the

Bolshevik government against harming U.S. citizens. "A course of reprisal," Phillips stressed, "would be certain to arouse in the United States an overwhelming public sentiment of indignation against the authorities at Moscow."[54]

In public hearings conducted during the following week, the Lusk Committee revealed its intentions to dismantle the Soviet Bureau and to pressure the federal government to initiate deportation proceedings against Martens. The committee began by questioning Martens' ancestry and his refusal to register as an enemy alien during U.S. involvement in the war. Although Nuorteva claimed, "Martens is no more a German than President Wilson is a Scotchman," the committee focused on Martens' German parentage and his registration in Great Britain in 1911 as an enemy alien. Meanwhile, through his sister he received notification that the Soviet government had granted his request for Russian citizenship. Under such circumstances, the committee concluded, Martens stood in violation of the presidential proclamation regarding enemy alien registration.[55]

The Lusk Committee also indicted the efforts of the Soviet Bureau to conduct a propaganda campaign on behalf of the Communist Party of Russia. In a statement epitomizing the logic of the committee's investigation, Lusk wrote:

> Bearing in mind that one of the objects of the regime which he [Martens] represents in this country is the overthrow of the system of government now existing here, *every act which he commits* in this country which is beneficial to the Bolshevist regime, *whether a direct violation of any existing statute in this country or not,* and is unquestionably an act of hostility against the government and the people of the United States.[56]

In the ensuing weeks, the committee continued to issue vague charges against Martens and the Soviet Bureau, oftentimes questioning the character of other individuals and groups by disclosing various letters and mailing lists. Resorting to the tactic of "guilt by association," Stevenson read into the record a number of prominent names appearing on the bureau's New York mailing list: Carleton J.H.Hayes, professor of history at Columbia University; Paul V.Kellogg, the editor of *Survey,* whom Stevenson claimed "did his midget best to keep America from going to war with Germany;" Lillian D.Wald, founder of the Henry Street Settlement; and Norman Thomas, popular advocate of conscientious objectors. Later revelations disclosed associations between the Soviet Bureau and a number of liberals and socialists, including Frank A.Vanderlip, Dudley Field Malone, Amos Pinchot, Gilbert Roe, and Lincoln Colcord.[57]

Martens attempted to continue trade negotiations with U.S. businessmen in the months following the raid, informing many firms "that the work of the Commercial Department of this Bureau continues unaffected by recent events." However, the combination of his preoccupation with the legal proceedings directed against himself, as well as the increased reluctance of American firms to submit themselves to the public scrutiny surrounding the bureau, led Martens to realize that his quest to establish economic ties between the two countries were nearing an unsuccessful conclusion. In November 1919 he admitted: "The raid on my office and subsequent press campaign…caused… substantial damage to myself, to the Government and to the people I represent." The damage was especially evident in terms of commercial relations, as several firms that had been negotiating contracts with Martens quickly severed all ties with the bureau.[58]

Concentrating on his effort to prohibit the Lusk Committee from obtaining his diplomatic papers, Martens refused to answer a summons to appear before the committee on November 14, 1919. In a letter to Lusk, the director of the Soviet Bureau identified the request as "an excess of the jurisdiction of your Committee, and without warrant in law under the rules of international law." Intent on presenting himself as the official representative of Soviet Russia, Martens considered the State Department to be "the sole authority vested with jurisdiction in the matter." Such defiance forced the committee to request an attachment against Martens, resulting in Justice L.A.Giegerich's order to the county sheriff that he apprehend the defiant Bolshevik representative and bring him before the Lusk Committee.[59]

Forced to appear before the committee, Martens testified on November 25 and 26 regarding his financial assets. While admitting to the existence of couriers who delivered up to $90,000 from Soviet Russia, Martens refused to divulge their names. Declared in contempt by Chairman Lusk, Martens again sought legal recourse by applying to the State Supreme Court for a cancellation of the subpoena. In an affidavit filed November 29, 1919, Martens and his attorney challenged the efforts of the committee on three counts. First, he asserted that the attempt to secure the papers transmitted between the bureau and the Soviet government did not fall within the scope of the committee's investigation of seditious activities in New York State. Second, declaring that the Lusk Committee was a legislative rather than a judicial body, Martens then argued that it had no subpoena power to compel him to produce his private papers. Finally, because the committee had sought an indictment against him personally for his alleged seditious activities, Martens held that the various subpoenas demanding his testimony violated state laws as well as his Fifth Amendment rights which protected individuals against self-incrimination. On November 30, 1919, acting on the affidavit, Justice Robert F.Wagner directed Lusk, Newton, and Stevenson to show cause why the subpoenas should not be vacated per the bureau's request. Furthermore, he questioned whether the committee should be prohibited from serving further papers on Martens or any other member of the staff of the Soviet Bureau.[60]

Following a series of hearings during which Dudley Field Malone and Deputy Attorney General Berger engaged in heated debate over the committee's actions, State Supreme Court Justice Samuel Greenbaum denied Martens' claim for diplomatic immunity, directing the head of the Soviet Bureau to appear before the committee to answer all questions put forth to him.[61] Martens, however, fled the jurisdiction of New York State and traveled to Washington, D.C., in late December, 1919, in a final effort to avoid relinquishing his papers to the Lusk Committee. Faced with deportation proceedings initiated by the Department of Labor and a warrant for his arrest issued by the Department of Justice, he remained in hiding in a hotel three blocks from Attorney General Palmer's office. Martens eventually agreed, on January 19, 1920, to appear before the Senate Judiciary Committee in exchange for the protection of its parole.[62]

Testifying about his activities in America, Martens reiterated that his mission's single goal was to enhance commercial trade between the U.S. and Soviet Russia. He continued to deny all allegations regarding his involvement in the distribution of radical propaganda throughout the country. His activities, the director of the bureau stressed, "being strictly confined to the presentation of facts about Russia, could not be regarded as improper or objectionable, inasmuch as the United States has not declared war on Russia...." Martens' counsel, former U.S. Senator Thomas W.Hardwick, likewise emphasized his client's innocence, denying charges that he "propagated or instigated, or even participated in any way, in any political activity in this country, or in any attempt to overthrow its government."[63]

The Senate committee disagreed. Citing the content of Lenin's "Letter to the American Workingmen," a document freely circulated by the Soviet Bureau, and Martens' frequent attendance and addresses at meetings where other speakers advocated the destruction of the capitalist system, the committee's counsel, Wade H.Ellis, attempted to prove Martens' participation in the radical drive for international revolution. At the conclusion of the investigation on March 29, 1920, committee chairman George H.Moses supported Attorney General Palmer's request for Martens' deportation. Three committee members—Senators Atlee Pomerene of Ohio, Frank B. Brandegee of Connecticut, and William E.Borah of Idaho—opposed the move, but the decision received vast support from other members of Congress. Nearly one year earlier, in May 1919, Senator William H. King of Utah and Representative Albert Johnson of Washington introduced a concurrent resolution calling for Martens' expulsion from this country, an issue King raised repeatedly during the remainder of the year. Convinced of the subversive nature of the Soviet Bureau's activities, King concluded: "It is time that these disturbers of our peace and enemies of our country and civilization should be driven from this land whose hospitality they have so grievously abused."[64]

At the conclusion of the hearings, Martens once again faced the prospect that the Department of Justice would arrest him. Realizing that the arrest "was to be a species of public entertainment for which the Department of Labor could not decently allow itself to be responsible," Assistant Secretary of Labor Louis Post seized the warrant from Attorney General Palmer and ordered Martens to quietly surrender himself at the Department of Labor offices. In doing so, Post asserted, the appropriate steps were taken "to frustrate, not the arrest, but an abusive, lawless, indecent and scandalous method of making it." Upon making the arrest, Post reviewed and granted Hardwick's application for Martens' parole pending conclusion of the case.[65]

Martens faced a serious charge. Federal officials viewed him as a radical alien intent on overthrowing the government of the U.S. by force or violence, a violation of the Immigration Acts of February 5, 1917 and October 16, 1918. In the course of the hearings, Martens' attorney argued that the acts exempted accredited representatives of foreign governments from the point in contention. Furthermore, Recht claimed, Martens was neither a member of the Communist Party nor was he engaged in revolutionary activities.[66] Secretary of Labor William B.Wilson disagreed. In his decision rendered on December 15, 1920, Wilson held Martens to be the representative of an unrecognized foreign government; therefore, he was not exempt from the standards of the Immigration Acts. Although Martens himself did not advocate the forcible overthrow of the U.S. government, nor was he proven to be a member of the Communist Party, his affiliation as the representative of a foreign government which sought the overthrow of the American system constituted grounds for deportation. As such, Wilson directed the Commissioner of General Immigration "to take said Ludwig C.A.K.Martens into custody and deport him at the expense of the Government of the United States."[67]

Once he learned of the U.S. government's decision, Soviet Foreign Minister Tchitcherin directed Martens to rescind all orders previously placed with American businessmen and return to Soviet Russia. Secretary of Labor Wilson, mindful of the possibility of future relations with the Bolsheviks, allowed the director of the Soviet Bureau to leave the country without the embarrassment of formal deportation. On January 22, 1921, Martens, his family, and a number of the Soviet Bureau's office staff left New York City aboard the "second Soviet ark," the *S.S.Stockholm*. Upon reaching his destination, the Department of Labor announced the cancellation of the deportation warrant. The case of Martens and the Soviet Bureau was closed.[68]

In retrospect, the activities of the Soviet Bureau, even more so than their words, belie the Lusk Committee's charges that Martens' organization fomented revolution in America. From the bureau's inception, Martens, Heller, and Nuorteva repeatedly denied allegations regarding the dissemination of radical propaganda and interference in U.S. internal affairs. Responding to critics who pointed to the international Comintern's stated goal of ultimately destroying the world capitalist system, Martens replied "We are not such fools as to think other governments can be overthrown as the result of outside interference."[69] Heller further developed the bureau's position in a letter to Pittsburgh shoe manufacturer James P. Mulvihill. "The Russian Soviet Government Bureau does not interfere in American affairs," he plainly stated. "Notwithstanding loose talk about the representatives bureau, [we have] consistently avoided even a semblance of such propaganda."[70]

Despite such pronouncements, Martens continued to face heightened scrutiny for the bureau's press releases describing the situation in Russia, the publication of a weekly information bulletin, and the circulation of Lenin's "Letter to the American Workingmen." In defense of his actions, Martens emphasized "All that I am doing is to tell the truth about Russia and in furtherance of that work to give the news, which in no instance is anti-American, to about 2,000 newspapers in various parts of the country." To claim that the Soviet Bureau or the Bolshevik government was agitating for the overthrow of the U.S.

government was, he claimed, false.[71] Even following the Lusk Committee's raid and subsequent public hearings concerning subversive activities, Soviet Bureau employees continued to deny such allegations. As late as November 1919, Heller announced, "I am under strict orders from the Lenin Government, as are Mr. Martens and all other official representatives of Soviet Russia, to refrain entirely from political propaganda." The bureau's only objective in the U.S., he stressed, was "to make it possible for Russia to obtain essentials for rebuilding" their country."[72]

However, the Soviet Bureau's denial of allegations regarding propaganda was not completely truthful. To the contrary, the Bolsheviks — through Martens—pressured for much more than a resumption of trade between the two countries. In reality, Martens and his staff viewed the establishment of commercial relations as the key to a greater goal of achieving official U.S. diplomatic recognition of the Bolshevik regime. Despite public pronouncements downplaying the bureau's interest in political recognition, Heller easily drew the connection between the resumption of trade and the onset of diplomatic relations. In his handwritten ledger, the commercial director concluded "that there is a market, an active, demanding market" in Russia, and the resumption of U.S. trade in that market "will sooner or later break down all political barriers, all barriers artificially created." Martens agreed with Heller's analysis, holding Russia's position to be "that recognition will follow after trade relations…are reestablished. We want recognition, but we understand the difficulties before us and when the time comes how to overcome them."[73] To that end, the Soviet Bureau undertook serious efforts to cultivate support for lowering existing trade barriers and resuming normal relations between the two nations. Although publicly opposed to the Soviet Bureau's stated mission, prominent businessmen and government officials alike privately supported this strategy to varying degrees, as has been previously explored.

At the state level, however, the Lusk Committee did not hold duplicitous positions in the bureau's activities. Regardless of his stated intentions, the committee held Martens' efforts in low regard. Despite their biased convictions, the committee did express an accurate understanding of the Soviet Bureau's overriding strategy: to obtain diplomatic recognition via commercial intercourse, with American businessmen encouraging government officials to pressure to the State Department into altering their official position on Bolshevik Russia. In the committee's final report, Lusk concluded that "the success of the propaganda which Martens has so skillfully employed is shown by the growing sentiment among members of Congress favoring the recognition of Soviet Russia." Through the efforts of Heller and the Commercial Department American businessmen have "bombarded" Congress with requests to establish formal relations with Russia. "By these methods," the report concluded, "legislators who pride themselves upon being independent thinkers have become unconscious tools of the Russian proletariat."[74] The subsequent federal investigation of Martens' endeavors, conducted by the Senate Foreign Relations Committee, ultimately reached the same conclusion. " [It is] inescapable," the SFRC stated, "that the entire fabric of trade negotiations which Martens unrolled was part of an ingenious scheme of propaganda to create sympathy, based upon cupidity" for the Bolshevik government."[75] The director of intelligence at Scotland Yard agreed with this assessment, finding the commercial activities of the Soviet Bureau to be "an insidious form of propaganda...no doubt intended to cover more illicit methods of furthering the Bolshevik cause."[76]

Contrary to the Lusk Committee's final report, as well as the conclusions reached by the U.S. Senate and British intelligence, the Soviet Bureau's endeavors were neither radical nor subversive in nature. That Martens defended the Bolshevik Revolution and spoke frequently at Communist Party rallies was certain; however, accusations that the Soviet Bureau channeled millions of dollars into a propaganda campaign designed to foment revolution in America were baseless. Records indicated that at times Martens lacked the necessary funds even to satisfy the Bureau's payroll and operating expenses. Furthermore, as a commercial operation, the Bureau enjoyed little success. Owing largely to the Lusk Committee's raid and subsequent investigations, Martens managed to sign a mere dozen contracts, of which only one was completed. Although correspondence and memoranda suggested that the Soviet Bureau had potential agreements with hundreds of American businesses, the Lusk Committee's attacks destroyed any chance of their fulfillment.

In simplest terms, revolutionary Russia faced the task of rebuilding that which World War One had devastated. As a result, Russia offered an enormous market for American businessmen to rid themselves of postwar accumulations in inventories. The Soviet Bureau attempted to alleviate both challenges by bringing the two together. Rather than radical activities, the representatives of the bureau could be accused of little more than behaving in a rational, pragmatic fashion, in the process repeatedly facing government obstacles and false accusations of subversion in their quest for an improvement in relations between the two countries. Louis Kantor, correspondent for the New York *Tribune,* captured the true nature of the Soviet Bureau in an article he wrote based upon his visit to Martens' offices one week following the Lusk Committee's raid:

> I was frankly disappointed with the Soviet offices. No long-haired men, no dreamers, and no idealists. Apparently only hard-headed businessmen, anxious to establish trade relations with Russia. I had an idea from somewhere that the Bolsheviki would diminish the hours of work, a sort of millennium, and yet Nuorteva's secretary spoke freely about her overtime work. The whole experience is frankly disillusioning. The offices of L.C.A.K.Martens are just ordinary business offices.[77]

Despite the Soviet Bureau's minuscule success in establishing trade relations and its non-existent efforts to incite revolution, New Yorkers nonetheless feared Martens' operation. Rather than the truth, they chose to believe the Lusk Committee's characterization of the Bureau's activities. The public hailed Lusk and Stevenson's efforts to protect the state and nation from the evil Martens and his cohorts represented. Having thus established a reputation for no-holds-barred tactics in their attack upon the Soviet Bureau, the committee looked forward to the future, obviously anticipating similar victories in months ahead. According to Stevenson's findings, the funding allegedly provided by the bureau comprised only one element of the subversive infrastructure present in New York. Education, he contended, presented a more dangerous foe, for schools created numerous opportunities for radical teachers to proselytize among young minds. The danger presented itself in two forms: teachers in public schools who oftentimes hid their political leanings from administrators and school boards, yet spread their beliefs among their students; and private schools that openly professed radical doctrines. Initially, the Lusk Committee set their sights on the latter, choosing to follow-up their raid on the Soviet Bureau with an even more elaborate attack on the Rand School of Social Science.

Chapter 5
The Rand School vs. the Lusk Committee

ALTHOUGH THE SOCIALIST PARTY OF AMERICA SERVED THE POLITICAL needs of many in the working class, party leaders understood the necessity to educate the masses as well. During the earliest years of the party, from 1901 until 1906, the American Socialist Society served that purpose by arranging lecture courses and classes for the study of economics and socialism, as well as aiding in the acculturation of newly-arrived immigrants. However, from its inception, the ultimate goal of the society was to create a permanent educational institution to meet these and other needs. Finally, in 1906, the society created the Rand School of Social Science with two stated purposes: first, to offer to the public facilities for the study of socialism and related subjects; and second, to offer socialists instruction and training in order to make them more efficient party functionaries.

Initially, the Rand School struggled to keep its doors open. Bounced around the Lower East Side for over a decade, the school finally found a permanent home in the People's House, a building located in Manhattan that the Society of the Commonwealth Center had recently acquired. Likewise, enrollment remained weak throughout the early years of the school's existence, at times barely reaching 250 students. However, from its modest origins the Rand School steadily grew; as the Socialist Party gained strength during the First World War, enrollment escalated, eventually exceeding 1,500 students in 1916, which created serious overcrowding and forced administrators to seek a new location for the school. By 1918, over 5,000 students registered for an average of twenty class sessions each, a figure that did not include single admissions to evening lectures, as well as extension and correspondence courses.

A fund established through a deed of trust executed by the late Carrie Rand, a veteran of the antislavery abolitionist movement, financed the Rand School from 1906 to 1921. However, the bulk of working capital came from student tuition fees, bookstore sales, donations, and ticket sales for balls and concerts. Although tuition varied among the courses, students paid an average of twenty cents per lecture or class session. In 1918 alone, tuition yielded over half of the $45,000 annual operating expenses of the school; bookstore profits generated an additional $10,000. Individual donations from former students and friends of the school, seldom exceeding $10 each, generated the balance. The Rand School proudly advertised that operating costs remained low in large part thanks to teachers and lecturers who rendered their services cheaply due to "their hearty devotion to the school's educational purpose." School records revealed that it never paid a salary of more than $2,500 annually to any instructor or school official.[1]

The administrative staff and faculty of the Rand School was surprisingly diverse, given the institution's close ties to the Socialist Party and inability to offer substantial salaries. In 1909 Algernon Lee and Bertha Mailly assumed the positions of Educational Director and Executive Secretary, respectively, charged with maintaining the daily operations of the school. The principal, full-time instructors included David P. Berenberg, a graduate of the City College of New York; Dr. Scott Nearing, a former faculty member at the University of Pennsylvania; and Alexander L. Trachtenberg, a graduate of Yale University.

Rather than permanent instructors, however, the Rand School relied upon numerous guest lecturers and temporary instructors, a list of which read like a "who's who" of prominent educators and liberal thinkers of the day. Professors from Columbia University, Brown University, New York University, Princeton University, and Dartmouth College frequently offered their services to the school, including renowned historian Charles Beard, sociologist Lester Ward, and biologist David Starr Jordan. Guest speakers included civil rights activists W.E.B. DuBois, A. Philip Randolph, and Chandler Owen; anthropologist Dr. Robert Lowry of the American Museum of Natural History; U.S. Congressman Meyer London; Florence Kelley, founder of the National Consumers' League; Owen Lovejoy, head of the National Child Labor Committee; and novelists Jack London and William Butler Yeats. Clearly, for a noticeably modest fee, the school exposed its students to a remarkable list of eminent speakers.[2]

Although the Rand School served primarily as an auxiliary to the Socialist Party, steady growth required diversification as the years progressed. By the fall of 1919, the school offered courses in natural science, philosophy, literature, drama, music, and the arts, in addition to the staple classes of history, economics, and political science.

Furthermore, to better serve the workers of New York City, regardless of their political affiliation, the Rand School began offering practical courses in grammar, correction of accent, public speaking, and hygiene.

Such courses fell into one of three main divisions at the school: the Local Department, the Workers' Training Course, and the Correspondence Department. The Local Department scheduled evening and weekend lecture series and individual class sessions for residents living within reach of the school; the timing allowed workers who could not participate during regular business hours to enjoy the school's educational benefits. The Workers' Training Course offered similar courses on a full-time basis, in the hope of preparing students for positions within the Socialist Party, labor unions, relief societies, and the radical press. Under this program, students attended classes full time for a period of six months at a cost of $75.00, which included tuition and textbooks. For an additional fee, students could live at the People's House while completing the program. The Correspondence Department, created in 1913, brought a national scope to the school's work. Directed by Berenberg, the department offered introductory courses on socialism for local groups and individuals in over two dozen states as far away as California, and in foreign countries such as Canada and Mexico. Within two years of its formation, over 2,000 students nationwide had taken one of the three courses offered through the department.[3]

A diverse faculty, combined with a varied course listing and format, revealed the teaching aims of the Rand School. As Lee explained in the *Bulletin for 1919±1920,* the school did not seek "red ink publicity; reporters who visit in the expectation of finding some lurid or bizarre material for a story are often sadly disappointed to find that the Rand School is really a school, with sane, healthy, good-humored, hard-working teachers and students." Dogmatism, sensationalism, and dry routine were unacceptable according to Lee. Above all else, the aim of the Rand School was "to cultivate in the students' minds a habit of intellectual courage, of open-minded inquiry, of self-critical thinking, to aid them in mastering right methods of study, and to introduce them to sources of knowledge— in a word, to educate rather than instruct." In subsequent legal proceedings, the school repeatedly defined itself as "distinctly an educational institution, auxiliary to the socialist movement." Despite the school's emphasis upon freedom of thought and open door policy to all students and instructors regardless of their political affiliation, however, critics refused to look beyond the Socialist Party's formal endorsement of the institution as proof of the teachers' and administrators' radical leanings.[4]

In conjunction with their normal course offerings and evening programs, the Rand School operated the Department of Labor Research, as well as a bookstore containing thousands of pamphlets and books, socialist and otherwise. Established in 1915, the Department of Labor Research quickly gained notoriety for its investigations into working conditions and strikes in New York and throughout the country. Labor unions across America repeatedly requested statistical reports from the department to assist them in their negotiations over wages and hours. Recognizing the benefits their research provided, the department began publishing *The American Labor Year Book* in 1917; by 1918, libraries, government offices, and corporations throughout the country began placing annual requests for the book. The aim of the Department of Labor Research, according to their promotional literature, was to establish a scientific link between the Rand School and the socialist movement in America. By investigating union and political activity, the department intended to help students find meaningful employment within the labor movement and Socialist Party, as well as help legislators and party officials prepare programs and policies favorable to their cause.[5]

The Rand Book Store served two important functions as an auxiliary to the school. Politically, it disseminated socialist, radical, and labor-oriented literature to the school's students, as well as to the general public. More importantly, especially during the early years of the school's struggle to survive, the bookstore generated thousands of dollars of income to offset the deficit created by the school's academic endeavors. Bookstore profits doubled from 1916 to 1917, reaching levels in excess of $19,000, and again by 1918, exceeding $39,000. Among the works carried by the store were standard socialist tracts, including biographies of Karl Marx and Eugene Debs, John Spargo's *Applied Socialism,* and Morris Hillquit's *History of Socialism in America;* works on political economy, including Thorstein Veblen's *Instinct of Workmanship,* and the writings of David Ricardo and John Stuart Mill; and literature on the labor movement, including studies on the Industrial Workers of the World and trade union movements. The store also sold pamphlets and books on controversial topics, such as women's suffrage, birth control, and evolution. However, the store's shelves also contained numerous works of fiction, drama, poetry, and art that appealed to the general public, regardless of their political leaning. Customers could even purchase works critical of socialism, such as Henrí Guyot's *Socialistic Fallacies,* although the store did not prominently display such books.[6]

On the eve of the Red Scare, the Rand School of Social Science was a flourishing educational institution. Enrollment had steadily increased since 1912, and the school was financially solvent, although donations and book store profits, more so than tuition, made self-sufficiency possible. As the educational arm for a movement strained for funds, the Rand School was, put simply, an overwhelming success. However, the school developed as more than a training ground for future party leaders; it offered a reasonably priced education for any interested person, regardless of their political affiliation. Although geared towards working class individuals who had time only for evening and weekend courses, all were welcome to enroll and participate in school activities.

Educational Director Lee characterized the student body, as well as the larger purpose of the school, in a subsequent legal deposition. "We are not just Socialists," he explained. "Our students come from all walks of life." However, he said, all students leave the school with "an informed, intelligent, constructive idealism that builds in a new and better way where the present structure fails and collapses." He equated the Rand School with "a great educational power plant" with its energies "dedicated to the cause of political freedom and economic justice" regardless of whether or not such goals are achieved through socialism or by other means.[7]

The first weapon of reactionaries is the mob. Long before the Lusk Committee conducted its official raid, the Rand School felt the wrath of the mob on numerous occasions. The first of four separate attacks upon the school took place on November 25, 1918, when a group of young men in military-style uniforms stormed the People's House following a socialist rally at Madison Square Garden. Organized by the American Defense Society, the men broke many of the building's windows, but failed to gain entrance before police dispersed the group. The following April mobs, again consisting primarily of discharged soldiers and sailors, swarmed the school as they chased Ralph Trott, president of the Soldiers, Sailors, and Marines' Protective Association, from Union Square to the People's House. While searching for "that damned Bolsheviki" the mob disrupted a public lecture and a student dance, attacking an innocent bystander with a black-jack at the latter. Although the police eventually responded to calls from school officials, the group had dispersed before the authorities arrived. Two days later another crowd of military men forced entry into the Rand School, where the New York City socialist aldermen were holding a caucus. A squad of policemen arrived as the mob tore down circulars, bulletins, and announcements found in the building; however, no arrests were made.[8]

As winter gave way to spring, and as economic and social turmoil mounted in the face of a growing socialist presence, the school once again became a prime target for citizens whipped into a frenzy by the growing red hysteria. On May Day, the largest attack on the Rand School to that date occurred when a uniformed crowd marched from Madison Square Garden to the school where a meeting of the Leather Workers' Union was in progress. Although school officials barricaded the doors and called for police assistance, the mob scaled fire escapes to enter the building on the top floors. In less than fifteen minutes, the military intruders ransacked the library, nailed an American flag to a makeshift flagpole on the roof of the school, and ordered everyone present into the street to sing the "The Star Spangled Banner." Much of the throng left to attack the offices of the New York *Call* before the police arrived; again, no arrests were made.[9]

Elected officials and newspaper editors throughout the nation applauded the public stance taken in New York City. Ole Hanson, the mayor of Seattle who successfully crushed an attempted general strike earlier in the year, offered to help "clean up" the radical problem in New York. He commented, "If the government doesn't clean them up, I will. We will hold meetings and have hanging places. You may be willing to take the trouble to deport these traitors, but I am ready to hang them to the first convenient light pole." The Washington *Post* captured the growing public hysteria in an editorial attacking the latitude given radical speakers under the guide of free speech: "Away with the red flag. The soapbox agitator who preaches violence should be summarily suppressed. Free speech has been outraged long enough. Let there be a few free treatments in the electric chair."[10]

In the midst of this growing anti-radical sentiment, Clayton Lusk, Archibald Stevenson, and the Joint Legislative Committee struck again. A well-established pattern of repression, combined with heightened public hysteria, convinced Lusk that his strategy of raiding and destroying radical strongholds, as he had done with the Soviet Bureau, was the proper approach to the threat. That his committee targeted the Rand School was no surprise. Since March, committee members repeatedly indicated that radicals within the educational system represented a particularly dangerous menace to American society; Stevenson's previous testimony before the Overman Committee corroborated their fears. In fact, in a report he prepared for the Military Intelligence Division of the U.S. Army a year earlier, Stevenson had specifically mentioned the Rand School as "the inspiration for the Socialist movement in America." Secret reports from operatives stationed within the school further convinced committee members of its subversive nature. Rather than students pursuing "constructive idealism," as the school's educational director professed, investigators discovered "agitators, propagandists, and organizers...trained to preach revolution, and financially supported by red sympathizers." From the perspective of the Lusk Committee, a raid upon the school represented a logical extension of their investigation into radicalism.[11]

Committee investigators were nothing if not prepared for their June 21st raid on the Rand School. For days in advance, operatives mingled among students and took note of the location of various offices in the People's House. Crudely drawn maps enabled the state police working with the Lusk Committee to plan the comprehensive raid. One day prior to the event, Lusk compiled a hastily-typed checklist he entitled "Program for the Raid." Among the items listed were three moving vans, fifteen balls of heavy twine, and five hundred evidence tags; he apparently expected to confiscate a significant number of documents. Also concerned for his safety, as well as for the protection of his operatives, Lusk requested three squads of uniformed policemen, revolver permits for his investigators, and identification badges for his operatives within the school.

Most intriguing were the final three items on the checklist: two dozen reporter credentials, instructions for the captains, and three rooms at the Prince George Hotel. The desire for a pool of journalists clearly indicated Lusk's intent to orchestrate a media circus during the raid; as he had demonstrated in the past, no press was bad press. The instructions for the captains conducting the raid was a direct result of the lesson Lusk learned from the heavy-handed tactics his men employed when they stormed the Soviet Bureau a week earlier. In order to avoid subsequent legal battles over Fourth Amendment questions of illegal search and seizure, Lusk wanted the Rand School raid to proceed in an orderly fashion. The printed instructions stressed courtesy and cooperation, as well as care in handling documents and furnishings at the school; no physical damage was to result. Finally, the three rooms at the hotel were to provide Lusk a location to receive the confiscated documents and review them for material essential to his committee's investigation before relinquishing them to the magistrate who signed the warrant, despite the fact that the warrant required the state police to immediately deliver all documents to the judge's chambers.[12]

Unlike the raid on the Soviet Bureau, for which Lusk obtained a search warrant from a local traffic court judge, the raid on the Rand School occurred under the watchful eye of Chief City Magistrate

William McAdoo. Mindful of the publicity generated by the shoddy search of Martens' offices, McAdoo closely scrutinized the committee's application. In his original affidavit and request for a warrant, Clarence L.Converse, one of the committee's chief investigators, listed excerpts from a variety of pamphlets and books he purchased at the Rand School Book Store a week earlier. Among the "revolutionary, seditious, and obscene statements" he found in the literature, Converse repeatedly referred to documents that advocated violence and bloodshed. Specifically, he quoted from Lenin's letter to American and British soldiers: "Comrades! Drop this dirty work. Turn your guns on your real enemies, the capitalists!" Refusing to blindly sign the warrant based solely on an affidavit, McAdoo interrogated Converse. In the subsequent exchange, Converse revealed that he had never attended a meeting at the school, nor had he spoken to anyone with the exception of asking how much he owed for a bundle of pamphlets he purchased at the bookstore. Although reluctant to issue the warrant, McAdoo eventually relented; however, he included specific stipulations to limit the scope of the raid. McAdoo permitted committee investigators to seize "all books, letters, papers, circulars and literature…having to do with anarchist, revolutionary, and Bolsheviki activities, and Socialists advocating violence." The magistrate added the final two words to the warrant, exclaiming he refused to "issue a warrant for Socialist books" unless they clearly called for violent action.[13]

Upon signing the warrant, McAdoo issued a strong, verbal warning to Converse and Deputy Attorney General Samuel Berger, who was also present at the hearing, regarding the committee's conduct. First, he cautioned that the warrant did not provide *carte blanche,* the Lusk Committee could not seize "innocuous papers or private accounts" that had nothing to do with violence. Furthermore, the committee was to inventory all of the materials seized and surrender them to McAdoo on Monday, two days after the Saturday raid. When Berger interjected that the sheer volume of material would preclude delivery to the judge's chambers, McAdoo sternly warned him to protect the integrity of the materials. "The papers seized are under my orders," he stated. "You must not do anything with them unless you acquaint me with it; you must not move them, and must not use them for any purpose without informing me." Finally, McAdoo admonished the Lusk Committee for its excessive use of force in the previous raid against the Soviet Bureau. As for the proposed raid on the Rand School, "only the amount of force necessary to get these papers is to be used," the judge concluded; "no unnecessary force and positively no destruction of property." McAdoo planned on running a taut ship.[14]

Within hours of receiving the warrant, the Lusk Committee staged "the biggest raid of the kind in the history of the city" and, clearly, "the most spectacular raid" undertaken by the committee. At 2:30 in the afternoon, fifty members of the New York State Troopers and the former American Protective Association divided into parties of two and began a well-planned search of the Rand School. Stevenson and Berger, both of whom were present, directed the troopers to examine the contents of the bookstore, library, publicity department, storeroom, and administrative offices of the school. In addition, Stevenson ordered one officer to take control of the telephone switchboard so to ascertain the names and telephone numbers of the persons contacting the Rand School during the raid. The raid "went off as smoothly as a well-rehearsed theatrical production," according to one report. Stevenson had one objective, "Names!", he told the reporters present at the raid. "That is what we want chiefly, names of all the parlor Bolsheviki, I.W.W.'s, and socialists we can get hold of. They will be a real help to us later on." Since his appearance before the Overman Committee six months earlier, Stevenson's goals remained unchanged.[15]

Rand School officials viewed the raid in a different light. Algernon Lee denounced it as "amusing and also annoying," and characterized Stevenson as "the greatest maker of Bolsheviki in America." S.John Block, counsel for the school, likewise warned, "If these people don't want Bolshevism in America, they had better stop trying to create it." He went on to decry the incident as an "indefensible, malicious action." The next day, Block clarified his statements, comparing the Lusk Committee's tactics to those that resulted in revolutions in other countries. "It is entirely within the realm of possibility," he cautioned, "that people may be goaded to extreme action in this country by a disregard of their rights by those who are in power and who do not know how to exercise that power."[16]

Perusing the fruit of their initial raid on the Rand School, the committee immediately announced its plan to detain all of the "parlor Reds" whose names were listed in the files and card indexes seized from the institution. Upon a cursory, overnight glance at the records, one committee member felt qualified to divide such radicals into three groups. "The first is a small minority who would resort to any extreme to carry out their programme of revolution," suggested State Senator Boylan. "The second is made up of loose-mouthed, mentally-unbalanced political reformers," he observed; "and the third consists of a depraved few drawn together by talk of free love and the nationalization of women." Despite drawing such distinctions, Boylan quickly added that all three groups represented subversive threats and should be dealt with accordingly.[17]

The raid was a tremendous success with one exception; in the office of the Society of the Commonwealth, state troopers located a large safe that was not mentioned in the original search warrant. Heeding Chief City Magistrate McAdoo's instructions, Berger and Stevenson left the safe untouched, but guarded by state police overnight, until Converse returned with a second search warrant. In his affidavit before McAdoo, the committee investigator told of a comment he overheard during the initial raid, when a school official allegedly said, "It's a good thing they haven't opened that big safe on the third floor." From the "jealousy with which it was guarded," as well as the comments he overheard, Converse concluded that the safe must contain seditious documents that "endangered human life and threatened grievous bodily injury or property destruction." McAdoo agreed, and quickly granted a second warrant allowing the investigators to open the safe, by force if necessary, and examine its contents.[18]

The next day, led by Berger and Stevenson, state troopers engaged the services of Vincent Thomas, "an expert safe opener," to crack the seven foot high safe. I.M.Sackin, counsel for the Commonwealth Center, summoned two policemen passing by on the street to guard the safe; however, upon reading the warrant, they deferred to Berger's authority as Deputy State Attorney General and refused to intervene. Thomas then used an automatic drill to open the safe in six minutes. Sackin directed Lee to make an inventory of all materials removed by the Lusk Committee. Records seized included a list of contributors to the Rand School, minutes of the board meetings of the American Socialist Society, and written evidence that the Rand School aided in the fund-raising drive for the defense of William Haywood and other I.W.W. leaders convicted in Chicago in the previous year. Stevenson delivered the papers to the committee's temporary headquarters in the Prince George Hotel, where Lusk and other members had already begun reviewing the materials seized in the initial raid. The next morning, state police who had been on guard at the Rand School since the initial raid left the premises; for the first time in three days, the People's House was quiet.[19]

Public response to the raid was swift. The first sign of a formal protest came late on June 21st, when the Conference of the Young Democracy concluded a three day convention at Rockaway Beach by passing a resolution condemning the Lusk Committee for their "czarist actions" against the school. Declaring the committee's behavior to be "an outrage against democratic ideals and American principles," conference organizers forwarded the resolutions to legislators in Albany in the hope that "such evils do not reoccur in the State of New York and that the citizens are allowed to enjoy their constitutional rights." Albert DeSilver, Director of the National Civil Liberties Bureau, offered a more detailed analysis of the events. To him, the idea that the school posed a radical threat was "nothing more or less than nonsense." However, he reserved his most scathing attack for the Chief City Magistrate McAdoo. "It should not be possible," DeSilver concluded, "for Mr. Stevenson to secure search warrants by such a simple method as having one of his subordinates make an oath to a bizarre conclusion;" the work of "silly busybodies who wish to pry into other people's private affairs unless proper cause can be shown" must end. Louis Waldman, a Socialist Assemblyman who would later be expelled from the State Assembly, likened the Lusk Committee's effort to force open the safe at the school to his "younger days in Russia, when the czar used such methods to deprive people of their liberties."[20]

Facing heat in the press, Lusk sought to regain the upper hand by publicly explaining and justifying the raid. As committee members continued poring over the documents they seized, he felt confident in reporting that the evidence would justify the raid. Furthermore, Lusk reiterated the broad goals of his committee. "What our committee hopes to do is to get at the cause of so much radicalism in this country and to do what we can toward effecting a remedy," he said. Lusk even invited leading Socialists and other radicals to appear before the committee for "a chance to be heard and to suggest remedies for the situation." By seeking constructive solutions through legal means, he concluded, "the great State of New York …is bound to go a great way toward solving these problems throughout the entire country." The promises of constructive measures and inclusive hearings were hollow, however. As with their raid on the Soviet Bureau, the Lusk Committee planned to introduce every piece of damning evidence possible in an attempt to close the Rand School's doors forever. Lusk revealed this strategy on the evening prior to the public hearing when, unwilling to wait for the spectacle to begin the next day, he informed reporters of a close connection he uncovered between the Rand School and the Soviet Bureau. The smear campaign was about to begin.[21]

Archibald Stevenson spent the entire first day of the public hearings reading into the record titles and excerpts from documents and pamphlets seized from the Rand School Book Store. Not surprisingly, the committee rejected Algernon Lee's request to testify at the hearing in defense of the school's operations. In a letter he sent to Lusk, Lee angrily denounced the raid on the school as little more than "a press agent's stunt" and demanded the opportunity to appear before an open session of the committee. Lusk's response to the outburst was equally terse. "Mr. Lee will have an opportunity to be heard if he has anything of constructive value to suggest," the committee chairman stated; "but we are not inclined to provide a forum for soap box oratory." Lusk intended to control the entire scenario, including who testified, the evidence presented, and if possible, the press accounts of the event.[22]

As the hearings continued the next day, committee members began to reveal evidence intended to associate the school with violent radicals. Upon establishing the link between the Rand School and the American Socialist Society, State Attorney General Charles Newton read into the record the corporate charter of the society. Specifically, he reported that a federal court had convicted and fined the society $3,000 under the federal espionage act for publishing Scott Nearing's pamphlet *The Great Madness*. Since the Rand School still employed Nearing and paid him over $600 for one month of lectures, Newton concluded that the institution harbored seditious writers. Stevenson then read into the record a complete list of lecturers at the school, as well as the compensation they received, in a thinly veiled effort at guilt by association.[23]

After a brief recess for lunch, Lusk opened the afternoon session of the public hearing by charging the Rand School with planning to foment revolution among African-Americans in an effort to overthrow the U.S. government. Intrigued by the accusation, newspaper reporters in the room eagerly awaited the evidence, which Lusk eventually provided in the form of an article by noted black socialist William A. Domingo. As editor of *The Emancipator* and contributing editor to *The Messenger,* Domingo frequently wrote articles detailing the poor economic and social conditions African-Americans faced. Early in June, he submitted an article entitled "Socialism Imperiled, or the Negro —a Potential Menace to American Radicalism" to the Rand School for possible publication. In it, he called for "white radicals to concentrate their efforts and propaganda upon the Negro race" in order to encourage their membership in radical organizations. Lusk wasted little time in blaming the Rand School for disseminating such propaganda clearly designed to encourage African-Americans to join the Socialist Party and "improve their lot in life by abolishing our form of government."[24]

Stevenson concluded the day's hearings by reading an article and a letter that he believed further indicated the revolutionary nature of the Rand School. The article came from *The Communist,* a left-wing socialist paper edited by John Reed, on sale at the school store. The letter, a copy of which the committee confiscated from Correspondence Director David Berenberg's desk during the raid, proved to be even more damning. Writing to a young man who requested literature for his fellow union members, Berenberg asked, "What are you going to do when the state robs you and your union and so makes you helpless to strike?" The answer, he wrote, was simple: "TAKE OVER THE STATE. Are the members of your local prepared to take over and conduct wisely and well the affairs of your town and county? Are you ready to meet the militia when the powers of the state and courts are against you? Are you arming yourself?" For Stevenson, the committee members, and reporters hungry for headlines, no other single piece of evidence better illustrated the Rand School's violent proclivities. Newspapers the following morning applauded the committee for its patriotic actions. The New York *Times,* in particular, congratulated Lusk for "proving conclusively" that the school's efforts were "determined and ruthless."[25]

However, as with many of the Lusk Committee's accusations, all was not as it appeared. In an attempt to clarify the Rand School's activities, executive secretary Bertha Mailly issued a press release the next day to answer many of Lusk and Stevenson's charges. Regarding the money paid to Nearing, Mailly claimed that no one employed by the school received anything more than "a modest salary." Specifically, the school paid Nearing for services rendered over a six month period at the school as well as outside the auspices of the institution. The committee's allusions to the Domingo article reflecting the school's propensity to foment revolution among African-Americans were equally misleading, Mailly claimed. While investigators did find the article in Berenberg's desk, they failed to mention also recovering a stamped, return envelope, along with a rejection letter, addressed to Domingo; the school had no intention of publishing the article. Finally, Mailly accused committee investigators of taking Berenberg's letter to union organizers in Ohio completely out of context. If Stevenson had bothered to read more of it into the record, the public would have ascertained the letter's true intent, for it concluded: "Are you arming yourself with the knowledge of the foundations of our society so that when these crises come to you, you will have an organization strong enough to have foreseen and forestalled them?" Rather than armed revolution, the letter promoted education. "These are the real facts," the school's executive secretary concluded; "but for some reason best known to it, the committee permitted witnesses to distort and misstate the facts." But all was not lost, Mailly proclaimed. Although "greatly outraged" that the Lusk Committee denied them a fair hearing, Rand School officials remained hopeful that the court system would right any wrongs. The time would come, Mailly warned, when both sides in the battle must "stand flatfootedly on the laws and Constitutions of the State of New York and the United States."[26]

Rand School officials did not wait long to begin their quest for legal redress. On June 28th counsel for the school, S. John Block, filed papers to vacate both search warrants on the grounds that McAdoo improperly issued them solely on the affidavit of a committee investigator. Although unlikely to result in a favorable outcome, Block felt it necessary to put the Lusk Committee on notice that the school would not simply close, as did the Soviet Bureau two weeks earlier. "We intend to see whether or not the courts would sanction the lynch-law methods which were followed by the men who raided the Rand School and the building of the Society of the Commonwealth Center," he told reporters. Once the school had a fair opportunity to present its arguments, "the gross illegality of the proceedings which were instituted against it will be manifest."[27]

One week later, Block requested an oral hearing before McAdoo on his petition to vacate the original search warrants, and lodged a protest regarding the disposition of the papers, which were still in the hands of the committee. At the hearing McAdoo relented, and ordered the Lusk Committee to immediately relinquish to him all documents obtained during the raid. "I have ordered the papers brought to my chambers forthwith," he stated; furthermore, he prohibited the committee from continuing to use the information in its hearings, and from revealing it to the press. However, Clayton Lusk denied ever receiving a formal court order; therefore, the committee retained possession of the papers, and continued to use them freely in their investigation. Eventually, the disposition of the papers fell into the hands of another judge. At the close of the hearing, McAdoo claimed he was ill and was leaving for the country for rest. Acting Chief Magistrate Charles E. Harris would have the final say in the matter. Frustrated by what he considered to be the Lusk Committee's open defiance of McAdoo's order, Block announced the next day his intention to expand the proceedings to punish officials who participated in the raid on the school.[28]

The school's defiance forced Lusk into uncharted waters. Two weeks earlier, a similar raid on the Soviet Bureau was sufficient to severely damage Martens' operation; within days the bureau had closed its doors. However, the Rand School fought back, as Block's legal maneuvering indicated. The Red Scare subtly took on a new character in July, 1919, as the drama slowly moved from committee hearings to legal hearings, and as the tactics shifted from spectacular raids to briefs and writs. Despite the new setting, the hysteria continued at a fevered pitch; and Lusk redoubled his determination to close the doors of the Rand School through any means necessary.

As Block and other attorneys for the school prepared their motions for a writ of prohibition that would vacate the original search warrants, the Lusk Committee set their own legal wheels in motion. To bolster the evidence obtained during the raid, the committee planted a secret operative among the school's student body to observe the activities taking place at the People's House throughout July. The reports of Operative No. 22, later identified as Benjamin Levy, detailed the meetings that occurred in the building, the new publications available at the book store, and the comments he overheard in passing. Although Levy never uncovered any dramatic plots to overthrow the American government, his investigations helped the committee to present a more complete picture of the school's allegedly revolutionary undertone.[29]

Based upon the evidence gathered by the committee and its agents, Attorney General Newton announced his intention to appear before the State Supreme Court and attempt to revoke the incorporation charter of the American Socialist Society, the school's parent organization, on two grounds: first, because of the society's federal conviction for publishing Nearing's pamphlet; and second, because the Lusk investigation revealed the Rand School to be a center for spreading Bolshevik propaganda. Within a week, Deputy Attorney General Berger had completed the necessary briefs, leaving Newton to decide whether to proceed with the action. The mere threat certainly attracted the Rand School's attention. When questioned by reporters about the move, Block contended there were no legal grounds for such proceedings; however, he noted, "As we have seen by experience, legal grounds may be ignored by those who seek to injure the school which is a law abiding and absolutely legal institution."[30]

On July 8th, Newton tested the waters, and received formal permission from State Supreme Court Justice Edward J. Gavegan to initiate proceedings to revoke the charter of the American Socialist Society and place the Rand School in the hands of a receiver. Since the

State Supreme Court could not hear the case until its October session, Newton requested a permanent injunction to close the school in the interim. In his deposition, Newton accused the school of "fostering class hatred" through "insidious and obscene propaganda." He supported his claims with many of the documents revealed by the Lusk Committee at its earlier public hearings, including the letter to union organizers in Ohio and the article by Domingo regarding Socialism among African-Americans. The State Attorney General's argument was persuasive; Gavegan agreed to the motion, and ordered defense attorneys to appear two days later to show cause why an injunction should not be granted and the school placed in the hands of a receiver with the intention of terminating its operations. What the Lusk Committee was unable to do through the result of a physical raid, it appeared ready to accomplish through legal proceedings.[31]

Facing possible extinction in less than a month, the Rand School and American Socialist Society turned to noted attorney Samuel Untermyer for assistance. Although he held no sympathy for socialism in principle, Untermyer firmly supported the school's right to profess and teach such ideas. "I am a pronounced anti-Socialist," he proclaimed, "but also a pronounced believer in free speech." So long as teachers and administrators at the Rand School promulgated their ideas through lawful means, Untermyer stood willing to defend their rights. If a true villain existed, he declared, it was the Lusk Committee, which "is doing incalculable harm by its unlawful methods and is driving law-abiding citizens into the arms of the radical wing of the party." For Untermyer, the Rand School cause was not only noble, but necessary. "I never have known anything as lawless as the Lusk Committee," he concluded; their "open contempt for law and order is a flagrant example of lawlessness."[32]

Untermyer wasted little time in retaliating against the Attorney General's efforts to close the school. He correctly assessed that the battle would be fought on two fronts: the State Supreme Court and the court of public opinion. In an open letter to the Lusk Committee, printed in newspapers throughout New York City, he criticized their "lawless and reckless" raid of the Rand School offices, as well as "the incredibly unlawful and despotic actions" of Clayton Lusk in particular. Untermyer deemed it his duty to keep the committee within the limits of the law that they repeatedly defied. Specifically, he demanded that the committee permit Algernon Lee to testify before them in an open, public hearing. Furthermore, he warned committee members to cease utilizing school documents as the basis for the "incompetent, unproved hearsay drivel" they regularly released to reporters. Such "extraordinary tactics" damaged the reputations of good men, Untermyer observed, and drove more people towards radicalism than did any action undertaken by the school. Such suppression of free speech must end immediately, he concluded; if the committee's "star-chamber proceedings" continued, they would do so at Lusk's own peril.[33]

Not known for backing down from a challenge, the Lusk Committee responded to Untermyer's comments with vigor. Despite evidence to the contrary, committee members suggested that Untermyer's services did not come cheaply; therefore, they concluded, the Rand School and American Socialist Society clearly had substantial financial backing, likely originating from American radicals, for their endeavors. Untermyer steadfastly denied such accusations; he repeatedly claimed "I am acting in this matter absolutely without compensation." When offered payment by the school, he declined the money. "I do not want any Socialist money, for I am bitterly opposed to the Socialists and all they stand for," he explained. Committee members also questioned Untermyer's judgment for taking up the school's defense. Assemblyman Louis M. Martin, Vice-Chairman of the Lusk Committee, commented adversely on the defense attorney's attempt "to make it appear that the American Socialist Society conducting the Rand School is an institution of eminent respectability, devoted to the public good." Given the society's previous conviction in federal court, Martin concluded, "Mr. Untermyer's notions of respectable character and mine differ materially."[34]

As the legal proceedings progressed, Untermyer assumed responsibility for the defense in both the matter of the Attorney General's efforts to revoke the charter of the American Socialist Society, as well as the Rand School's attempt to vacate the search warrants upon which the Lusk Committee based the original raids. Appearing before State Supreme Court Justice John E. McAvoy on July 10, Untermyer opposed an injunction to close the school pending a formal hearing on the society's charter; such a move would cause irreparable harm to the school before the case was ever heard, he contended. In a surprise move, he requested an immediate trial to answer Newton's charges against the society. "My suggestion is that we go to trial tomorrow morning and give this school a chance," he argued; "or that in the event the trial of the Attorney General's main action is put off until October, that this motion go over until the trial." Clearly caught off guard, Deputy Attorney General Samuel Berger opposed such a move. "I object to going to trial tomorrow," he pleaded; "I will not be able to go on with the trial until October, but I am prepared to argue this motion [for an injunction] now."[35]

The ensuing heated debate between Berger and Justice McAvoy foretold of the struggle the State faced in the coming weeks. When McAvoy indicated that an injunction threatened to close the school and destroy a business corporation, Berger responded that such action was necessary in order to prevent the school from continuing to disseminate seditious literature. "How long has that been going on?" McAvoy inquired. Berger's reply of "two years" enraged the judge. "Where has the Attorney General been in the meantime?" he asked; if the Rand School's lecturers and administrators represent that great of a menace, he concluded, "lock them up under existing law." Although McAvoy officially reserved judgment on the State's request for a temporary injunction, wishing to weigh the various briefs and arguments before rendering a decision, his testy exchange with Berger indicated his growing reluctance to issue one.[36]

Later that afternoon, fireworks again erupted in McAvoy's courtroom when the judge heard oral arguments on Untermyer's writ to prohibit Newton from making use of any materials seized during the raid on the school. The briefs that each side subsequently filed with the court characterized the larger battle between the Rand School and the Lusk Committee. Untermyer based his argument on two sound legal principles. First, he claimed that Justice McAdoo issued the original search warrants on insufficient affidavits provided by biased witnesses, specifically committee investigator Clarence Converse. Second, Untermyer claimed the committee violated the New York Code of Criminal Procedure by refusing to relinquish the seized documents to the judge who issued the warrants.[37]

Newton based his response to defense counsel's protests in rhetorical rather than legal terms, a tactic often employed by the Lusk Committee to curry public favor through a fear of radicalism. "The committee is engaged in a most important public work," Newton contended, as if to excuse the investigators from any failure to follow technicalities of the law. To him, as well as to others who continued to fan the flames of hysteria, the ends clearly justified the means. "Sinister and insidious forces in this State and elsewhere are endeavoring to undermine the most sacred institutions of our land, forces whose ideals are foreign to American principles," he concluded; therefore, such action was necessary.[38]

Untermyer disagreed. The Lusk Committee's continued use of the documents they obtained illegally threatened "to harm the school's public image," he exclaimed, and was "as damaging as the proposed injunction to close the institution." In a fevered pitch he accused Newton of presenting bits and pieces of evidence to the press, and thus "tearing reputations to tatters." Deputy Attorney General Berger immediately came to his superior's defense. "This case is brought by the Attorney General against the American Socialist Society," he explained; "Mr. Newton has no apology to make for being here." Untermyer vehemently protested. "He will have to apologize," the defense attorney concluded. "This is not the first time public office has been prostituted or a public officer prosecuted." Berger objected to such references; and McAvoy subsequently ordered Untermyer to sit. The judge later commented that he had seldom seen two attorneys as "red-faced and passionate about their cause."[39]

Justice McAvoy's decisions, issued the next day, gave the Rand School and the American Socialist Society partial victories. First, he refused to issue an injunction to close the school, and then he ordered the trial regarding the charter of the society to take place before him beginning July 28. Berger was to file the State's complaint, and Untermyer his answer, no later than July 21; the defense would then receive the bill of particulars no later than three days preceding the trial. As for the documents and publications seized during the raid, McAvoy ordered that "all the papers that have been and are to be used in connection with these proceedings must remain in the custody of the Court and not given out to anybody." Although not the writ of prohibition he desired, Untermyer did achieve an important victory; his risky strategy to call for an immediate trial, combined with McAvoy's decision to take possession of the records, made it exceedingly difficult for the Lusk Committee and the State Attorney General's office to use the papers seized from the Rand School to further smear the institution in the press before they had their day in court.[40]

Support for the Rand School legal defense grew in the intervening three weeks. School officials immediately undertook a nationwide campaign to raise funds for their cause. At a mass rally held on the night of July 11, 1919, they collected nearly $1,000. Speakers at the event included Algernon Lee and Scott Nearing, representing the school; Paula Cohen, the Vice-President for the International Ladies Garment Workers Union; Charles W.Ervin, editor of the New York *Call;* Socialist Alderman B. Charney Vladeck, manager of the *Jewish Daily Forward,* and Norman Thomas, of the National Civil Liberties Bureau. Throughout the evening, repeated mentions of the Stevenson's and Lusk's names drew hisses and boos from the crowd. Lee jokingly proposed a resolution thanking the Lusk Committee for the free publicity the Rand School received as a result of the raid.[41]

At another meeting held two days later, one speaker compared the Lusk Committee's raid to an outright burglary of school property. Communist Labor Party organizer James Larkin, who was himself arrested and indicted for criminal anarchy, later challenged the aptitude of committee members who, he suggested "are about as low a type of mentality as ever cussed the human heart." As the meetings continued in the ensuing weeks, one of many themes became increasingly clear: supporters believed that persecution of the school at the hands of government authorities would continue unabated unless the courts resolved the issue soundly in their favor.[42]

Subsequent advertisements in newspapers throughout New York City urged "all public-spirited citizens to assist the Rand School in its desperate fight" by sending financial contributions. Many heeded the call. One contributor wrote, "I am not a Socialist, but I am a firm believer in free speech. I believe there is a place for the Socialist Party and for the work the Rand School is doing. Now and then they may be over-radical, but the time needs radicalism; it will do us good." Another person offered five dollars "to assist in opposing those misguided prosecutors who, if left unrestrained, would speedily bring all law into contempt by denying the most elementary protection to those whose opinions differ from theirs." A professor of theology sent a check "as a slight token of the indignation I feel at the present official methods of repressing free speech in this country."[43]

Even businessmen and veterans came to the defense of the school, with some donations reaching as high as $100. One veteran of the First World War justified his contribution in a letter he sent to Senator Lusk. Having received a military bonus from the State of Massachusetts "to promote the spirit of patriotism and loyalty," he donated the money to the Rand School in order to defend the democratic principles for which he fought "against the autocratic attacks of your committee. I shall deem it a favor," he concluded the letter, "if you will add my name to the list of Liberals and Radicals which I understand you are compiling from the mailing lists of your victims." The defense fund grew throughout July and, more importantly, the doors of the Rand School remained open. Lee later commented "we found that we had many more friends than we had thought."[44]

The national press also began to question seriously the actions of both the Lusk Committee and the State Attorney General; to some, the repeated attacks upon the Rand School appeared increasingly personal and the accusations equally far-fetched. Editors of *The Nation* declared the evidence against the school to be "so weak and flimsy that the whole proceeding must be regarded as a peculiarly vicious and vindictive piece of rail-roading." Editors of *The Public* concurred; according to them, the Lusk Committee suffered "from a rush of authority to the head, and has turned itself into an inquisition." The whole investigation, they concluded "is conducted after the approved manner of the bigots of the Middle Ages." A New York *World* editorial called for the committee to "halt the witch hunt." In becoming judge, jury and prosecuting attorney, the editor concluded, the committee forgot its proper function; "it is solely a committee of investigation, with limited powers, which it seems none to well qualified to exercise."[45]

On July 29, the day before the trial was to begin, Untermyer subpoenaed Lusk, Stevenson, Converse, Newton, and Berger, as well as Chief City Magistrate Harris. He also attempted to serve a subpoena on City Magistrate McAdoo, but was informed by the housekeeper that he had "just left for somewhere in Maine." With the exception of McAdoo, Untermyer arranged to have the entire cast responsible for what he termed "the persecution of freedom of thought" present in the courtroom. To defend the Rand School's activities, he arranged an equally impressive witness list including lecturers who taught at the school, former students, social reformers, and people active within the socialist movement. The prosecution, however, had other ideas. Newton informed reporters on the eve of the trial that he planned to present a motion to postpone the action until October, as well as reintroduce his motion for an injunction to close the Rand School in the interim. When questioned about this decision, he announced the discovery of "new, potentially damaging evidence" against the Rand School, the review of which required several more weeks of investigation and witness interviews. The events of the next day revealed an alternative reason for the Attorney General's motion—a simple lack of preparedness.[46]

The trial lasted all of one day. After Justice McAvoy gaveled the session to order, Deputy Attorney General Berger formally requested a delay in the proceedings until October, so that the State could amend its complaint to include new evidence and allegations against the Rand School, as well as examine witnesses in other states. Untermyer strongly protested the delay on the grounds that the school was preparing for its fall term, and postponement would leave 5,000 registered students in limbo. More importantly, without immediate judicial relief, the false accusations directed against the school threatened to close its doors. "Libels affecting the school have been scattered throughout the country," he explained; "unless we get the hearing we are legally entitled to, the purpose of our enemies, who want to destroy the school, will be accomplished." In a bold move, similar to his previous call for an immediate trial three weeks earlier, Untermyer consented to answer any new charges the Attorney General could "stir up or invent" and "to go on trial this minute with those additional charges in the complaint."[47]

The defense attorney was particularly scathing in his attack on the Attorney General for the obvious delay tactic. "We are not going to let this man escape the immediate trial of this action, if we can avoid it," Untermyer declared. He feared, in particular, that the pattern of unlawful conduct by the State against the Rand School would persist unless an accounting before a court of law occurred without delay. "There is no rule he has not defied. The Attorney General's case," Untermyer concluded, "is the finest example of criminal lawlessness and the strongest incitement to disrespect of the law that I have ever known." Untermyer even waived the defense right to a bill of particulars. Actually, the prosecutor's attempted delay came as little surprise to Untermyer, who had received a telephone call from Deputy Attorney General Berger nearly a week earlier announcing his intention to do so. But while Untermyer's theatrics may have been planned, his message was serious. "We will not allow the Attorney General to play fast and loose with the court," Associate Defense Counsel S.John Block announced. Put simply, Untermyer called the prosecution's bluff.[48]

The ensuing debate between McAvoy and Berger sealed the State's fate regarding their attempt to postpone the case. When the judge asked why the Deputy Attorney General wanted to break a previous agreement to try the case at that time, Berger suggested a "number of matters" he wished to offer in affidavit form. Growing impatient with the delays, McAvoy refused to read additional affidavits; "just tell me what the matters are," he said. When Berger began to reply, "We would prefer..." McAvoy's patience had reached its limits. "No doubt you would prefer," he bellowed at the Deputy Attorney General, "but I'm asking for your rea sons, and I want an answer before we proceed any further." When a stunned Berger again explained that the State required at least a month's postponement to revise the charges, McAvoy called for an immediate trial. On Untermyer's motion, he dismissed all charges against the Rand School and the American Socialist Society. The case was over.[49]

As he left the courtroom, Untermyer offered a brief statement to the dozens of reporters who had covered the events surrounding the Rand School since the initial raid by the Lusk Committee over a month earlier. To him, the day's proceedings were no surprise. "The outcome was the logical outgrowth of this scandalous suit," he stated; "It was apparent from the day the action was begun that the Attorney General never intended to try it, and no matter how many actions he may begin in the future, in my judgment he never will try them." The entire episode, however, held a greater meaning for the country than simply keeping one school in New York City open. Individual constitutional rights and civil liberties were at stake, Untermyer argued. "If people's homes and offices can be ransacked, their safes opened by expert safebreakers, and their documents crated away to be used in an inquiry," he concluded, "there is no longer hope for freedom in this country." With such comments, Untermyer attempted to alert New Yorkers to the idea that the cure for radical thought may be as dangerous as the radical thought itself.[50]

In his closing thoughts on the entire episode, associate defense counsel S.John Block reiterated Untermyer's sentiments. "If this were not such an outrageous proceeding," he commented, "it would indeed be ridiculous." In his view, the proceedings against the Rand School by the Attorney General were "vicious and malicious." Yet, while the school had "nothing to fear" from the proceedings, Block worried that the attacks would continue. "I hope," he concluded, "that the people of the State of New York will not allow the Attorney General or the Lusk Committee to continuing wasting money for political adventuring." Block was prophetic in his fear, for neither Newton nor the Lusk Committee were finished.[51]

Despite the setback, Newton announced his intention to re-file charges against the American Socialist Society and the Rand School when the regular October session of the State Supreme Court met two months later. As a precursor of events to come, he proposed a new line of attack against radical institutions, legislative action. After the trial he informed reporters "If the court decides that the acts of this corporation are not in the interest of good government but that there is no law which authorizes the State to deal with them, then it will be my duty to recommend to the Legislature the enactment of laws to protect our institutions." Where the Lusk Committee raids and legal proceedings failed, laws governing teacher loyalty and licensing of private schools may succeed. The only question was whether a reactionary state legislature could overcome the will of a progressive governor.[52]

Chapter 6
From the Courtroom to the Legislature

DOWN, BUT NOT OUT, ATTORNEY GENERAL NEWTON CONTINUED TO attack the Rand School in the press throughout August and September as he prepared to re-file legal papers to close the institution. Most notable were his comments before a meeting of the National Association of Attorneys General on September 2, 1919. The message was a familiar one: associate the Rand School with other allegedly radical organizations that were more overt in their efforts, and then demand the school's closure because of such affiliations. The Rand School worked "hand in hand with the Martens-Bolshevist bureau," Newton charged; "this institution, whose charter I aim to revoke, is nothing more or less than a school of radicalism, a preparatory school for the I.W.W. and other extremely violent organizations." However, having faced defeat in the courtroom less than two months earlier, the Attorney General consciously introduced a new element into his campaign against the school, education legislation. Where the courts failed, the state legislature could succeed, he claimed; therefore, he called upon the politicians in Albany to pass laws that guaranteed "intensive instruction in the ideals and traditions of America in the schools." From police raids to courtroom battles, and now to the legislative chambers in Albany, the Red Scare in New York was entering its final stage.[1]

As the winter of 1919–1920 passed, public opinion regarding the efforts of Lusk, as well as of U.S. Attorney General A. Mitchell Palmer who began conducting his own raids of socialist and radical meeting places in November, covered the entire spectrum. Conservative news editors, including those at the New York *Times,* suggested that the Lusk Committee had not gone far enough in it efforts to stymie the Bolshevik menace facing the country. "The evidence of far-reaching anarchist activity has been spread before the country for months," the editors claimed; but while "something is always *going* to be done about it, not much *has* been done about it." In the absence of a clear victory for Americanism, "sensational raids and great thunder in the index impress nobody." The Lusk Committee's failure to close a small private school was an embarrassing testament to the power of the state, the *Times* editors concluded. "In the contest of intelligence between the police and the bomb-planters, the latter seem to have won." A month later, the newspaper adopted Newton's stance regarding educational reform. If institutions such as the Rand School cannot be closed by force or by legal proceedings, the time had arrived to pass new laws. The propaganda and teaching material uncovered at the school "makes real Americans hot with anger," the *Times* observed. "Poisons like this must not be vended or given away; they are mental wood alcohol."[2]

At the other end of the spectrum, men such as Walter Lippman, editor of *New Republic;* Professor Zechariah A.Chaffee of Harvard University Law School; Norman Hapgood, former American minister to Denmark; and Laurence Housman, British playwright, continued to publicly oppose the work of the Lusk Committee. At a luncheon of the League of Free Nations Association on February 28, 1920, Lippman noted the committee's inability to deal with the revolutionary conditions at work in America. "The plain fact is," he said, "that they have advertised more revolution than could exist, and caught fewer violent revolutionists than do exist." In a satirical review of the committee's endeavors, Lippman mocked their sense of self-importance, lamented their actions, and warned others of the repercussions. "There are some people in this country who believe they were chosen by God and the Union League Club to save the country from contamination," he observed. "Because they believed the country was going to rack and ruin they took any lawless measure to carry out their ideas." Lippman specifically accused the Lusk Committee of manipulating the news, character assassination, and violating "every principle of fair play." He concluded, "These men used the Government in the last few months in a more lawless fashion than it had been used in a century."[3] Increasingly, other New Yorkers, particularly journalists and educators, came to agree with Lippman that the Lusk Committee's disregard for the law, bordering on contempt, represented a greater threat to American institutions than did any position taken by the Rand School.

Facing such criticism, Lusk abandoned the committee's initial tactics of physical raids, private hearings, public revelations, and legal proceedings, and chose to adopt the Attorney General's new position emphasizing legislative action to bring about educational reform, one purpose of which would be to close the Rand School once and for all.

That Lusk would turn to his colleagues in Albany to assist in this endeavor came as no surprise. As the 143rd session of the State Legislature opened on January 7th, Assembly Speaker Thaddeus Sweet initiated proceedings to expel the five duly-elected Socialist Party members from the body. His reasoning was simple; as members of a political party whose doctrines were inimical to the best interests of the State of New York, they were disqualified from service in the assembly. The fact that Samuel DeWitt, Charles Solomon, Samuel Orr, Louis Waldman, and August Claessens represented nearly 30,000 citizens in the New York City vicinity appeared to be of little concern to Sweet, especially since most of the constituents comprised ethnic enclaves of first-and second-generation immigrants largely from southeast Europe. To the applause of the guests in the gallery, the State Assembly voted 140 to 6 to suspend the five Socialists pending a judiciary committee inquiry and a final vote on their qualifications. Despite an immediate wave of state and nationwide outrage over the event, Sweet and his colleagues stayed the course, and April Fool's Day voted overwhelmingly to dismiss all five men from the assembly. In the State Legislature, Lusk clearly found allies willing to tackle the radical threat facing the country, especially since the courts would not. Confident that he had discovered a means by which to finally close the Rand School, Lusk set about his work.[4]

In late January, 1920, the Lusk Committee held public hearings to discuss ideas concerning educational reform in New York State. Most of the educators and administrators they invited to speak favored an Americanization program in the public schools, higher standards for instructors, and higher salaries. There was also strong sentiment for a compulsory education program for foreign-born adults under 45 years of age. Frank Dickinson Blodgett, president of Adelphi College in Brooklyn, a women's liberal arts institution, testified that who teaches was of greater importance than what they teach. "If there is any place on earth where we should test a person's patriotism, Americanism, and all around good behavior," he concluded, "it is for anybody going into the teaching profession." While Blodgett believed the number of radicals teaching in the state was "the exception and not the rule," he still favored a new law to silence the few "who make a good deal of noise if they set out about it."[5]

John Jacob Coss, an assistant professor of philosophy at Columbia University, agreed with Blodgett's assessment. "I think that it would be very advantageous to make sure that the character and personality of every teacher is of the very highest type," he suggested, "character in the sense of positive manliness and patriotism." As the hearings continued the next day, Elmer Elsworth Brown, the chancellor of New York University, echoed such sentiments. "Everything should be done to assure the public of the fact that the teachers are loyal Americans," he stated; "only true patriots can enlighten immigrant students as to what are the real characteristics, qualities, and advantages of the American government."[6]

Subsequent public hearings focused on elementary and secondary education, specifically in New York City. William L.Ettinger, the superintendent for the city's public school system, reiterated the opinions expressed by college administrators; character, specifically patriotic character, was an essential ingredient for effective teaching. "The proper kind of teaching means the proper kind of Americanization," he stressed, "and you cannot be too careful in selecting your teacher." Socialism, anarchism, and other forms of radicalism, he concluded, were not appropriate ideologies for public school teachers to espouse. To those critics who claimed that teachers could separate their job from the politics, the superintendent strenuously disagreed. "The teacher is always a teacher," he said; "everything that teacher gives utterance to after three o'clock has a reflex on the classroom, just as much as if he stood in front of his class."[7]

Anning S.Prawl, president of the New York City Board of Education, lamented the board's inability to dismiss teachers who supported radical doctrines; state legislation was necessary to ensure that un-American teachers were removed from their jobs. Associate Superintendent John L. Tildsley agreed; only an organized state program, enforced by law, he contended, could ensure "American teachers who produce thoroughly American boys and girls." Like Ettinger and Prawl, Tildsley described the ideal teacher as one "who is moderate in his point of view, well-trained, a good thinker, and is steeped in American ideals." Regardless of the educational level, elementary, secondary, or collegiate, consensus abounded at the Lusk Committee hearings; quality teaching required 100 per cent Americanism, and current laws failed to guarantee that.[8]

On March 17, 1920, Clayton Lusk submitted his committee's preliminary report, as well as their recommendations for legislation, to the Senate and Assembly. According to the report, the committee specifically opposed any repressive measures to combat the radical menace; instead, they focused on constructive measures designed to enlarge the educational program of the state and elevate the teaching standards. Among the committee's greatest concerns was the questionable loyalty of public school teachers. Their year long investigation revealed several teachers who, despite being trained and licensed, held membership in revolutionary organizations dedicated to overthrowing the American government. Inasmuch as character and patriotism were essential qualities for effective teaching, the committee proposed a bill requiring a mandatory certificate of loyalty for all public school teachers. The plan required all currently employed teachers and future applicants to submit to an examination before the State Commissioners of Education regarding their moral character and loyalty to the state and nation. Refusal to obtain the certification was grounds for immediate dismissal.[9]

Equally distressing to the Lusk Committee were private institutions, such as the Rand School, which fell outside the scope of the existing state education laws. Having failed to close the school by means of physical raid and legal proceedings, the committee seized the opportunity to do so through legislation. In their report, they proposed a bill requiring a state license for all private, secular schools operating within New York. The bill forced private institutions to file an application with the Regents of the University of the State of New York. If the Regents found the school to be operating in a manner "detrimental to the public interest," they would deny or revoke the license, as well as encourage the attorney general to prosecute those schools that continued to operate without one. Exempt from the proposed legislation were religious schools throughout the state.[10]

Based upon the public hearings they held in January, the Lusk Committee also recognized the need for special classes aimed directly at immigrants who they believed were most susceptible to the radical propaganda disseminated by socialists, communists, and anarchists. Therefore, they proposed mandatory Americanization classes at factories and community centers, where they were most likely to reach first-generation immigrants. In addition, the committee recommended special courses to be offered at State Normal Schools to train teachers to conduct effective Americanization courses. Finally, should all of the educational measures fail to achieve their goals, and radicalism remain a threat to the state, the Lusk Committee called for the creation of a special bureau, under the direction of the Attorney General, to continue the investigation into revolutionary organizations and prosecute those groups and individuals who violate the state's twenty year old criminal anarchy statute.[11]

The immediate response to the committee's proposals appeared favorable. Assembly Speaker Sweet and Senate President pro tem

J.Henry Walters commented that the legislation would pass in record time given its "paramount importance." The New York *Tribune* also strongly supported the measures, especially the school licensing law, which, it claimed, would "close the Rand School permanently." An editorial in the New York *Times* agreed with the *Tribune's* assessment. "The Lusk Committee has done valuable work for the public," the editors concluded. "Its investigations have been fruitful; its recommendations are wise."[12]

However, not all were happy with the proposals. When State Senator Henry M.Sage of Albany presided over a public hearing of the Joint Finance Committee of the State Legislature on March 31, 1920, to discuss the bills, battle lines were drawn. The strongest opponent to the measures was attorney S.John Block on behalf of the Rand School. The bills, he claimed, threatened to "deny the American mind knowledge" and "force into secrecy those who refuse to fall in line." In addition, the Reverend F.H. Johnson, representing thirty Protestant churches in New York City; Captain Harold Riegelman of the United Neighborhood Settlement Houses; and Edward C.Byblcki, Chairman of the Emergency Education Conference of the Central Federated Union, specifically criticized the private school licensing measure, out of fear that authorities could arbitrarily close their educational branches simply by denying them a license.[13]

On April 13, 1920, the State Senate prepared to vote on the five "Lusk Bills," as they had come to be known in the press. Debate in the chamber was intense. The strongest opposition to the measures came from Senators George F.Thompson of Niagara, Frederick S.Davenport of Oneida, Stephen Gibbs of Erie, and W.Copeland Dodge of New York City, a small but vocal group of Democrats representing the growing number of critics who in the spring of 1920 began to take issue with the excesses of the political hysteria generated by the Lusk Committee. Thompson led the charge when he questioned the alleged patriotism underlying the committee's endeavors; to him, the motivation for the Lusk bills was a "desire to restrict the education of the laboring classes to teaching them how to labor and serve the little clique that usually has a decisive say" in political and business matters. Just as alarming, Thompson contended, was the power the bills granted to the Board of Regents "to define what constitutes patriotism and loyalty to the Government." The thought behind the proposals was obvious, he concluded: "Let us take a club to the workers." Davenport, who also taught political economy at Hamilton College, criticized the bills as an attempt at "goose stepping the mind" and "licensing thought and private and public opinion." Gibbs and Dodge specifically questioned the wide scope of the licensing bill. Gibbs feared the bill would affect courses run by the Young Men's and Young Women's Christian Associations. Dodge worried that Masonic schools could be closed under the auspices of the bill. Such attacks against the Lusk bills, although widespread and varied, shared one characteristic, a small but growing concern over civil liberties and the rights of individuals in the face of an increasingly powerful and repressive state government.[14]

The strongest support for the measures came from President pro tem Walters, committee member and Democratic Senator John J.Boylan, and Lusk himself. Lusk bristled at critics who questioned whether the radical threat was great enough to warrant such laws. "Of course it is," he responded; "any man who says the country is not in danger is uninformed, unintelligent or disloyal." Urged on by Lusk's Republican colleagues, three of the original five proposals passed in the State Senate: the bill creating a special secret service to continue the State's investigation into radicalism (31–20), the bill calling for public school teacher certification (43 to 8), and the bill for private school licensing (32 to 18). With such measures in place, the New York *Times* reported, it was only a matter of time before the Rand School and other similar institutions were "put out of business."[15]

With the wounds from the Socialist expulsions of the preceding January still fresh, the State Assembly considered the three bills on April 15th. Debate was as fierce as expected, with a number of opponents challenging outright the constitutionality of the measures. Assemblyman William S.Evans of the Bronx labeled the educational proposals "repressive and foolish" legislation, which would have no impact on socialism in the state. Radicalism was waning, he contended, until the Assembly "revived its life" with the expulsion trial. Specifically, Evans blamed "one or two men" with political ambition "who thought the time was ripe to follow in the footsteps of the Governor of Massachusetts." In response to the accusation, Assemblyman Martin G.McCue of New York City issued a veiled warning to his colleague, whom he considered to be "the greatest advocate of radical socialism that ever stepped across the threshold of this House." Clearly, McCue claimed, "all the Socialists have not yet been expelled from the Assembly; the ones we threw out were not half as radical as you, Evans." Despite such heated exchanges, Assembly passage of the bills was never in doubt. The school licensing measure passed overwhelmingly (100 to 30), as did teacher loyalty certification measure (136 to 4), and the bill to create a special investigative division under the auspices of the Attorney General (101 to 26). The bills now awaited approval or veto by Governor Alfred Smith.[16]

Smith's approval was not as certain as supporters of the measures hoped. In a state where Republicans overwhelmingly controlled both houses of the legislature, Smith was a staunch, progressive Democrat, cut from the same cloth as Woodrow Wilson and Robert LaFollette. Although originally a loyal Tammany Hall politician, Smith became a defender of good government and efficiency as he rose through the ranks to become Speaker of the Assembly in 1911, and eventually elected governor in 1919. Supporters of the Lusk bills realized they faced a hurdle in Smith; critics understood that he represented the last, best hope to defeat the measures. Most important, Smith recognized his precarious position, and summoned all of his political savvy to find a solution.

In late April, Professor William H.Giddings of Columbia University wrote to Smith expressing his displeasure over the school licensing and teacher certification bills. The New York *Times* published excerpts from the letter, as well as allowed Lusk an opportunity for rebuttal. "These measures are not Americanism," Giddings wrote; rather, "they are repugnant to everything that the people of this land have been trying for ten generations to establish as distinctly American." Should the bills become laws, he warned, history will condemn them. "They will be repudiated," he concluded, "and I do not hesitate to predict that everyone responsible for them will at no distant time deeply regret his action."[17]

Lusk strongly disagreed with Professor Giddings assessment. Referring specifically to the case of the Rand School, the senator justified the educational measures passed under his name. "However good the purpose of its founder, and however eminent and respectable men have lec tured there in times past, the obvious question is what is the school doing at the present time?" he asked. "Someone must determine what course of instruction is in the public interests and what course is detrimental," Lusk claimed. "Shall this determination be left to felons convicted of disloyalty to our government, or to the Board of Regents of the University of the State of New York?" To Lusk, the answer was obvious; state supervision provided the only reasonable solution.[18]

Public pressure on Governor Smith continued to mount throughout May as he contemplated his decision on the Lusk bills. Speaking at an open meeting of the National Civic Federation on May 11, 1920, Archibald Stevenson and Samuel Berger defended the measures as both necessary and morally justified. Stevenson attacked the Rand School in particular, claiming it continued the same activities that resulted in its conviction during the war. "The opponents of the bills are organizing, and give the impression that they are representing public opinion," he observed; "sadly, the good people of the State are falling for it." Berger, who had fought to close the Rand School for nearly a year, wanted the debates to end and conclusive action to be taken. "The time has come," he proclaimed, "when all the people ought to put themselves in one camp or the other; let all the criminal anarchists go in one camp and those believing in the Constitution go in the other." According to the deputy attorney general, continued talks simply allowed the radical elements in the state to organize stronger opposition to the bills. "The time has arrived," he concluded, "when we should put a stop to this coddling of anti-American doctrines."[19]

Despite Berger's vigorous defense of the measures, the balance of public opinion regarding the Lusk bills continued to waver. At that moment of uncertainty, a politically astute Governor Smith seized the opportunity to conduct a public executive hearing on the measures. The hearing took place in Albany on May 14, 1920. At the gathering, Berger again stressed the importance of the bills, as well as defended the year-long Lusk Committee investigation that resulted in them. "There is an imperative need for such statutes if New York is to curb sedition and radicalism effectively," he pleaded. Financier and Union League Club member Henry A. Wise Wood, another strong defender of the proposals, raised Governor Smith's ire when he read sexually explicit excerpts from *Married Love,* a textbook allegedly used by the Rand School. "You don't realize the rottenness of these people," Wood exclaimed; "the Rand School is comprised of moral perverts and social defectives." Mabel Washburn, a concerned citizen present at the hearing, agreed with Wood. She later wrote Smith, urging him to "contain the powerful wickedness" of the Rand School, whom she accused of "degeneracy, blasphemy, and incest," by supporting the bills. Former Senate Majority Leader Elon Brown joined the procession when he condemned the school for "attempting to poison the well springs of patriotism" and seeking "to destroy the Constitution and laws of the State."[20]

Opposition came from a number of sources, led by constitutional lawyer Louis Marshall, who had previously defended the Socialists expelled from the Assembly. "These bills affect the fundamentals of our governmental system and attack the liberty of the system," he observed. "They are so reactionary that no parallel can be found in American history." The fact that socialism represented an unsound doctrine was, to Marshall, irrelevant. "The question is," he stressed, "whether the thought of the State of New York shall be put in a straitjacket." According to Marshall, the Lusk bills were nothing more than the result of hysteria; yet their passage presented a grave threat to the American principles of freedom of speech and thought. Nothing was worse, he contended, than a government willing to pass judgment on the thoughts of individuals. "In a moment of hysteria shall we forget all that America stands for and adopt the hated Prussian system?" he asked. "The sooner we shift off this hysteria, the better it will be for the entire State." While some critics, including Brown, criticized Marshall's remarks as "cheap constitutional law," Governor Smith later wrote that his words "rang true."[21]

While Marshall indicted the entire set of proposals, other critics focused their comments on specific aspects of them. Mrs. William H. Rockwell, chair of the national board of the Young Women's Christian Association, feared that the school-licensing proposal threatened to "kill all the good work of the Y.W.C.A." Likewise, the Teachers' Union of New York sent a written statement to the Governor offering ten reasons why the loyalty bill was antithetical to quality teaching, and represented a grave threat to freedom of speech and freedom of thought. Finally, Algernon Lee, representing both the Rand School and the state headquarters of the Socialist Party, criticized the legislation for creating the very radicalism that the Lusk Committee claimed to fight. In the absence of real solutions to the economic and social problems that workers face in New York, he warned, "these bills serve only to incite the resort to secret organization and lawless violence."[22]

The day of hearings served their purpose. On principle, Smith had long opposed the Lusk proposals, as he had opposed the expulsion of the five socialist assemblymen in January. However, Smith the politician needed to gauge public opinion before rendering his final decision. The result of the hearings, combined with the hundreds of letters and telegrams he received in opposition to the bills, made the decision an easy one for him. Over the next five days he drafted strongly worded veto messages for each of the measures, and finally released them to the press on May 19, 1920. The school licensing bill, he wrote, "is unsound and vicious; it strikes at the very foundation of one of the most cardinal institutions of our nation: the fundamental right of the people to enjoy full liberty in the domain of idea and speech." The teacher loyalty bill was equally repugnant to Smith. He found that it discriminated against teachers and limited their freedom of thought.

Education would suffer under such a law, he concluded, as only those weak of mind and spirit could become teachers in that system.[23]

Clayton Lusk, who had been a fixture in the press for the previous twelve months, was conspicuously unavailable for comment. Archibald Stevenson had but one reaction to Smith's vetoes: "It was a foregone conclusion." However, S.John Block, now State Chairman of the Socialist Party, was elated. "Eternal vigilance is still the price of liberty in the State of New York," he observed. Block went on to characterize Lusk and his colleagues as "stupid politicians" interested only in furthering their own political careers. Others tempered their celebration with caution. In a surprisingly prophetic statement, Louis Waldman and Charles Solomon, two of the excluded socialist assemblymen, expressed gratification for the governor's decision, but warned "his veto did not end the fight; it is far from being over." Both Governor Smith and the Rand School soon learned just how resilient the Red Scare hysteria truly was.[24]

As Algernon Lee and Bertha Mailly prepared to begin the fall term at the Rand School, Alfred Smith faced a difficult political challenge in his reelection bid against the Republican challenger, Nathan L.Miller. In November, Smith lost to president-elect Warren Harding as much as he did to Miller. Harding's election signaled not only the beginning of a Republican ascendancy that dominated the country for the decade of the Twenties, but also a rejection of the progressive idealism associated with former President Wilson and his supporters. "Normalcy" became the operative word; and Alfred Smith represented anything but normalcy. Miller defeated Smith by 75,000 votes on a day when Harding carried New York State by a margin of nearly two million votes. The closeness of the contest, in the face of an overwhelming reactionary national shift towards the Republican Party prompted one supporter to send a telegram to Smith congratulating him on his remarkable feat. "Even in defeat," the man wrote, "you came nearer to swimming up Niagara Falls than any man I have ever seen." Smith's narrow defeat proved even more disheartening for the Rand School; having survived numerous attacks by the Lusk Committee, the school now faced the prospect of a Republican governor, as well as Republican majorities in both the Assembly and Senate.[25]

Following Miller's inauguration on January 1, 1921, the tide appeared to change. Three days later, at Miller's behest, the Republican caucus selected Lusk as the new president pro tem of the State Senate, a move that surprised many, even in his own party, considering he had only two years of experience in Albany. Later the same afternoon, with

Archibald Stevenson at his side, Lusk announced his decision to reintroduce two of the committee's original bills: teacher loyalty certification and private school licensing. Even more so than during the previous year's hearings on the proposals, their reintroduction created rigid divisions along party lines, as well as generated an acrimonious spirit that spilled over into other legislative debates as well. In early February, during a discussion of Governor Miller's transit plan for New York City, Senator James J. Walker, the Democratic minority leader and long-time critic of Lusk, called the president pro tem a "political juggler and a sleight-of-hand man." One month later, while debating funds for the State Hospital System, Walker labeled Lusk a "sorehead." The president pro tem responded, "Oh, you remind me of the river steamboat which had a whistle bigger than its boiler and every time they tried to blow the whistle the boat stopped."[26]

In the midst of name-calling and partisan stubbornness, the two Lusk bills finally appeared on the legislative docket in slightly amended form on April 6, 1921. The school licensing bill again provided that all private schools be reviewed and licensed by the Board of Regents; however, exceptions to the law now included schools operated by fraternal orders as well as religious sects. Also, the new version of the bill specifically defined "conduct detrimental to society" as "the teaching of doctrines which advocate the overthrow of the government by force, violence, or unlawful means." The bill concerning teacher certification also underwent change between 1920 and 1921. Although loyalty remained the most important consideration when issuing a license, the bill now instructed the Commissioners of Education also to take into greater account the moral character of all applicants.[27]

Opposition to the measures mounted in the coming days. On April 9th, labor organizations throughout New York City met at the Emergency Educational Conference to coordinate their efforts in a campaign to defeat the bills. Representatives from the Amalgamated Clothing Workers, Amalgamated Textile Workers, and two teachers' unions present at the meeting agreed to form the "Executive Committee of 17" to organize the protest. In an official statement issued at the close of the conference, the participants announced their decision to send numerous labor leaders to the Senate hearings on the bills set for April 12th. The cause, they declared, was crucial. "Labor believes that all its efforts tending toward the enlightenment of its people will be destroyed if these bills become law," they claimed. Furthermore, they charged, "the humiliating conditions" imposed upon teachers by the loyalty certification proposal threatened to diminish the already low quality of education that workers' families currently received.[28]

Despite such protests, Senate debate over the bills was swift. Partisan wrangling, more so than serious discussion of the constitutional issues at stake, dominated the session. Senator Nathan Straus, Jr., sarcastically commented, "Flap-doodle legislation of this kind has become the hobby of Senator Lusk." Senator Frederick Davenport, noting the longevity of the Red Scare, attributed the measures to the "nonsensical post-war hysteria" that continued to grip the nation nearly three year's after the armistice. Only Senator Salvatore Cotillo spoke of the principles at stake should the bills pass. "While not necessarily involving an infringement of free speech," he concluded, the measures "nevertheless are incompatible with the great principle of American liberty." Such meager protests were insignificant in the face of a Republican majority determined to pass the bills. Even the long-time Lusk critic Senator Walker later admitted, "we simply didn't have the votes."[29]

On the afternoon of April 14, 1921, the Senate passed both the school licensing measure (40 to 7) and the teacher certification program (43 to 7). To speed Assembly consideration of the bills, Governor Miller submitted an emergency message. On April 16, with little discussion, the Assembly passed both measures (school licensing, 81 to 50; teacher certification, 90 to 43). The New York *Times* applauded the government's efforts. In an editorial on April 19 it suggested that, if Miller's successes were representative of a reactionary course, then "Give us reactionaries!"[30]

Prior to signing the bills, which everyone expected him to do, Miller decided to hold a public hearing similar to Smith's executive chamber public hearing a year earlier. Although he intended to use the forum as a display of public support for the bills, Miller encountered strenuous opposition from citizens who believed the governor had railroaded repressive legislation through a compliant, reactionary legislature. Two days before the hearings, nineteen clergymen and publishers sent a letter to Miller asking that he veto the measures. Religious leaders still feared that the government could selectively enforce the school-licensing proposal against their educational centers. Publishers raised concerns that suppression of speech and thought was only one step removed from suppression of the press. Both agreed that while "the word 'un-American' has doubtless been too freely and loosely used, we submit that if any measure merits that designation, as judged by the spirit of our Government and the history of our liberties, these measures are un-American." Miller wanted public support for the bills; however, as similar protests arose, he faced a difficult situation.[31]

Representatives from over twenty civic, educational, and labor organizations attended the public hearing on April 26 to protest the bills. Morris Hillquit, representing the Rand School and the Socialist Party, declared the measures "unconstitutional, unenforceable, unreasonable, unAmerican and unnecessary." The possibility of an espionage system of enforcement, with teachers spying on teachers, alarmed Hillquit and other critics as well. Such a program of oaths and licensing, he claimed, was unprecedented in America. "I challenge the authors or proponents of these bills," he concluded, "to show anything like them in the statute books of any State in the Union or any country in this world with a claim to civilization." Although some present at the hearing, including Lusk, spoke in favor of the proposals, Hillquit's oratory carried the day. Unlike Smith's hearing a year earlier, Miller left the session still clamoring for public support of the educational measures he fully intended to sign into law.[32]

Jockeying for position continued throughout the ensuing week. On May 1, 1921, Lusk and Stevenson defended the bills before a rally at Carnegie Hall coordinated by the American Defense Society. F.W. Galbraith, National Commander of the American Legion, appeared at the meeting to offer his support. The American Legion, he stated, was prepared "to survey every school teacher and every school in the United States, and get the teachers' records" once the governor approved the measures. "If we find them disloyal we will tell you, and you can kick them out," he informed Lusk; "we have had enough of this." Some educators agreed with Galbraith, and felt the time had come to pass legislation to protect the students. Gilbert Raynor, the principal of Commercial High School in Brooklyn, urged passage of the bills in order to protect "the little red school house, but not the 'red' school teacher." Another school administrator saw "one or two objectionable features" in the measures, but felt "half a loaf was better than none." Aaron Dotey of the executive committee of the Teachers' Council recommended passage of the bills in order to protect impressionable students from "poison-tongued teachers."[33]

Equally vociferous were those who implored Miller to veto the educational proposals. In the week following the public hearing, the governor received dozens of letters and telegrams further explaining the harm such measures would create. S.John Block continued the attack that his socialist colleague, Hillquit, initiated at the hearing. The bills, he informed Miller, were "unwise, unsound, impractical, un-American and unconstitutional." Their passage, he warned, would transform the state's educational system into "a gross spectacle." Harold Riegelman, the attorney for the United Neighborhood Houses of New York City who attended hearings to protest the Lusk bills the previous spring, reiterated Block's claims. "These proposals," he wrote, "which embody provisions so grotesque and so inconsistent with the most treasured of American principles, are unnecessary, vicious in principle, and reactionary and extreme beyond any possible academic justification." Edward T.Devine, an editor for *Survey* magazine, considered the bills "obnoxious to the whole spirit of the English and American common law, and to the traditions which have been cherished by lovers of freedom." Letter upon letter expressed similar concerns and criticisms of the Lusk bills to Governor Miller. He soon realized the futility deriving from any effort to construct a majority in favor of his impending decision.[34]

But that realization did not stop him; although public support was weak at best, Governor Miller finally signed the education bills into law on May 9, 1921, coincidentally the same day the Lusk Committee filed its final report with the State Legislature. However, unlike the strongly worded veto message that Smith wrote in 1920, Miller felt it necessary to fully explain his approval, as well as to allay the concerns of those who worried that the laws might harm innocent citizens. In his memorandum accompanying the school-licensing bill, Miller explained how "no one need fear the result of this measure, unless he wishes to teach criminal sedition or to practice fraud." As for teacher certification, he emphasized the "dignity and solemn responsibility" a loyalty oath entailed. In his view, the laws did not curb the freedoms of law-abiding individuals and organizations. Violators of the laws, he concluded, "seek license, not liberty," and deserve to be punished. The New York *Times* praised the significance and eloquence of the governor's decision. "Passage of the laws," the editor concluded, "means that the Rand School of Social Science, in New York City, will soon be abolished." The brazen prediction, however, proved to be premature.[35]

When the Rand School prepared to open its doors without the prerequisite private school license on September 26 for the start of the fall term, school officials announced their intention to fight the law, which they perceived as aimed directly at destroying their institution. "It is absolutely necessary," the Board of Directors concluded in a resolution, "to challenge this high-handed and oppressive legislation; it must be tested to the last step." Educational Director Algernon Lee announced his willingness to risk imprisonment for sixty days rather than forego the opening of the school. The school's attorney, Morris Hillquit, hoped that conviction, fine, and imprisonment would not become necessary. He planned to challenge the law as violating three fundamental principles: freedom of speech, the traditional exemption of teaching from legal prohibitions, and the principle of property rights.[36]

As the first day of classes rapidly approached, the *Rand School News* informed prospective students and faculty of the plan to conduct business as usual in defiance of the licensing law. "The responsibility for testing its constitutionality rests upon the Rand School," Lee told the students; "the responsibility is accepted." The Educational Director was not worried, as he felt Lusk's crusade had lost much of its steam. "We do not feel that there is much of a chance of Senator Lusk sending a uniformed policeman around to close our doors," he stated, "particularly in view of the fact that he has already had so much publicity concerning his new set of silverware," a direct reference to the alleged bribe the senator recently received from the New York City Detectives Association in return for sponsoring legislation to establish a larger pension fund to benefit retired detectives. Lee also noted the return of a saner disposition among some legal authorities following the post-war hysteria that gripped the country the preceding three years.[37]

The day before classes were to begin, the American Socialist Society gave state authorities every possible reason to enforce the statute when they passed a resolution reaffirming the Rand School's adherence to the Socialist Party doctrine. In addition, the society appointed four new directors to their board, including perennial Lusk Committee critics S.John Block, Morris Hillquit, and I.M.Sackin. However, instead of prosecuting the Rand School, state officials vacillated. On the same day as the meeting of the American Socialist Society, the Board of Regents announced that they would take no action against the Rand School pending a decision as to which authority held responsibility for the enforcement of the school licensing law. Chester S.Lord, Chancellor for the Regents, declared that he knew nothing of the enforcement procedures, specifically whether his agency, the State Attorney General, or city officials were to act.[38]

As Rand School activities began without incident on September 26th, Dr. Frank G.Gilbert, Assistant Commissioner of Education, announced from Albany that he planned to meet with Attorney General Newton the next day to discuss an immediate plan of action. "We are going to proceed at once," he stated to reporters, "probably by injunction." However, in a surprising move, Gilbert revisited the debate over the constitutionality of the school licensing law. "The Rand School authorities in New York are no more anxious than we to determine if the law is unconstitutional," he concluded, "for we do not want to go on and compel other schools to take out a license if the law is unsound." By raising such questions, Gilbert opened the door and gave hope to those critics who wanted the legislature to repeal the Lusk laws, but believed such a move to be unlikely.[39]

The door opened wider following Newton's conference with Gilbert. On September 27, the Attorney General announced that he would take no steps against the Rand School until the courts determined the constitutionality of the Lusk laws. Newton planned to initiate proceedings before the Appellate Division of the State Supreme Court as soon as possible, in order to attain a speedy decision in the matter. "The State education authorities have agreed with me that a test of the constitutionality of this law is the proper course to pursue," he explained. "This course," he noted, "will forestall any complaints of unfairness in dealing with the Rand School and similar institutions." Despite his newfound concern for fairness towards the Rand School, Newton's desire to close its doors permanently remained his foremost goal. "The State will employ every agency within its command to sustain the validity of the law," he concluded.[40]

Hillquit agreed with the Attorney General's assessment that court proceedings provided a possible remedy. That the Rand School conducted classes without a license in open defiance of the law was obvious, he admitted in an agreed statement of facts. "We admit the facts in the case and declare that the reason therefore is that the law requiring all schools to take out a license is unconstitutional," Hillquit informed reporters; "as the matter now stands, the legality of the law will have to be passed upon by the courts before any further action is taken." Eventually Newton filed suit on October 24, 1921; the second round of the *People of the State of New York v. American Socialist Society* was set.[41]

In preparation for the trial, school officials once again rallied support for their legal defense. At the school's New Year's Eve Ball, Hillquit unveiled a bust of Eugene Debs and read a message from the founder of the Socialist Party to the 10,000 guests present at the dance. From his home in Terre Haute, Indiana, Debs encouraged defenders of the school to fight for its existence. "The Rand School has been persecuted as myself and others have been persecuted for telling and teaching the truth," he wrote. Specifically he blamed Lusk and "the other political tools of capitalism" for attempting to close the school. However, he predicted, "they will not be any more successful than was the attempt to suppress my voice by placing me in the prison at Atlanta." Amidst the cheers of the crowd, Hillquit read Debs' encouraging closing words: "Every one who loves liberty should rally to the support of the Rand School. Courage, comrades, on with the fight. We win."[42]

Following several delays due to illness and other unrelated circumstances, both sides filed briefs on May 4, 1922. Since the burden of proof regarding constitutionality rested with the defense, Deputy Attorney General Berger in the State's brief simply stood on the exact wording of the school licensing law, which clearly stated that "no license shall be granted" to any school that appears to advocate the overthrow of the government "by force, violence or unlawful means." He also quoted from the final report of the Lusk Committee, which detailed the American Socialist Society's previous conviction for publishing Nearing's pamphlet. "The State," he argued, "has every right to guard against criminal offenses that would harm the safety, peace, order, morals, and general welfare of its citizens." The doctrines taught at the Rand School, Berger concluded, represented just such criminal offenses.[43]

Hillquit challenged the law on the same grounds he announced the previous September. With regard to property rights, he argued that the law was too broadly defined, and interfered with the intellectual property rights associated with traditional academic disciplines. Put simply, the law granted the State too much oversight concerning curriculum and written materials. Hillquit indicated that the law applied to the teaching of spelling, grammar, math, and science, as much as it applied to economics, history, and sociology. Arts, crafts, and sports also fell under the State's supervision, as did instruction in dancing, swimming, and singing. "The list is endless," he argued, and "no such classes can be taught without first obtaining a license from the State."[44]

Hillquit then questioned the State's ability to legislate restrictions upon "common business and callings of life" such as teaching. "The doctrine is well established," he argued, "that the ordinary trades and pursuits which have been followed in the community from time immemorial, must be free to all alike without hindrance or restriction." One could not seriously suggest that teaching was not a common calling, Hillquit observed. Berger interrupted; "how can teaching criminal anarchy be considered a common calling?" he asked. A presumption of innocence was paramount, Hillquit replied. "No right should be more jealously guarded against arbitrary interference and restrictions on the part of the Legislature than the broad and general right to teach," he contended.[45]

Finally, should his first two arguments fail to sway the court, Hillquit emphasized the overriding importance of free speech. "Every person with an experience or a message has the right to impart or convey the same to anyone who cares to take advantage of the opportunity," he concluded. Free speech concerns outweighed all others, according to Hillquit; and on those grounds alone, the court should declare the school licensing law unconstitutional.[46]

The court disagreed. On July 14, 1922, following two months of deliberation, they upheld the Lusk law requiring private school licensing by a 4–1 vote, thus permitting the State to apply for an injunction against the Rand School. The majority opinion, written by Justice Edgar S.K.Merrell, made no mention of the allegedly radical doctrines taught at the Rand School; rather, it addressed the law in the abstract. Specifically, the decision emphasized that any organization had proper recourse to seek relief through the courts should the State arbitrarily deny them a license without good cause. "Every right of the defendant is guaranteed by the provisions of the statute," the ruling proclaimed. Furthermore, the justices concurred that regulation of private schools fell well within the proper exercise of the police power of the State "to protect the peace, health, public safety and security of its citizens." In essence, the court ruled that the State had the power to control private schools, up to and including closing them for teaching questionable material. The potential harm deriving from the arbitrary or improper exercise of that power was insignificant, according to the court, so long as the school could appeal the decision and correct the wrongdoing.[47]

Hillquit was flabbergasted by the far-reaching implications of the decision, and immediately announced his intention to appeal. The court agreed to allow the Rand School to continue operating until the appeal had been settled. "The decision is of extraordinary public importance," he told reporters. "It is, so far as I know, the first adjudication by an authoritative American tribunal which sanctions the institution of preliminary censorship." Hillquit warned that time-honored constitutional safeguards, such as freedom of press and speech, would soon give way "to oppressive class despotism and to the most dangerous forms of political chicanery" should the Lusk laws stand. The fight he vowed to wage was not simply on behalf of the Rand School, or even the Socialist Party. "It is a fight," he concluded, "to preserve the most fundamental civic rights of American citizenship."[48]

While the Rand School battled the school licensing law, the Teachers' Union of New York City took aim at the loyalty oath required of all public school teachers. Between May and December, 1921, authorities enforced the measure by administering two oaths to all instructors throughout the state. However, as reports began to mount that some individuals lied when taking the oath and continued to teach radical ideas to their students, the State Commissioner of Education, Dr. Frank P.Graves, ordered principals to prepare secret reports on the morality and loyalty of their employees. For that purpose, the State Department of Education prepared forms upon which a principal could vouch for a teacher's character through first-hand knowledge, reliable second-hand knowledge, or not at all.[49]

Graves also created the State Advisory Council on the Qualification of Teachers to hear cases of alleged disloyalty. He appointed Archibald Stevenson chair of the committee. In a subsequent interview, Stevenson outlined the procedures of the council. "The teachers who come before us are not under charges and are not being tried," he explained. Rather, he compared the process to one of selecting members for a club. "The committee makes a careful scrutiny into the fitness of the candidate." The state commissioner made the final decision on whether or not to dismiss a teacher based upon the council's findings and recommendations. Graves reiterated Stevenson's comments when he promised that all teachers who appear before the council "will have the full opportunity to defend themselves with due regard to all legal rights."[50]

The Teachers' Union had little faith in the process, particularly due to Stevenson's involvement on the council. Dr. Henry R.Linville, president of the union, formally protested the commissioner's decision to "establish a spying system within the schools." The result of such a system, he warned, would be "lower spiritual and intellectual quality" among the teachers employed in the schools. Regarding the council in particular, Linville accused its members of holding "partisan and unfavorable attitudes to any teacher accused of holding any view other than one of complete reaction." In simple terms, he claimed, the advisory council was "little more than a new Lusk Committee." Within a week, the Board of Education of New York City joined the Teachers' Union in condemning the qualification process. Board President George J.Ryan denounced the "secret inquiry" conducted by the council. "There is no need for it," he claimed. If any reports on individual teachers were necessary, he observed, the board was in the best position to provide accurate information directly to the commissioner without interference from a council.[51]

Ignoring the debate swirling about them, the Advisory Council on Teachers' Qualifications began conducting hearings on May 16, 1922. Stevenson summoned four teachers to appear and answer questions concerning negative evidence of their loyalty. He refused to open the proceedings to the public, nor did he allow attorneys to be present, on the grounds that they were only investigations, not trials. Linville later decried the "secret tribunal" and vowed to fight to open the hearings to the public. At his urging, Sarah Hyams, a cooking instructor at P.S. 68 in Manhattan whom the advisory council had summoned, refused to answer any questions. Her lawyer, Gilbert Roe, accused the council of "terrorizing teachers behind closed doors" on the basis of "secret, illegal, and unnecessary reports." He promised to force a courtroom challenge to the Lusk law.[52]

As the days and weeks passed, protests regarding the council's activities mounted. Even the typically conservative New York *Times*, long a defender of the Lusk Committee and its endeavors, questioned the need for a council to judge the loyalty of teachers. By June, the newspaper declared, "whatever usefulness the committee had has ended." Walter Foster, President of the High School Teachers' Association, also implored Graves to discontinue the Advisory Council. "Damaging statements reflect very unfavorably upon the reputation and character of the teachers under suspicion," he noted; even when dismissed, as happened in the vast majority of cases, the stigma associated with the accusation remained. "The teachers concerned live under a cloud forever," he lamented. Over the next week, six additional teachers and one principal summoned before the council to answer a variety of questions on their political beliefs refused to appear. Frustrated by such defiance, Advisory Council member William McAuliffe pledged to continue his work and expose disloyalty among teachers wherever he finds it. "One who occupies the exalted position of teacher should not hesitate," he stated, "to answer any questions relative to his character or his loyalty to the government." Teachers should welcome the investigations, he reasoned, in order to defend themselves against potentially serious charges.[53]

By October 1922, opposition to the teacher loyalty law was as intense as the Rand School's fight against the private school licensing law. Based upon evidence uncovered by the Advisory Council's investigations, the State Commissioner had withheld teaching certificates from twenty public school teachers since May. The

Teachers' Union president was outraged; despite repeated efforts to learn why Graves denied the certificates, none of the teachers received a reply. "It appears," Linville said, "that unknown committees are sitting in judgment; and unknown persons have made unknown charges." As the November elections approached, public school teachers had less protection from the Advisory Committee than students had from allegedly disloyal instructors. "The stated purpose of the Lusk law has been forgotten," Linville concluded.[54]

Neither a final court battle to preserve the Rand School, nor a legal challenge to the loyalty oath program, ever materialized. As the Teachers' Union battled the Advisory Council, and the Rand School's lawyers waited to argue their case before the State Court of Appeals, the political scene in Albany underwent notable changes. Hoping to return to the governor's mansion in 1923, Alfred Smith began campaigning in earnest in the late summer of 1922. He made public debate concerning the Lusk laws a cornerstone of his effort to unseat Miller. Hoping to take advantage of the precarious position in which Miller placed himself when he signed the legislation, Smith repeatedly challenged the governor to explain to the people his support of the measures. At a rally on November 2, 1922, Smith observed that "Governor Miller may be able to explain it, although up to this minute he has refused to do it, and it is fitting and proper at this place that I should ask him what group of people in this State desired this un-American and undemocratic legislation." Smith differed from Miller on numerous other issues as well, including the question of government reorganization, a topic that attracted the attention of many voters later that November. Smith's reelection was never in serious doubt. As he described in his autobiography, by late 1922, the citizens of New York had lost interest in President Harding's normalcy and begun focusing on issues of local interest once again. Smith defeated Miller by 387,000 votes that fall, the largest margin of victory in the New York governor's race to that point in history.[55]

Smith made it perfectly clear that, upon his return to Albany, first on his agenda was the repeal of the Lusk laws. Many legislators, including a few who originally defended the measures, began to support his view. Speaking before the City Club of Cleveland on December 16, 1922, the new Democratic majority leader in the Senate, James J. Walker, informed reporters that he would lead the repeal of the Lusk laws in the upcoming session. The public also began to rally behind Smith's call to repeal the laws. On December 29, the Social Service Commission of the Episcopal Diocese of New York announced its unanimous decision to work for the repeal of the laws. The Reverend Charles K. Gilbert said the effort would commence immediately. "We have always believed that the laws are unnecessary and quite out of harmony with the spirit of our country," he stated. "We were in touch with the bills from the very start, during Governor Smith's Administration; and although we felt that the prospect of repealing the laws during the term of Governor Miller was slight, the prospect is brighter now." Charles Brent, the Catholic Bishop of Western New York, also urged Smith to fight for repeal of laws he considered "a grave infringement on the very principles of democratic thought and life." Coordination was the key, according to M. Carey Thomas, president of Bryn Mawr College. While opposition to the laws was admirable, she said, the forces must organize if they wish to repeal "the hideous Lusk laws."[56]

Smith heeded Thomas' advice. On January 3, 1923, in his annual message to the State Legislature, the governor officially proposed the repeal of the Lusk laws, which he considered "vicious" and "wrong in principle." "Interference with personal liberty, censorship of thought, word, act or teaching," he concluded, "encourages intolerance and bigotry in the minds of the few directed against the many." Later in the same session, Lusk assumed the position of minority leader in the Senate and began criticizing much of Smith's legislative agenda, particularly his plan for government reorganization. Sensing that Lusk's power, if not his sense of self-worth, had greatly diminished in Miller's absence, Smith wasted little time in attacking Lusk and regaining the upper hand. "Senator Lusk had a good deal to do with the raping of State affairs for the last two years," the new governor informed reporters, "and he did his job so well that it sent his party to the scrap heap by an unprecedented plurality; that is all I have to say about that."[57]

Concerned very little with Lusk's posturing, Smith orchestrated the repeal. Action was swift, as on January 8, Senator Bernard Downing introduced two bills to revoke the educational laws. Simultaneously, public sentiment continued to swell in favor of Smith's position. At a meeting of the New York City Women's Club on January 11, Senator Benjamin Antin, the chairman of the Senate Committee on Education, received a standing ovation when he predicted that the Lusk laws "were destined for an early burial."[58]

Lusk refused to end his crusade, however. On January 18th he informed reporters of his intention to fight and save the laws bearing his name. "The only charitable view to take is that the Governor is not thinking clearly on these subjects," he said; "I hope he comes to his senses before he does irreparable harm to our democratic institutions." Upon hearing the comments, Smith again brushed off Lusk as little more than a nuisance. "This is politics—just little politics," the governor noted. "I will leave it to the people to judge between myself and Lusk as to who is the better exponent of democratic government." In Smith's mind, the answer was clear. "The people spoke pretty decisively on this question in the last election," he observed. "Let Lusk run for Governor and see how long it would take him to get elected; that is my answer to Lusk."[59]

Although shrinking in number, a few individuals continued to defend the Lusk laws. Edward Riggs, a reporter for the New York *Tribune*, implored the governor to enforce the measures and, if necessary, "jump all the radicals out of the country." In an appearance before the National Republican Club of New York City, Henry A.Wise Wood chastised Smith for his efforts to repeal the laws. The governor based his position, Wood concluded, on favors he owed the immigrant community for electing him to office. "Smith does not believe that the State should be given any control over educational institutions of a private nature, even though these be teaching sedition and anarchy," Wood lamented. "This, I presume, is part of the price which Mr. Smith agreed to pay for his re-election by the un-American and alien-hearted community." Wood's comments drew only faint applause from the crowd.[60]

Wood's efforts not withstanding, public opposition to the measures continued to grow throughout January and February. As winter drew to a close, the recently formed Citizens' Committee for the Repeal of the Lusk Laws issued an open letter urging Governor Smith and members of the State Legislature to act swiftly in order to end "the deadening influence" the laws had upon education. J.Gresham Machen of the Princeton Theological Seminary also criticized the laws in a letter to the editor of the New York *Times* on February 26. He warned, "the citizens of our State are in constant danger of the government's intolerable interference with private life which a real enforcement of the laws would mean." Action must be taken to repeal the measures before they create the very danger they purport to combat. "The trouble is," he concluded, "the Lusk laws, far from being conservative, really involve a radical collectivism of the most oppressive kind."[61]

Finally, on February 27, 1923, the Senate passed Downing's two repeal bills by a 26 to 22 vote each. To the very end, Lusk continued to fight the repeal, charging the Democratic Party with merely courting the subversive vote. He cautioned his colleagues, "You are now nursing at your bosom traitors and radicals who plot the destruction of our Government." Lusk went on to claim that the American Legion, the U.S. Army Command, and the Teachers' Council favored retention of the laws. However, many senators felt little need to heed his warning; to them, the laws had outlived their usefulness and had never been effective. Downing noted, "Conditions which furnished an excuse for an enactment of these laws no longer exist today; the country is again on an even keel." The Lusk laws were never efficient, he claimed. "The only thing they did was to favor hypocrisy, lip service and lying." Clayton Lusk, Senator Downing concluded, was now simply "chasing shadows."[62]

The final legislative hurdle to repeal the Lusk laws was set for the third week of March. Most observers anticipated a contentious debate in the Republican-controlled Assembly. The New York *Times* considered it "doubtful" that the repeal measures would even pass through committee unscathed. Speaker of the Assembly Thomas Machold privately assured his colleagues that he would do everything in his power to save the education laws. To everyone's surprise, however, the repeal measures not only passed through committee, but also received the endorsement of eighteen Republican assemblymen whom the party leadership was unable to control. Although Speaker Machold was visibly disappointed, he urged his colleagues to vote their conscience, and reluctantly intimated that the measures would pass.[63]

Unwilling to assume their passage, Smith continued to rally support for repeal of the Lusk laws. "They are bad and should be repealed," he informed reporters. Those who support the laws "make no allowance for human difference of opinion, for the right of every citizen to advocate his opinions lawfully and honestly and, most of all, for the fact that real political progress comes from the expression and exchange of conflicting opinions." Smith received further support from Oswald Garrison Villard, editor of *The Nation,* who condemned "Luskers" for "preaching Americanism to others" while not having "the faintest idea about American principles." Vassar College President H.N.MacCracken congratulated the governor for his "courageous stance" on the issue. Victory appeared close at hand; but not until one final twist took place.[64]

On April 10, 1923, as the State Assembly prepared to vote on the repeal measures, five Democrats and eight Republicans who voted in favor of the Lusk laws in 1921 and who represented largely conservative, upstate constituencies left the chamber and refused to cast votes. Although eight Republicans joined a majority of Democratic members in support of the repeal, the Lusk law survived by identical votes of 71 to 66. Everyone on both sides of the aisle was stunned by the outcome. Speaker Machold later commented he "was surprised, but pleased." Sol Ullman, who along with his colleague James Walker, led the fight for the repeal measures, moved to have the vote reconsidered and laid on the table. Majority Leader Simon Adler consented to the motion; thus presenting the Democrats with one more opportunity to pass the repeal measures in two weeks. On April 24, the final vote occurred without debate. Again with the aid of eight Republicans, as well as by securing the support of every Democrat in the chamber, the repeal measures passed by votes of 76 to 71. All that remained was for Smith to affix his signature, and the Lusk laws would be history.[65]

Despite his convictions, Smith held a one day public hearing on May 22 to allow supporters of the Lusk laws one final opportunity to voice their opinions. Dwight Draman of the Allied Patriotic Societies warned of an impending red revolution in America in the absence of laws to safeguard the country's institutions. When others claimed that the Lusk laws had done no harm, Governor Smith interjected, "They have most certainly done a lot of harm; they have reversed our old ideas of freedom of thought, freedom of expression and freedom of conscience." In an assessment that could have applied to the entire Red Scare, he said of the Lusk laws "You cannot instill patriotism into the hearts of the people by binding them to the earth and telling them that they must not think." Dr. Linville of the Teachers' Union agreed. "There is no patriotism in repressing free thought and free speech," he concluded. "These laws are not only repressive, restrictive, and to an extent utterly repellent, but they are un-American."[66]

Three days later, Governor Smith kept his re-election campaign promise and repealed the same Lusk laws he had vetoed three years earlier. In the message accompanying his signature, he declared the school licensing and loyalty certification laws to be "repugnant to the fundamentals of American democracy." Offering his apologies to the teachers who suffered as a result of the Lusk Committee's endeavors, Smith acknowledged, "freedom of opinion and freedom of speech were by these laws unduly shackled, and an unjust discrimination was made against the members of a great profession." Meanwhile, 150 miles away in New York City, Algernon Lee and Bertha Mailly prepared the commencement ceremonies for another class of graduates. Having survived raids, legal action, and repressive laws, it was business as usual at the Rand School.[67]

The Lusk Committee's decision to initiate a legislative attack against the Rand School was logical, yet risky. Having failed in their effort to close the school by means of a physical raid and legal proceedings, committee members hoped that their largely reactionary colleagues in the Assembly and the Senate would respond to the committee's final report by passing laws designed to accomplish that task. Lusk's assessment was correct. Although Governor Smith vetoed the first set of bills, the state legislature did pass them in both 1920 and again in 1921. Even the repeal measures of 1923 were defeated on one occasion before the Democrats secured enough support for a second vote.

However, the legislature could not pass laws aimed directly at the Rand School alone. Furthermore, Lusk came to believe Stevenson's assertion, supported by committee hearings and stated clearly in the final report, that public schools were not immune from radical proselytizing. As a result, the Lusk bills touched all private and public schools in New York State, not just the Rand School. Lusk banked his hopes on the idea that protecting school children from radical influences would convince New Yorkers to ignore the potential violations of civil liberties inherent in the measures. He and his committee were wrong. Not only did the Rand School continue the fight they had begun the previous June following the initial raid, but thousands of public school teachers also joined them. Stevenson recognized the potential for such opposition when he wrote the committee's final report. In a note to himself "to be considered in writing the report" he concluded, "Most of these people who want freedom of speech are educators."[68]

The Lusk laws were also shackled by timing. As the Jazz Age unfolded, fewer and fewer New Yorkers continued to believe that "red revolution" was imminent. Vocal opposition to the measures was small, but growing between 1921 and 1923. When Governor Smith signed the repeal bills in 1923, most New Yorkers who did not openly condemn the Lusk laws simply no longer cared. When the New York *Times*, which had long supported the Lusk Committee's endeavors, began questioning the laws out of a fear that limitations on freedom of speech were only one step removed from similar restraints on freedom of the press, the die was cast. Opposition and apathy eroded any remaining support for the Lusk laws, and the Red Scare in New York came to a close.

Conclusion

THE EFFORTS OF THE LUSK COMMITTEE TO COMBAT RADICALISM IN New York State beginning in 1919 mirrored the events of the larger Red Scare that gripped the country in the ensuing months. The public's fear of radicalism, as well as the ability of political and civic leaders to manipulate that fear for their own gain, explained the harsh methods employed in New York and elsewhere from June, 1919, through January, 1920. However, while the national hunt for communist plots abated in early 1920, the crusade merely took on new form, in terms of both focus and methods, in the Empire State, and continued to hold the public's attention for over another three years. Only when public perceptions concerning civil liberties began to transform, and politicians grew incapable of controlling such views, did the Red Scare in New York come to a close.

For most of the nation, the Red Scare reached its zenith in January, 1920. For the previous year, bomb scares, violent labor uprisings, and the formation of two communist parties dominated thoughts and actions throughout the country. The arrival of Ludwig Martens and his creation of the commercially-oriented Soviet Bureau in New York City further served to alarm an already frightened public who came to view him as the harbinger of revolution in America. Dynamic headlines alerted Americans to the threat that radicalism presented, as well as to the solutions voiced by opportunistic politicians. The simple answer was one for which the public clamored: repression. The Lusk Committee was more than happy to oblige. Its raids upon the Soviet Bureau and the Rand School of Social Science in June, 1919, followed the typical pattern of physical repression. The use of dozens of state troopers, local police, and bomb squad units; cutting telephone lines or commandeering the switchboard in order to monitor incoming calls; seizing all papers, regardless of the limitations prescribed by the search warrant; destroying personal property; and, in the case of the Rand School,

128 CONCLUSION

employing the services of a safecracker, became standard procedure to combat the radical threat. In fact, U.S. Attorney General A.Mitchell Palmer watched the activities unfolding in New York with great interest as he prepared for his own series of raids the subsequent winter.[1]

Such methods succeeded in closing the Soviet Bureau without so much as a whimper from the general public, most of whom believed the committee's highly unlikely accusation that Ludwig Martens ran the bureau as a front for financing the dissemination of radical propaganda in America. Equally destructive was the impact of the raid upon the true operations of the bureau, establishing business relations with American firms and industrialists. In the days following the raid, prominent businessmen throughout the country scurried to denounce Martens, as well as to deny any potential ties between the bureau and their companies. Within one week, the bureau closed its doors never to open them again; within a year, Martens left America, never to return again. Trade relations between the U.S. and Soviet Russia remained limited for another thirteen years.

Public tolerance of the Lusk Committee's heavy-handed tactics, as well as those employed around the country by other agencies, stemmed from their perception of the radical threat. That hindsight exposed the threat to be baseless was irrelevant at the time. In the summer of 1919, fear of radicalism and its agents was rational, not hysterical, given the warnings issued by political and civic leaders and spread by newspapers eager for headlines to increase their circulation in the absence of war. Only when public perceptions changed, whether through self-revelation or when political leaders ceased manipulating public fear, would the Red Scare end.

Nationally, public perceptions began to change following Attorney General Palmer's spectacular arrest of over 4,000 suspected radicals in 33 cities on the evening of January 2, 1920. Absent an adequate number of arrest warrants, agents from the Department of Justice detained anyone present in, or simply passing by, the meeting halls, of suspected branches of the Communist Party. The conditions under which authorities placed their captives were deplorable. Poor sanitation, a lack of heat, and inadequate food, combined with frequent beatings and intense interrogations, led some to commit suicide while others went insane. In a few cases, authorities detained suspected radicals for over a month without informing the families of their whereabouts. Combined with previous arrests, Palmer announced to a cheering public his plan to deport nearly 3,000 foreign radicals over the next year.[2]

Although many applauded the attorney general for his efforts, a growing number of magazine and newspaper editors, as well as officials within the government began to question the unconstitutional methods at the core of them. Eventually, twelve of the country's most respected attorneys, including Felix Frankfurter and Zechariah Chafee, Jr., jointly authored the *Report Upon the Illegal Practices of the United States Department of Justice*. In it, they charged Palmer with violating the civil liberties of the men detained in the raids. Specifically, the report cited the lack of proper arrest warrants, the inhumane conditions of their detainment, and entrapment. The report included photographs of many alleged radicals who appeared beaten and bloodied. Within weeks, public support began to transform into resistance.[3]

Despite Palmer's protests to the contrary, few appeared interested in his defense of the Department of Justice's actions. Within the year, Assistant Secretary of Labor Louis Post, the man who served as final arbiter in deportation cases, dismissed charges against all but 500 radicals. Eventually, he deported the remaining individuals; but the 500 were a far cry from the thousands Palmer predicted. When the attorney general's prediction of a nationwide radical uprising the following May Day failed to materialize, the public came to consider him a man who cried wolf once too often. Across the nation, the Red Scare appeared to wane.[4]

Three more years were to pass, however, before the fear subsided in New York, where public perceptions were slower to change. One of the most important reasons for the persistence of the fear was that more foreigners were concentrated in New York City than in any other city in the nation. Owing to their large numbers, aliens established tight-knit communities within the city that enabled them to retain the dress, language, and customs from their homeland. Many native New Yorkers interpreted the failure to assimilate foreigners as evidence of the latter's desire to destroy American traditions. The prevalence of communist and socialist meeting halls, as well as foreign-language newspapers, convinced New Yorkers that their perceptions were accurate.

An increasing reluctance among political officials to abandon the anti-radical crusade further enabled the fear to persist among New Yorkers through 1923. As much as U.S. Attorney General Palmer saw the Red Scare as a vehicle by which he could become the Democratic Party's presidential candidate in 1920, Clayton Lusk and others involved with the committee's endeavors sought higher office as well. In some cases, the strategy worked. One committee member became a U.S. Congressman while another became a State Supreme Court

Justice. Lusk, himself, served briefly as acting Lieutenant Governor and acting Governor in 1922, and clearly had gubernatorial aspirations of his own. The key, particularly for a freshman senator from Cortland, was to remain in the public eye, and especially to be seen as the defender of the American way of life.[5]

Clayton Lusk capitalized on this perception in order to justify his committee's endeavors. However, the failure of the Rand School raid demanded new tactics on his part. Rather than closing its doors, the raid served only to encourage the school to challenge the Lusk Committee, and to use the publicity to its advantage. Enrollment at the institution actually increased in the wake of the raid, a fact that frustrated Lusk and other committee members to no end. Having repeatedly informed the citizens of New York that the Rand School represented the vehicle through which the largest amount of radical propaganda originated, Lusk had little choice but to continue his campaign to close it, or appear foolish for the failed effort and most likely ruin his own political aspirations.

Lusk's verbal attacks upon the institution and its administrators, which assumed a more personal nature as time passed, hinted at the importance he placed upon the case. In a memorandum to his special counsel, Archibald Stevenson, Lusk described the school's educational director, Algernon Lee, as "the most dangerous of the group." While Morris Hillquit was "a fool, consumed with vanity," Lusk wrote "Lee is not; he is a great undercover power...crafty and hypnotic." To Lusk, the answer was simple. "If we get Lee," he concluded, "we get everything." In a subsequent letter to Governor Alfred Smith, Lusk suggested arresting and trying Lee as a traitor for his work on behalf of the Rand School.[6]

Algernon Lee recognized Lusk's determination to continue his attacks upon the Rand School, thus extending the life of the Red Scare despite the failure of the initial raid, and reciprocated the senator's animosity with vigor. Two weeks following the initial raid, Lee informed some of the regular students to begin carrying baseball bats in order to defend the institution against future attacks by the committee. According to one informant, Lee commented "the Luskers will get such a f***ing from us that they will be sorry they ever started this." Following the initial legal proceedings to revoke the charter of the American Socialist Society and close the school, Lee described Lusk as a "bum and a loafer looking to spend the workingman's money." After the legal challenge failed, Lee joked that his pursuer "soon will become a member of the Rand School so he can get some education and an $18.00 a week job."[7]

Searching for new tactics to combat the radicalism specifically embodied by the Rand School, Lusk turned to the courts. The committee continued to engage in minor raids through November, 1919, but it practically abandoned the highly publicized assaults of June in favor of legal proceedings to close the school. Cutting telephone lines and seizing boxes of papers gave way to writs and depositions. Although still repressive in nature, the form of repression appeared more palatable to some citizens who had become increasingly critical of the committee's physical attacks upon the Soviet Bureau and Rand School. Throughout the remainder of 1919, State Attorney General Charles Newton, working with materials obtained largely from the Lusk Committee, struggled to revoke the charter of the school's parent organization, the American Socialist Society. His maneuvering eventually fell short, and the Rand School remained open; however, his effort kept the Lusk Committee on the front-page of newspapers, and as a result kept the Red Scare fresh in the minds of New York's citizens.

As the court proceedings concluded, Lusk sought a new strategy to continue his attack upon the Rand School. Algernon Lee never doubted for a second that the battle was far from over. Commenting on the school's victory in the courts, he noted that it was but one of "several chapters in the long story. of the persecutions piling up for future historians to consider." Raids and courts have failed, but "the powers behind the Lusk Committee will seek other means for effecting their evil purposes," Lee said. "We cannot tell where and when the next blow will fall, but we feel confident that in spite of the mobs and in spite of persecution the future belongs to us." He was correct in his assessment; Lusk would not surrender the fight, especially in an election year. The answer Lusk sought rested among his colleagues in the State Legislature. What physical raids and court cases failed to accomplish, laws would.[8]

Ironically, the legislative battles over the Lusk Laws, more so than the physical raids, triggered a negative public response which would eventually bring the Red Scare to a conclusion in New York as well. This was in part due to timing; with the Red Scare practically finished at the national level, New Yorkers desired a return to normalcy as well. They were anxious to move on with their lives, absent the tiring progressive crusades, world conflicts, and endless, seemingly unfounded concerns over radical revolution. However, of greater significance was the far-reaching nature of the laws. The legislature aimed them not only at the Rand School, but at all schools, both public and private. None of the state's 30,000 teachers were immune from their standards. As a result, the repression of the Red Scare reached more people than it ever had before.

Public reaction to the measures, particularly when they became law in 1921, was swift, vocal, and reflective of the growing attention paid to civil liberties. Critics of the laws mentioned "the grave infringement on the very principles of democratic thought and life" and the importance of free speech and freedom of teaching, "fundamentals without which no country can be called a democracy." Even the typically conservative New York *Times* chastised the State Legislature for imposing loyalty oaths upon public school teachers. Measures that impeded freedom of thought, they eventually concluded, were but one step away from censoring freedom of the press. Governor Smith, who eventually repealed the law in 1923, saw in the Lusk Laws an even greater threat to civil liberties. "The laws," he commented, "are un-democratic and un-American, for if you censor thought, you must censor speech; and if you censor speech, you must censor press. Where is it to end?" he asked.[9]

It was this growing public recognition of the importance of civil liberties, fostered in part by the actions of Lusk, Stevenson, and Palmer, which proved to be the final blow to the committee's endeavors. As more citizens came to realize that arbitrary attacks upon fundamental rights such as freedom of thought and speech weakened their rights as well, they began to actively oppose state-sponsored repression. Writing in the *Boston Law Review* in 1943, Robert E. Cushman argued that public awareness of civil liberties was the key to maintaining them. "The ultimate responsibility for the protection of freedom of speech and press," he wrote, "rests upon people like ourselves, the ordinary citizens. Freedom of speech and freedom of press will be effectively preserved in this country only if people themselves value these vital civil liberties and demand that they be protected." Such forces were at work in 1923 when the people of New York overwhelmingly demanded the protection of those rights they had been willing to deny others just months earlier. Specifically, Dr. Henry Linville, President of the Teachers Union in New York, wrote, "If it had not been that public opinion brought about the repeal of the Lusk Laws, teachers would have been stigmatized as unworthy for the rest of their lives." The sheer volume of letters and telegrams to the governor supporting the repeal of the Lusk Laws in 1923, four times as many messages that defended the laws, reinforced the fact that the sleeping public was awakened by the threat the measures represented.[10]

Surprisingly, however, historians seldom address the role that public perceptions of civil liberties played in bringing a conclusion to the Red Scare. Only Michael Heale, in *American Anticommunism,* contends that public attention began to focus on civil liberties at the same time as the red tide began to ebb. Murray Levin, in *Political Hysteria in America,* mentions the importance of the development of a "counter community" to combat the repressive tendencies of self-interested political leaders; however, he fails to identify or explain how this counter community developed in relation to the post-World War I Red Scare. Most scholars, including Heale, Levin, Robert Murray, Robert Goldstein, acknowledge a public backlash to the Palmer raids, but fail to draw the connection between the reaction and a significant decline in the repression. None mention that the Red Scare continued in New York State for an additional three years beyond the traditionally-accepted conclusion to the episode.[11]

The work of the Lusk Committee after January, 1920, cannot be ignored or adjudged a curious anomaly, however. By changing the committee's focus almost entirely to education, as well as by modifying its tactics to more benign forms of repression, such as legal and legislative proceedings, Clayton Lusk managed to keep the Red Scare foremost in many New Yorkers minds long after the Palmer raids took place. Through his manipulation of public perceptions, he convinced the citizens of New York, especially those in upstate rural areas, that the Rand School was a serious threat to the well-being of the state and nation. Whereas Palmer failed to keep the Red Scare front-page news after 1920, the freshman state senator from Cortland, New York, planted his committee's endeavors firmly in the minds of millions of New Yorkers until 1923, a full two years *after* the committee had filed its final report.

The shift in methods and target were for obvious reasons. As the public became more attuned to issues of civil liberties, Lusk's initial tactics, such as raids and confiscation of materials, appeared increasingly heavy-handed and less tolerable, especially when they failed to uncover a serious radical threat. Legal and legislative proceedings had an air of propriety and constitutional safeguards, and were thus more acceptable to the public. The new, benign methods of repression the committee practiced became an established pattern for investigating radicalism during subsequent communist scares, up to and including the work of Senator Joseph McCarthy in the early 1950s.

Hysterical responses to perceived threats were not limited to Red Scares and Cold War fears, however. The ultimate strategy introduced by the Lusk Committee to combat the radical threat facing New York and the nation—namely, enacting legislation to outlaw the threat—also proved useful in the wake of the September 11, 2001 terrorist attacks on the World Trade Center twin towers. In three instances eerily similar to the Lusk Committee's efforts, the New York State legislature quickly moved to pass laws designed to capitalize on public hysteria in order to broaden the state's police powers in the aftermath of 9–11. Less than one week after the attacks, a special session of the legislature passed a series of bills dubbed "Anti-Terrorist Act I" that included severe penalties for false bomb threats, solicitation of terrorist activities, or harboring a terrorist. Although additional proposals on roving wiretaps failed to pass, the message delivered by New York's lawmakers and Governor George Pataki, who signed the measures to take effect immediately, was clear excess in defense of Americanism and national security was acceptable.[12]

Five assemblymen opposed the measures, including Martin Luster, a Democrat from Trumansburg, who lamented "This process has totally undermined our notion of democracy at a time when we are most concerned about it." However, the vast majority of legislators supported the measures, even those who questioned the breadth of powers they bestowed upon the state. "Is it overkill?" Assembly Speaker Sheldon Silver asked. "It may very well be," he followed; "but at this time I think it is very important to show the unity of our purpose and not question political motivation." State Senate Majority Leader Joseph Bruno was even more adamant in his defense of the measures, despite the concerns over civil liberties voiced by the small number of dissenters. "There's a natural concern by some people that you don't want to overreact and go too far in dealing with people's civil liberties," he conceded. But "from my point of view, now is the time if we are going to overreact."[13]

Subsequent efforts by New York State legislators to introduce additional anti-terrorist measures in 2002 and 2003, including the suspension of the statute of limitations, a broader allowance for wiretaps, limitations on the Fourth Amendment guarantees against unreasonable searches, and permission to view suspects' tax returns, generated even greater concerns. In a bitter one-day debate, culminating with a quick vote in the State Senate, some Republican senators accused the bill's Democratic opponents of being unpatriotic. Senator William Larkin, Jr. labeled all those who cast no-votes, "un-American," and claimed that several of the critics had never served in military combat. Smacking of the Red Scare hysteria generated in the 1920s and again in the 1950s, Senator Michael Balboni played on public fears, charging that the bill's opponents would suffer if an attack occurred in the absence of such measures. Governor Pataki, who gave permission for the State Senate to suspend its rules and conduct an abbreviated debate followed by an immediate vote, appeared on the senate floor after the decision to defend what he termed "unquestionably the most important bill that will be taken up this year. We've got to be proactive," the governor added, "and do everything in our power to protect the people of New York."[14]

Opponents of the measures based their position on defense of the U.S. Constitution, claiming it would be un-American not to question a bill that challenged fundamental civil liberties. "Any time we start fiddling around and striking parts of the Constitution," said Senator Kevin Parker of Brooklyn, "I get a ticklish feeling in my stomach." Several critics also accused the governor of a grand-standing publicity stunt, in his effort to rush the bill through the senate with little debate. Senator Thomas Duane of Manhattan labeled the process "absurd." "That's why we are a laughingstock," he said of his fellow senators. However, defenders of the measures chose to ignore such complaints as little more than unpatriotic semantics. In a statement reminiscent of Senator Lusk's challenges to his colleagues at the height of the Red Scare eighty-four years earlier, Senator Balboni concluded, "Don't stand on technicalities, stand on principle."[15]

The Lusk Committee left its mark on future episodes of political repression not only through the strategies they developed in the wake of growing public concerns over their initially heavy-handed tactics, but also in terms of targets. The committee's decision eventually to focus their entire efforts on education stemmed from changes in public perceptions of the communist menace, as well as Lusk's desire to keep the work of his committee in the limelight. As New Yorkers began to question the extent of the radical threat in late 1919, Lusk sought an issue behind which most, if not all, citizens would rally. He found that issue in education. What person, he thought, would not take every step necessary to protect their children from radicalism in the classroom? As a result, the Lusk Committee devoted over one-half of its final report to an investigation of education in New York State, and recommendations on legislative remedies to the radical threat present in both public and private schools. The committee's single-minded focus on education beginning in 1920 became the standard for future efforts to combat radicalism, particularly in New York State, where the state legislature appointed two more committees to investigate the potential use of loyalty oaths among teachers.[16]

However, while Lusk established two important precedents for future investigations into the radical threat, he also crossed the line when he broadened his attack to include all private schools and public school teachers. As the committee's new form of political repression slowly enveloped more people between 1920 and 1923, opposition to Lusk's tactics, targets, and eventually his motives, steadily grew. Soon, the public's distaste for Lusk and the work of his committee exceeded their fear of an alleged radical threat that never seemed to materialize. Smith's re-election as governor in 1922 signaled the beginning of the end for the Lusk Committee's foray into radicalism; by May, 1923, the Red Scare had truly ended.

The specific legacies of the Lusk Committee, beyond its broad impact upon the methods and targets of political repression in America, were numerous. Although its direct impact upon Soviet-U.S. economic trade is open to debate, the Lusk Committee clearly forestalled many potentially significant transactions when it forced the Soviet Bureau to close in June, 1919. Included among the hundreds of firms who expressed a willingness to conduct business with the Bolsheviks were industrial and utility giants, such as Ford Motor Company, Goodyear Rubber Company, U.S. Steel, and General Electric, all of whom were in a position to initiate thousands, if not millions, of dollars worth of trade with Lenin's regime. In Martens' absence, efforts to establish U.S.-Soviet trade floundered until the mid-1920s, and only then succeeded to a minor degree through the use of concessions from the Soviet government. Following a brief upsurge between 1928 and 1930, when the U.S. became the chief supplier of machine tools and parts at the outset of the Soviet Union's first Five-Year Plan, trade quickly dwindled during the Great Depression.[17]

The Rand School fared better as a result of the Lusk Committee's investigation. Although, as Algernon Lee repeatedly stated, "eternal vigilance is the price of liberty," eternal publicity became the school's path to success. The notoriety the school gained from the attacks upon it generated enrollment and donations. The Rand School continued to operate as one of the leading workers' education centers until 1956, when financial considerations finally forced the institution to cease offering classes. The school's library remained open until 1977, when it was incorporated into the Tamiment Institute of New York University, which houses to this day one of the foremost collections of radical pamphlets and special collections in the country.

Archibald Stevenson, the special counsel who was as much responsible for the formation of the Lusk Committee as was Senator Lusk, continued his crusade against radicalism for another fifteen years. Undaunted by the failure of both the Overman Committee and the Lusk Committee to achieve a lasting victory over the red menace, Stevenson spent much of the Great Depression protesting America's recognition of the Soviet Union, as well as criticizing many of Roosevelt's New Deal programs. In his last concerted anti-communist effort, he sought to have Communist Party leader Earl Browder banned from the radio airwaves as the 1930s came to a close. Eventually, Stevenson retired to New Canaan, Connecticut, where he served as a selectman and continued his personal research into constitutional law. However, when he died in 1961, newspaper headlines remembered Stevenson for the fame he achieved with the Lusk Committee: "Communist Foe Succumbs at 77."[18]

The speed of Clayton Lusk's fall from public grace exceeded his rise to fame. Upon Nathan Miller's election as governor in 1920, Lusk appeared set on the fast track to the executive mansion in Albany himself. As president *pro tem* in just his second term as a state senator, Lusk had become one of the most influential men in New York. Even the New York *Times* reported that, should Miller not seek re-election in 1922, Lusk appeared a virtual lock for the Republican nomination for governor. However, in the wake of Miller's defeat at the hands of Alfred Smith, as well as the repeal of the Lusk Laws, the senator's career suffered. Subsequent revelations concerning a chest of silver flatware that Lusk allegedly received as a bribe from the New York City Detectives Association in return for favorable legislation, as well as charges that he received a substantial retainer fee to assist a bankrupt brokerage firm under investigation by state authorities, raised the eyebrows of many citizens and colleagues who had previously supported Lusk's war on radicalism. When he eventually voted against movie censorship legislation that he himself authored, allegedly in return for a $10,000 bribe from studio executives, his bright political future was ruined. On July 14, 1924, the three-time senator and once rising star in the New York State Republican Party announced he would not run for re-election in November; he lived the remainder of his life in relative obscurity on his farm in Cortland, where he passed away in 1959.[19]

The story of the Lusk Committee and the role it played in the Red Scare came full circle on August 12, 1925. For Benjamin Glassberg, that morning began like every other since he was dismissed from his teaching position at Commercial High School six years earlier for spreading radical doctrines to his students. However, this day held hope; he was to learn of the State Department of Education's decision regarding his appeal for reinstatement to his job. Surely, he thought, the calming influence of normalcy coupled with the prosperity of the Jazz Age would result in his return to the classroom. He was mistaken. That afternoon, Dr. Frank Gilbert announced the department's support of the New York City Board of Education's original dismissal of Glassberg for conduct unbecoming a teacher; he would not return to the classroom. In subsequent years, Glassberg would assume a nondescript post as a local relief administrator in Milwaukee during the Great Depression. Front-page news at the height of the Red Scare, Glassberg's case was now little more than a footnote to the repression that spread across New York between 1919 and 1923. However, it became a symbol of the Red Scare's most lasting legacy—the harm it did to the hundreds of teachers who were named, investigated, and subsequently tainted under the short-lived Lusk Laws, and the unquantifiable thousands more who no doubt spoke guardedly and consciously altered their classroom lessons lest they become the next Benajmin Glassberg, before changing public perceptions brought the episode to a long overdue conclusion.[20]

Appendix 1
Firms and Individual Agents Attempting to Conduct Business via the Soviet Bureau*

I.Aaronson (NY)
J.W.Abbott (NY)
Abbott Ball Co. (CT)
Abbott Laboratories (IL)
Abendroth Brothers (NY)
Acason Motor Trucks (MI)
Acme Knit Goods Novelty Co. (NY)
Acme Shear Co. (CT)
Acushnet Mill Corp. (MA)
B.F.Adams (NY)
Adams Co. (IA)
Admiral Hay Press Co. (NY)
Adrian Knitting Co. (MI)
Advance Rumely Thresher Co. (IN)
Aermeter Co. (IL)
Aerothrust Engine Co. (IN)
L.Agoos and Co. (MA)
Agrippa Mfg. Corp. (NY)
Ajax Rubber Co. (NY)
Akron-Selle Co. (OH)
Alaska Packers Association (CA)
Alexander Bros. (NY)
Leo Alexander and Co. (NY)
W.D.Allen's Co. (NY)
N.R.Allen's Sons Co. (WI)
Alliance Machine Co. (OH)
Allied Machinery Co. of America (NY)
Allied Manufacturers Export Corp. (MA)
Alpine Knitting Mills (PA)
A.J.Alsdorf Corp.
Aluminum Goods Manufacturing Co. (WI)
Ambrosia Chocolate Co. (WI)
American Agricultural Chemical Co. (NY)
American Alcohol Co.(NY)

American Aniline Products, Inc. (NY)
American Asphalt Association (MO)
American Bleached Goods Co. (NY)
American Blower Co. (NY)
American Bosch Magneto Co. (MA)
American Brass Co. (NY)
American Car Co. (PA)
American Car and Foundry Export Co.
American Cast Iron Pipe Co. (NY)
American Chain Co. (NY)
American Distilling Co. IL)
American-European Industries Inc. (NY)
American Envelope and Paper Co. (NY)
American Food Products Co.
American Fork and Hoe Co. (OH)
American Graphite Co. (NY)
American Hoist and Derrick Co. (NY)
American Horse Shoe Works (NJ)
American Hosiery Co. (CT)
American Insulated Wire and Cable Co. (IL)
American International Corp. (NY)
American Lead Pencil Co. (NY)
American Linoleum Manufacturing Co.
American Manufacturing Co.
American Milling Co. (IL)
American Mining Tool Co. (IA)
American Motors, Inc. (NY)
American Pad and Textile Co. (OH)
American Paper Export Inc. (NY)
American Paper Exporters (MO)
American Potash Co. (NE)
American Sewer Pipe Co. (OH)
American Six Automobiles

---

*Compiled from correspondence, memorandums, and mailing lists found in CF, L0032, Box 1, D165/4, Folders A4–7, B3, B7. Although extensive, the list is not complete. Several records were lost after the raid on the Soviet Bureau. Some evidence indicates the list of firms wishing to conduct business with the Bureau may have been twice as long.

American Spinning Co. (NY)
American Steam Pump Co. (MI)
American Steel Export Co. (NY)
American Sterlizer Co. (PA)
American Sterlizer Co. (NY)
American Thermos Bottle Co. (NY)
American Tobacco Co. (NY)
American Tool Works Co. (OH)
American Transformer Co. (NJ)
American Tube and Stamping Co. (CT)
American Tube Works (NY)
American Type Founders (NJ)
American Valve Co. (NY)
American Vanadium (NY)
American Wire Fabrics Co. (NY)
American Wood Working Machinery Co. (NY)
Max Ames Machine Co. (NY)
Oliver Ames and Sons Corp. (MA)
Amitale Corp. (NY)
Amory, Browne and Co. (NY)
William H.Anderson and Co. (NY)
Anderson Tool and Supply Co. (MI)
Ansco Co. (NY)
Anthaus Trading Co.
Apex Spark Plug Co. (IN)
Appleton Wire Works (WI)
A.P.W.Paper Co. (NY)
Arabel Manufacturing Co. (NY)
Armour and Co. (IL)
Armour Leather Co. (IL)
Armstrong Cork Co. (NY)
Armstrong Manufacturing Co. (NY)
Arnold and Co. (IL)
Arnold, Hoffman and Co., Inc. (NY)
Arnold Print Works (NY)
E.N.Arnold Shoe Co. (MA)
Atlantic Bag Co. (NY)
Atlas Co. (NY)
Atlas Tack Co. (MA)
Atwater Manufacturing Co. (CT)
Audiffren Refrigerating Machine Co. (NY)
Aultman and Taylor Machinery Co. (NY)
Austin Co., Inc. (IL)
Austin Manufacturing Co. (NY)
Austin Manufacturing Co. (IL)
Automatic Button Co. (NY)
Automatic Transportation Co. (NY)
Automobile Products Corp. (NY)
Automotive Products Corp. (NY)

Avery Co. (IL)
B.F.Avery and Sons (KY)
B.A.Babbitt (NY)
Bachman and Co. (NY)
Baeder, Adamson and Co. (NY)
Baer Bros. (NY)
Bail Bros. Glass Mfg. Co. (IN)
Joshua L.Bailey and Co. (NY)
Baker Chemical Co. (NJ)
A.D.Baker Co. (OH)
Walter Baker and Co., Ltd. (MA)
Baker Manufacturing Co. (IN)
R & LBaker, New York Corp. (NY)
Balfour, Guthrie and Co. (CA)
Balfour, Williamson and Co. (NY)
Charles J.Ball (NY)
Baltimore Pearl Hominy Co. (MD)
Banting Manufacturing Co. (OH)
Barcale Manufacturing Co. (NY)
Wm. C.Barker (NY)
Barr Shipping Co. (NY)
William Barrell and Co. (NY)
Barstow Stove Co. (RI)
Bartley Crucible Co. (NJ)
Bateman Manufacturing Co. (NY)
J.E.Bates and Co. (NY)
Batuibak Brass Co. (MI)
Baugh Chemical Co. (MD)
Baum and Bender (NJ)
Bausche and Lomb Optical Co.
Bay State Milling Co. (MN)
Bay State Threading Works (MA)
Beacon Falls Rubber Shoe Co. (MA)
R.H.Beaumont Co. (PA)
Beaver Companies (NY)
N.Beck (NY)
Beckwith Co. (MI)
Beckwith-Chandler Co. (NY)
Beggs and Cobb, Inc. (MA)
Herman Behr and Co. (NY)
David Belais (NY)
Belcher and Loomis Hardware Co. (RI)
Belden Manufacturing Co. (IL)
Benedict Manufacturing Co. (NY)
Berg Bros. (NY)
Berg Co. (WI)
Berger Manufacturing Co. (NY)
Berlin Construction Co., Inc. (NY)
Eline Berlow Commercial Agency

APPENDIX 1 141

C.A.Bernstein (NY)
N.Bernstein (NY)
A.Hall Berry (NY)
Bertelson and Peterson
Engineering Co. (MA)
Bessemer Gas Engine Co. (NY)
Best-Clymer Manufacturing Co. (MO)
Bethlehem Motors Corp. (NY)
Bethlehem
Steel Co.Bettendorf Co. (IA)
Frank S.Betz Co. (IN)
Binney and Smith Co. (NY)
James H.Birch (NJ)
Bishop and Babcock Co. (NY)
Bishop Guta-Percha Co. (NY)
Bishop's Service (NY)
George W.Blabon Co. (PA & NY)
Blackstone Manufacturing Co. (NY)
Blake and Johnson Co. (CT)
Blake Pump and Condenser Co. (MA)
Fabyan Bliss and Co. (NY)
Berle C.Bloom (NY)
M.Blumenthal (NY)
Bobroff Foreign Trading and
Engineering Co. (NY)
J.R.Bockendorff and Co., Inc. (NY)
E.C.Boise (NY)
Boker Cutlery and Hardware Co. (NY)
Bomack Paper Corp. (NY)
A.Bonn (NY)
Bonner and Barnewell (NY)
Boot and Shoe Recorder
Publishing Co. (MA)
Theodore Booth Rubber Co. (MD)
M.C.D.Borden and Sons (NY)
Borden's Condensed Milk Sales Co. (NY)
Bossert Corp. (NY)
Boston Corp. (NY)
Boston Molasses Co. (MA)
Boston Thread Co. (MA)
Boston Varnish Co. (MA)
Boston Woven Hose and Rubber Co. (MA)
Botany Worsted Mills(NY)
Bourne-Fuller Co. (NY)
Bovaird and Seyeang Mfg. Co. (PA)
Bowen Products Corp. (NY)
David Bradley Mfg. Works (IL)
Bradley Pulverizer Co. (PA)
F.A.Brady, Inc. (NY)
Brand Breadhead Worsted Mills (NY)

Joseph Branner and Co. (MD)
Braude-Goodman Shoe Co. (MA)
Brecht Co. (NY)
Brennan Packing Co. (IL)
Bridgeport Chain Co. (CT)
Bridgeport Rolling Mills (CT)
H.Brimberg (NY)
Bristol Brass Corp. (NY)
Brockway Motor Truck Co. (NY)
A.M.Brooks (IL)
M.S.Brooks and Sons (CT)
Brooks Uniform Co. (NY)
Broom and Newman (NY)
A. & F.Brown Co. (NY)
C.D.Brown and Co.
Brown Hoisting Machine Co. (OH)
Brown Shoe Co. (NY)
Brown Whales Co. (MA)
Bryant Electric Co. (CT)
Buckeye Aluminum Co. (NY)
Buffalo Pitts Co. (NY)
Bullard Machine Tool Co. (CT)
Burnham and
Merrill Co. (ME)
Burns and Bassick Co. (NY)
Bush, Beach and Gent, Inc. (NY)
Cairo Thread Works (NY)
California Fruit Growers Exchange (CA)
California Packing Corp. (CA)
Cannon Mills (NY)
Cape Ann Fish Net Co. (MA)
Capewell Horse Rail Co. (CT)
Carborundum Co. (NY)
Carolina Junk and Hide Co. (NC)
Carpenter Steel Co. (PA)
C.L.Carter (NY)
Carter, Macy and Co., Inc. (NY)
Carus Chemical Co.Carver-
Beaver Yarn Co., Inc. (NY)
J.I. Case Plow Works(WI)
J.I. Case Threshing Machine Co. (WI)
Castle Tobacco Works(PA)
Catlin and Co. (NY)
Cattaraucus Cutlery Co. (NY)
Central Rope Mfg. Co., Inc. (NY)
Central Scientific Co. (IL)
Certain-teed Products Corp. (NY)
Chalmers Knitting Co. (NY)
J.V.Chanutin (NY)
Charlottesville Woolen Mills (VA)

Chatham Manufacturing Co. (NC)
Chatham Shirt Co. (NY)
Chicago Pneumatic Tool Co. (NY)
Chicago Spring Butt Co. (IL)
S.Churchill (NY)
E.Clemens Horst Co. (NY)
Cleveland Brass and Copper Mills (OH)
Cleveland Twist Drill Co. (OH)
Clift and Goodrich (NY)
Clifton Manufacturing Co. (SC)
Clyde Mills (NY)
Colgate and Co. (NY)
Collins and Co. (NY)
Columbian Bronze Corp. (NY)
Columbian Chemical Co. (PA)
Columbian Enameling & Stamping Co. (IN)
Columbus McKinnon Chain Co. (OH)
Commercial Acceptance Trust Co. (IL)
Robert W.Coneybear (IL)
Connecticut Brass and Mfg. Corp. (CT)
Connecticut Steel Corp. (NY)
Consolidated Rendering Co. (NY)
Consolidated Safety Pin Co. (NJ)
Consolidated Steel Corp. (NY)
Consolidated Tea Co. (NY)
Contecook Mills (NY)
Continental Rubber Works (PA)
Cooper and Cooper (NY)
Corbitt Motor Truck Co. (NC)
Corn Products Refining Co. (NY)
H.W.Cotton, Inc. (NY)
C.B.Cottrell and Sons Co. (RI)
Coulter and McKenzie Machine Co. (CT)
Cowan Trucking Co. (MA)
Mark Cowen (NY)
Crane and Co. (IL)
Crescent Forge and Shovel Co. (IL)
Crescent Trading Co. (NY)
Cribben and Sexton Co. (IL)
Ralph Croft (NY)
Crompton Co. (RI)
Crompton and Knowles Loom Works (MA)
Cronk and Carrier Mfg. Co. (NY)
W.W.Cross and Co., Inc. (MA)
Crown Optical Co. (NY)
Crystal Knitting Mills, Inc. (NY)
Cudahy Brothers, Inc. (WI)
Cudahy Packing Co. (IL)

Cumberland Steel Co.(MD)
James Cunningham, Son and Co. (NY)
Howard L.Curry Co. (NY)
Curtis and Curtis Co. (CT)
Cushman-Hollis Co. (ME)
Cyclops Steel Co. (NY)
Damascus Manufacturing Co. (NY)
Dangler Stove Co. (NY)
R.B.Davis Co. (NJ)
Davis Machine Tool Co., Inc. (NJ)
Davis Manufacturing Co. (NY)
Henry N.Day and Co., Inc. (NY)
J.H.Decker and Son Co. (NY)
Deere and Co. (IL)
Defiance Machine Works (NY)
Deforest Sheet and Tin Plate Co. (OH)
Delvin Sales Co. (WI)
William Demuth and Co. (NY)
Dennison Manufacturing Co. (NY)
Carl Dernberg and Son (IL)
Detroit Electric Car Co. (MI)
Detroit Stove Works (NY)
R. & J.Dick (NJ)
Dickinson and Co. (IL)
F.D.Dirwick and Co., Inc. (NY)
Henry Disston and Sons, Inc. (PA)
Elais Diswick (NY)
Eugene Ditzgen Co., Inc. (NY)
Joseph Dixon Crucible Co. (NJ)
John and James Dobson, Inc. (PA)
Doherry and Wadsworth Co. (NY)
Jacob Dold Packing Co. (NY)
Dominion Brush Manufacturing Co. (Canada)
Doninger and Co. (NY)
A.Dougherty (NY)
Douglas Co. (IA)
B.F.Drakenfeld and Co., Inc. (NY)
S.R.Dresser Manufacturing Co. (PA)
Driver-Harris Co. (NJ)
Drueding Brothers Co. (PA)
Dry Milk Co. (NY)
Duckwell Belting and Hose Co. (IN)
Duesenberg Motors Corp. (NY)
Duff Manufacturing Co. (NY)
Dunbar Molasses and Syrup Co. (NY)
Dundee Textile Co. (NJ)
R.G.Dunn and Co. (NY)
Duplex Channel Pin Co. (NY)
Duplex Printing Press Co. (MI)

APPENDIX 1   143

Duplex Truck Co. (MI)
C.D.Durkee and Co. (NY)
W.H.Duval and Co. (NY)
E.I.duPont de Nemours Export Co. (NY)
J.H. and C.K.Eagle (NY)
Charles M.Eakle (NY)
Eastern Talc Co. (MA)
East Side Packing Co. (IL)
Eberhard Faber (NY)
Economy Fuse and Mfg. Co. (IL)
P.M.Edwards Co., Inc. (NY)
Eimer and Amend (NY)
Einstein-Wolff Co. (NY)
Sigmund Eisner Co. (NJ)
Elber Co. (OH)
Elder Manufacturing Co. (MO)
Electric Hose and Rubber Co. (DE)
Electric Wheel Co. (IL)
Electro Dental Manufacturing Co. (PA)
Max Elkind and Simon Fagan (NY)
B.K.Elliott Co. (PA)
Elliott Frog and Switch Co. (IL)
Ellis Steel Cushion Tire Co. (MA)
John B. Ellison and Sons (PA)
Elwell-Parker Electric Co. (NY)
Emerson-Brantingham Implement Co. (NY)
Emerson International Inc. (NY)
Emery Candle Co. (NY)
Emlenton Refining Co. (PA)
Empire Cream Seperator Co. (NJ)
Empire Manufacturing Co. (NY)
Empire Manufacturing Co. (IL)
Enterprise Co. (NY)
Erwin Cotton Mills Co. (NC)
Estes Mills (MA)
Ever Ready Specialty Co. (NY)
Exporters Drygoods Exchange (NY)
Exporters Purchasing Association (NY)
A.W.Faber (NJ)
N.K.Fairbank Co. (IL)
Fairbanks Co. (NY)
Falk Co. (WI)
D.J.Faour and Brothers (NY)
A.B.Farquhar Co. Ltd. (NY)
Fashion Childrens Dress Co. (NY)
Federal Glass Co. (OH)
Federal Plate Glass Co. of 111. (IL)
Federal Motor Truck Co. (MI)
Federal Rope Co. (NY)
Nathaniel Feingolf (NY)

Fellows Gear Shaper Co. (VT)
S.Fels and Sons (NY)
Felt and Tarrant Manufacturing Co. (NY)
F.I.A.T. (NY)
Marshall
Field and Co. (NY)
Finch Manufacturing Co. (PA)
Findelsen and Kropf
Mfg. Co. (IL)
Fischmann and Co. (NY)
Fish Clearing House (WA)
Fisk Rubber Co. (MA)
M.D.Fitzgerald (NJ)
Fitzsimons Co. (OH)
Flash Chemical Co. (MA)
Charles R.Flint and Co. (NY)
Florence Manufacturing Co. (NY)
S.Fole and Sons (NY)
Ford Corporation (NY)
Ford Motor Co. (MI)
Ford Roofing Products Co. (MO)
Foreign Products Co., Inc. (NY)
Forstmann and Huffmann Co. (NJ)
Foster Wheel Drive Auto Co. (WI)
Franco-American Food Co. (NJ)
Franklin Manufacturing Co. (NY)
Frederick Motor Truck Co. (NY)
Free Sewing Machine Co. (IL)
Frick Co., Inc. (PA)
Frye and Co. (WA)
Fuld and Match Knitting Co. (NY)
Futterman and Co. (NY)
William Galdonay Co. (IA)
Gardener Governor Co. (NY)
Garford Manufacturing Co. (OH)
Garford Motor Truck Co. (OH)
Garland Manufacturing Co. (ME)
Gas Oil Stove Co. (MI)
Abraham Gash (NY)
Gaston, Williams & Wigmore, Inc. (NY)
Gaynor Glass Works (NJ)
Gehl Brothers Mfg. Co. (NY)
Geisman, Nusliner and Brightman (NY)
General Asbestos and Rubber Co. (NY)
General Asbestos and Rubber Co. (NC)
General Electric Co. (NY)
General Fastener Co. (MA)
General Motors Truck Co. (NY)
General Ordnance Co. (NY)
Getz Brothers and Co. (CA)

144 APPENDIX 1

Gilbert and Barker Mfg. Co. (NY)
Gilbert Knitting Co. (NY)
Robert Gill (NY)
Gill Brothers Co. (OH)
Gillette Safety Razor Co. (MA)
J.E.Gilson Co. (WI)
Globe Soap Co. (OH)
Globe Stove and Range Co. (NY)
Glover Machine WorksGlunhanck and Hill (NY)
Leo Goldblatt (IL)
Goldstein and Newburger (NY)
Goodall Worsted Co. (ME)
Goodell-Pratt Co. (MA)
Goodman Manufacturing Co. (IL)
Goodyear Rubber Co. (NY)
Gordon Tire and Rubber Co. (NY)
Goshen Shirt Mfg. Co. (IL)
Goss Printing Press Co. (IL)
Grace American International Co. (NY)
Grafton Johnson (IN)
Grand Rapids Underwear Co. (MI)
Robert Grant Iron and Steel Co. (NY)
Grasselli Chemical Co. (NY)
Graton and Knight Manufacturing Co. (MA)
Frank B.Graves Co. (NY)
R.Z.Graves, Inc. (PA)
Great Republic Tire and Rubber Mfg. Co. (OK)
Great Western Electric Chemical Co. (NY)
Green and Daniels Co., Inc. (RI)
Green Fuel Economiser Co. (NY)
Maurice Greenberg (NY)
Greenfield Tap and Die Corp. (MA)
Greenlee Brothers and Co. (IL)
Benjamin Griffen (NY)
Guggenheim and Co. (CA)
I.Gumport and Sons, Inc. (NY)
W. and L.E.Gurley Machinery (NY)
A.S.Haight and Co. (NY)
Hale, Hartwell and Co. (NY)
Hamilton Manufacturing Co. (WI)
Hammer Brothers White Lead Co. (IL)
Hammond Multiplex Typewriter Co. (NY)
Hanet Hat Co. (NY)
Hansen and Dieckmann(NY)
Harding, Tilton and Co. (MA)
Harris Construction Co. (CT)

Harris and Stern (NY)
Harrisburg Pipe & Pipe Bending Co. (PA)
Hart-Parr Co. (IA)
Hartford City Paper Co. (IN)
Hartley Silk Co., Inc. (NY)
John Hassall, Inc. (NY)
Hawkeys Tire and Rubber Co. (IA)
Haynes Automobile Co. (NY)
C.B.Hayward and Co. (NY)
Hazard Manufacturing Co. (PA)
R.P.Hazzard Co. (NY)
Heald Machine Co. (MA)
Heath and Milligan Mfg. Co. (IL)
Heckanam Mills Co. (CT)
John O.Heinze Co. (OH)
Helenholz Mitten Co. (WI)
Henry and Wright Mfg. Co. (CT)
Joseph N.Herman Shoe Co. (MA)
Hershey Chocolate Co. (PA)
Hewitt Rubber Co. (NY)
E.B.Hindley and Co.(NJ)
Hires Turner Glass Co. (NY)
Hodgman Rubber Co. (NY)
Walter Hodkins (MA)
R.Hoe and Co. (NY)
Hoefer Manufacturing Co. (IL)
S.L.Hoffman and Co. (NY)
Holbrook Brothers (NY)
Holbrook, Cabot and Rollins Corp. (NY)
Hollingsworth and Co. (MA)
Homes Brothers Co. (MA)
Hood Rubber Co. (MA)
W.T.Hoofnagle (NY)
C.N.Hooper (IL)
William E.Hooper and Sons Co. (NY)
Hoopes and Townsend Co. (PA)
Hope Webbing Co. (RI)
Horse Twist Drill and Machine Co. (MA)
E.Clemens Horst (CA)
Horton and Diago S. en C. (NY)
Hospital Supply Co. (NY)
J.W. and A.Howard Co. (PA)
B.H.Howell and Son Co. (NY)
G.W.Hume Co. (CA)
Frank W.Hunt and Co. (MA)
Hunt-Rankin Leather Co. (MA)
Charles N.Hunter (NY)
Hunter Mfg. and Commission Co. (NY)
Hunter Pressed Steel Co. (PA)
Hunter Saw and Machine Co. (PA)

APPENDIX 1   145

Miss M.B.Huson, M.D. (NY)
A.G.Hyde and Sons (NY)
Illinois Tool Works (IL)
Imperial Glass Co. (OH)
Incandescent Supply Co. (NY)
Indian Refining Co. (NY)
Indiana Truck Corp. (NY)
Industrial Works (MI)
E.Ingram Co. (CT)
Innis, Speidon and Co., Inc. (NY)
International Cotton Mills (MA)
International Harvester Co. (IL)
International High Speed Steel Co. (NJ)
International Machine Tools Co. (IN)
Int'l Mfs. Sales Co. of America, Inc. (NY)
International Oxygen Co. (NJ)
International Packing Corp. (CA)
International Paper Co. (NY)
International Silver Co. (NY)
Interstate Pulp and Paper Co. (NY)
Intertype Corp. (NY)
Interwoven Stocking Co. (NJ)
S.Jacobs (NY)
Jeffrey Manufacturing Co. (OH)
H.W.Johns-Manville Co. (NY)
Johnson Brokerage Co. (PA)
Endicott Johnson Shoe o.J.S.Johnston Co. (NY)
H.S.Jones (NY)
Jones and Laughlin Steel Co. (NY)
Julian School Co. (NY)
J.W.Salvage (NY)
Kalamazoo Stove Co. (MI)
Katzenbach and Bullock Co. (NY)
Emil Kaufmann Co. (NY)
Preston B.Keith Shoe Co. (NY)
Keller and Tamm Manufacturing Co. (MO)
Kelloggs and Miller (NY)
Kelly-Sprigfield Motor Truck Co. (OH)
Kempsmith Manufacturing Co.
Kentucky Wagon Manufacturing Co. (KY)
Keystone Type Foundry Supply House (PA)
Keystone Watch Case Co. (NJ)
K–G Welding and Cutting Co., Inc. (NY)
Kimble Glass Co. (NY)
J.A.Kirsch and Co. (NY)
A.Klipstein and Co. (NY)
Knickerbocker Knitting Works (NY)

Knox Motors Associates (NY)
Knox Woolen Co. (ME)
Kohler Co. (WI)
Koken Barbers' Supply Co. (MO)
Kokomo Rubber Co. (IN)
Korein Brothers (NY)
N.C.Kousnetzoff (NY)
James B.Kuane (NY)
George E.Kunhardt (MA)
La Golondrina Co. (OH)
Edward L.Ladew Co. (NY)
Lakeside Forge Co. (PA)
Lakshmi International Merchandising Co. (NY)
Lamborn and Co. (NY)
Lancaster Glass Co. (OH)
Landeck Lumber Co. (FL)
John J.Lattermann Sheet Mfg. Co. (NY)
John Lauson Manufacturing Co. (WI)
Frederick Lausser and Son (NY)
Lautz Brothers and Co. (NY)
Lawrence Brothers (IL)
John Lawrie and Sons (IL)
F.H.Lawson Co. (OH)
Daniel Leary (NY)
H.Leben Co. (NY)
Lee Tire and Rubber Co. (NY)
Charles Leffler and Co. (NY)
Lehigh Machine Co. Levine and Greenbaum (NY)
Levinson and Shapiro (NY)
Levy Overall Manufacturing Co. (OH)
Lewis Manufacturing Co. (MA)
Liberty Commerce Corp. (NY)
Liberty Tire and Rubber Co. (PA)
Lidgerwood Manufacturing Co. (NY)
S.Liebovitz and Son, Inc. (NY)
Limoneira Co. (CA)
A.J.Lindemann and Hoverson Co. (WI)
Linen Thread Co. (NY)
Linograph Co. (IA)
J. and G.Lippmann (NY)
Little Giant Co. (MI)
B.Litzenberger (IN)
Lockwood Co. (NY)
Locomobile Company of America (CT)
Lodge and Shipley Co. (OH)
Long Wear Rubber Co. (OH)
Ludlow-Saylor Wire Co. (MO)
Ludlow Valve Manufacturing Co. (NY)

146 APPENDIX 1

Ludlum Steel Co. (NY)
Luitwieler Pumping Engine Co. (NY)
Lundham and Moore (NY)
Luther Grinder Manufacturing Co. (WI)
Lux Manufacturing Co. (NJ)
Lynchburg Foundry Co. (PA)
Maclead Co. (OH)
Macomber and Whyte Rope Co. (WI)
James Magee Webbing Co. (PA)
Magee Carpet Co. (PA)
Jospeh Meisel Co. (NY)
Majestic Machine & Tool Co., Inc. (NY)
Majestic Mills Paper Co., Inc. (NY)
Mallinckrodt Chemical Works (NY)
Mangus Co. (NY)
Manning, Maxwell and Morre, Inc. (NY)
Manufacturers Clearing House Association (IL)
Manufacturers Iron and Steel Co. (NY)
Marathon Tire and Rubber Co. (OH)
Marietta Paint and Color Co. (OH)
Marion Steam Shovel Co. (OH)
Maris Brothers (PA)
Market Warehouse Co.Markt and Hammacher (NY)
Marlboro Cotton Mills (SC)
Marlowe and Iwaya Co. (NY)
Martin-Senour Co. (IL)
Maryland Co. (MD)
Charles Maschwitz, Jr., Inc. (NY)
Massey, Harris Harvester Co. (NY)
Mast, Foos and Co. (OH)
Mathieson Alkali Works, Inc. (VA)
Max Grinding Wheel Corp. (MA)
David Maydale Hammer Co. (NY)
F.Mayer Boot and Shoe Co. (WI)
Mechanical Appliance Co. (WI)
A.Mecky Co. (PA)
Mendelssohn Brothers (Canada)
H.D.Merblum Co. (NY)
Mercer Pottery Co. (NJ)
Mercury Chemical Co. (NY)
Messinger Manufacturing Co. (PA)
Mesta Machine Co. (PA)
F. and J.Meyer (NY)
Meyer Brothers Sales Co. (NY)
Louis Meyer and Son (NY)
Mianus Motor Works (CT)
Michaels, Stern and Co. (NY)
Michelin Tire Co. (NJ)

Michigan Copper and Brass Co. (MI)
Michigan Refining and Preserving Co. (MI)
Michigan Wire Cloth Co. (MI)
Miller Supply Co. (WV)
Millers Falls Co. (NY)
Jason H.Millikin and Sons (MA)
Milwaukee Shaper Co. (WI)
Miner-Edgar Co. (NY)
Minford, Lueder and Co. (NY)
Mishawaka Woolen Manufacturing Co. (IN)
M.Mishel and Co. (MA)
Missouri Meerschaum Co. (MO)
Henry Mittelberger (MI)
Modern Machinery Exchange (NY)
Mohawk Valley Cap Factory (NY)
Moline Malleable Iron Co. (IL)
Moline Plow Co. (IL)
Mollc Typrewriter Co. (WI)
Monarch Knitting Co., Ltd. (NY)
Monitor Stove Co. (OH)
Monroe Calculating Machine Co. (NY)
Moore Motor Vehicle Co. (IL)
John Morrell and Co. (IA)
Morris and Company (IL)
Morris Glass Co. (NY)
Morse Twist Drill and Machine Co. (MA)
Moskowitz Brothers (NY)
William F.Mosser Co. (MA)
James P.Mulvihill Shoe Co. (PA)
F.E. Myers and Brothers (OH)
McCall Co. (NY)
S.R. and I.C.McConnell Co. (IA)
W.H.McElwain Co. (MA)
McKeesport Tin Plate Co. (PA)
McKesson and Robbins (NY)
McKibben, Driscoll & Dorsey, Inc. (MN)
Nairn Linoleum Co. (NJ)
Napier Saw Works, Inc. (MA)
National Acme Co. (OH)
National Blank Book Co. (NY)
National Brass Co. (MI)
National Carbon Co. (OH)
National Lead Co. (NY)
National Leather Belting Co. (NY)
National Manufacturing Export Co. (NY)
National Marine Lamp (CT)National Merchandise Co. (NY)
National Oats Co. (MO)

APPENDIX 1   147

National Sanitary Co. (OH)
National Sewing Machine Co. (NY)
National Shoe Co.National Standard Co. (NY)
National Storage Co.
National Wire Wheel Works, Inc. (NY)
National Woolen Co. (OH)
Natwill Co. (NY)
Lawrence Neebe, Inc. (NY)
N.O.Nelson Manufacturing Co. (MO)
Nemours Trading Corp. (NY)
A.E.Nettleton Co. (NY)
New Departure Manufacturing Co. (CT)
New Hide Manufacturing Co. (PA)
New Jersey Car Spring & Rubber Co., Inc. (NJ)
New York Export Purchasing Co. (NY)
New York Leather Belting Co. (NY)
New York Merchandise Co. (NY)
New York Rubber Co. (NY)
Niagara Alkalai Co. (NY)
Nicholson File Co. (RI)
Nilson Tractor Co. (MN)
Ninety Six Cotton Mills (SC)
Harry Noble (NY)
Noble Electric Steel Co. (CA)
Nordberg Manufacturing Co. (WI)
Nordyke and Marmon Co. (IN)
North American Copper Co. (NY)
Northwestern Knitting Co. (MN)
Nunn, Bush and Weldon Shoe Co. (WI)
R.D.Nuttall Co. (PA)
Nyanza Mills (MA)
O. and J.Machine Co. (MA)
Oak Knitting Co. (NY)
Oelbaum Brothers and Bauer (NY)
Official Manufacturing Co. (WI)
Ohio Valley Pulley Works (KY)
Ohio Wire Goods Manufacturing Co. (OH)
Old Reliable Motor Truck Corp. (NY)
Oliver Typewriter Co. (NY)
Maurice O'Meara Co. (NY)
Onondaga Pottery Co. (NY)
Openheimer Casing Co. Oppenheimer and Berliner (NY)
Oriental Trading Co. of America (NY)
Ostemoor Co. (NY)
W.R.Ostrader and Co. (NY)
Otto Engine Manufacturing Co. (PA)
Pacific and Eastern Steamship Co. (NY)
Packard Motor Co. (MI)
Page-Storm Drop Forge Co. (MA)
Palmolive Co. (NY)
Charles Parker Co. (NY)
Parsons Paper Co. (MA)
Patent Button Co. (CT)
Paterson Parchment Paper Co. (NJ)
Patterson, Gottfried & Hunter, Inc. (NY)
Patterson-Sargent Co. (NY)
Peninsular Stove Co. (MI)
Peoria Cordage Co. (IL)
Pepperell Manufacturing Co. (ME)
Perlman and Co. (NY)
Peru Plow and Wheel Co. (IL)
Petigor Bramson Co. (NY)
Pettit, Marshall and Co. (NY)
Charles Pfizer and Co., Inc. (NY)
Phillips Wire Co. (NY)
Physicians & Hospital Equipment Co. (NY)
Pittsburgh Plate Glass Co. (PA)
Pittsburgh Steel Co. (NY)
Plant Brothers and Co. (NH)
Plottel Raincoat Co. (NY)
Polack Tire and Rubber Co. (NY)
J.T.Polk Co. (IN)
J.W.Polly (NY)
Power Equipment Co., Inc.(NY)
Precious Castings Co. (NY)
Prest-O-Lite Co., Inc. (NY)
Preston Shirt Co. (NY)
W.M.Pringle and Co. (NY)
Proctor & Gamble Distributing Co. (OH)
Isaac Prouty Shoe Co.Puritan Fibre Co. (MA)
Pussey and Jones Co. (DE)
Rahn-Lerman Co. (OH)
Rawlins Clenzene Co. (MO)
Fred Reed Corp. (NY)
Reisman, Rothman and Beiber (NY)
Reliable Glove Co. (NY)
Reliance Yarn Co. (CT)
Republic Rubber Co. (NY)
Republic Varnish Co. (NJ)
Rhodes Engineering Co. (NY)
E.E.Rich (NY)
Rickitts and Shaw (NY)
Lindsay J.Riggins Co. (NY)
J.L. and D.S.Riker (NY)
H.Rippen (NJ)
A.Rosalsky and Brother (NY)

Rosenfeld-Kessam Co. (NY)
Rosen-Reichardt Brokerage Co. (MO)
Rosensweig, Pincus and Hollender (NY)
E.W.Rosenthal and Co. (GA)
Rower and Bearak (MA)
John D.Russ (IL)
Russell and Co. (NY)
Russian Star Co. (NY)
Daniel Saks, Inc. (NY)
Salant and Salant (NY)
Sanders Dental Supply Co. (Canada)
Gustave H.Schiff (NY)
Louis Schlessinger and Co. (NY)
S.Robert Schwartz and Brother (NY)
Scientific Utilities Co. (NY)
Sears, Roebuck and Co. (IL)
Seller Distributing Co. (MI)
Sheffield Farms-Slawson Decker Co.
Sherman Brothers Co. (IL)
Siff Brothers Co. (NY)
Signal Accessories Co. (NY)
C.T.Silver, Inc. (NY)
Silver Manufacturing Co. (OH)
William M.Smith (NY)
W.Smith Grubber Co. (MN)
J.L.Sommer Manufacturing Co. (NJ)
Southseas Import and Export Co. (NY)
B.Souto Co. (NY)
Standard Shoe Co. (MA)
Steel Sole Shoe Co.Herman Stein (NY)
Sterling, Geneen Corp. (NY)
Charles T.Stork and Co. (NY)
Strohmeyer and Arpe Co. (NY)
Submarine Salvage Co. (NY)
Surpless, Dunn and Co. (NY)
Samuel M.Sutliff (NJ)
Swift and Co. (IL)
Taber, Wheeler Co. (MA)
Talcum Puff Co. (NY)
Taylor, Clapp and Beall (NY)
N.B.Thayer and Co. (MA)
Thayer, Everet, Terhune (NY)
W.B.Thompson (LA)
Tindel-Morris Co. (DE)
Tobacco Products Export Corp. (NY)

Twin Rock Drill Co., Inc. (NY)
Union Card and Paper Co. (NY)
Union Smelting and Refining Co. (NY)
United Clothing Co. (NY)
United Skirt Co. (NY)
U.S. Chain & Forging Co. (PA)
U.S. Distributing Co. (MI)
U.S. Manufacturers' Export Corp. (NY)
U.S. Packing Co. (IL)
U.S. Provision Export Corp. (IL)
U.S. Rubber Co. (NY)
U.S. Steel Export Co.U.S. Steel Products Co. (NY)
Victor, Achelis and Frederick (NY)
Virginia Wagon Co. (VA)
Boris A.Wachernin (PA)
Lewis Walther Manufacturing Co. (PA)
Washburn-Crusby Co. (NY)
Weber Engine Co. (MO)
F.S.Webster Co. (NY)
Weinberg and Posner Engineering Co. (NY)
Wellington, Sears and Co. (NY)
Wentworth Hat Manufacturing Co. (WI)
Western Electric Co.(NY)
Western Electric Export Co. (NY)
Western Knitting Mills (NY)
Weyenberg Shoe Manufacturing Co. (WI)
White Co. (OH)
Clarence Whitman and Son, Inc.(NY)
Benjamin Whittaker (NY)
Wiebusch and Hilger, Ltd. (NY)
Joseph Wild and Co. (NY)
R.C.Williams and Co. (NY)
Williams, Clark and Co. (MA)
Wilmarth and Morman Co.Wilson and Co. (IL)
Isaac Winkler Brothers and Co. (OH)
J.Wolkind and Co., Inc. (NY)
W.J.Wollman and Co. (NY)
Wolverine Tractor Co. (MI)
J.S.Woodhouse Co. (NY)
Workman and Silver Import Co. (NY)
Wright's Underwear Co. (NY)
Wyandotte Worsted Co. (NY)
Young, Corley and Dolan (NY)

Walter J. Townsend and Co. (NY)
Trans-Oceanic Commercial Corp. (NY)
Youroveta Home and Foreign Trade (NY)
Yu Ess Manufacturing Corp. (NY)

Appendix 2
Contracts Concluded by the Soviet Bureau*

Date	Company	Product	Amount
7 May 1919	Weyenberg Shoe Mfg. Co.[a]	Shoes	$226,710
10 May 1919	F. Mayer Boot/Shoe Co.[b]	Boots	$1,201,250
7 Jul 1919	Milwaukee Shaper Co.[b]	Machinery	$45,071
23 Jul 1919	Eline Berlow Agency	Boots	$3,000,000
24 Jul 1919	Fischmann and Co.	Clothing	$3,000,000
30 Jul 1919	Kempsmith Mfg. Co.[b]	Machinery	$97,470
Aug 1919	Steel Sole Shoe Co.[b]	Boots	$58,750
16 Sep 1919	National Storage Co.[c]	Mdse.	$10,000,000
29 Sep 1919	Weinberg and Posner	Machinery	$3,000,000
27 Oct 1919	Lehigh Machine Co.	Presses	$3,000,000
22 Jan 1920	Morris and Co.	Food	$10,000,000
n.d.	Anthaus Trading Co.[d]	Shoes	$10,164

Total: 12 contracts, $33,639,415

[a]Weyenberg Shoe Manufacturing Co. negotiated a contract with the Soviet Bureau, but later encountered difficulties concerning the fluctuating market price of leather as well as the ninety-day clause regarding the procurement of an export license.

[b]These four firms conducted their business with the bureau via the commercial agent, Bobroff Foreign Trading and Engineering Co.

[c]National Storage Co. delivered a shipment of "assorted merchandise" to Petrograd but, according to Martens, "could not meet the terms of the deal"; therefore, the Bolsheviks terminated the contract.

[d]Anthaus Trading Co., which delivered 5,500 pairs of shoes to Petrograd, was the only firm to receive payment on a completed contract.

---

*'Compiled from information found in United States, Senate, *Russian Propaganda,* 71; Weyenberg Shoe Manufacturing Co., Contract, May 7, 1919, LCF, L0032, Box 1, D165/4, FolderA7.

Appendix 3
Lecturers, Rand School of Social Science, 1905–1920*

Dr. G.B.L.Arner, statistician, formerly of Dartmouth College.
Prof. Charles A.Beard, historian, formerly of Columbia University.
Samuel Beardsley, of the International Jewelry Workers' Union.
August Claessens, New York State Assemblyman.
Evans Clark, lecturer on municipal affairs, formerly of Princeton University.
Dr. John Dillon, formerly New York State Commissioner of Food and Markets.
Dr. W.E.B.DuBois, sociologist and expert on race relations.
James Duncan, of the International Association of Machinists.
Robert Ferrari, lawyer and criminologist.
Prof. Willard C.Fisher, economist, of New York University.
John Fitch, industrial expert, of the New York School of Philanthropy.
Elizabeth Gurley Flynn, labor activist, member of the Industrial Workers of the World.
Charlotte Perkins Gilman, writer on suffrage and feminism.
Alice Henry, of the Women's Trade Union League.
Morris Hillquit, lawyer and expert on socialism.
Rev. John Haynes Holmes, of the Church of the Messiah.
Dr. I.A.Hourwich, statistician and authority on Russian economic conditions.
Dr. Frederic Howe, U.S. Commissioner of Immigration.

Prof. David Starr Jordan, biologist, of Leland Stanford University.
Florence Kelley, founder of the National Consumers' League

---

*List of Instructors, Rand School of Social Science, LCF, L0038, Box 1, Reel 5, Folder 11

Dr. P.A.Levene, physiological chemist, of the Rockefeller Institute.
Jack London, novelist.
Meyer London, U.S. Congressman.
Owen Lovejoy, of the National Child Labor Committee.
Dr. Robert Lowy, anthropologist, of the American Museum of Natural History.
Mary MacArthur, of the British Woman's Trade Union League.
James H.Maurer, President of the Pennsylvania State Federation of Labor.
Duncan McDonald, President of the Illinois State Federation of Labor.
Scott Nearing, anti-war activist, formerly of the University of Pennsylvania.
Chandler Owen, civil rights activist, co-editor of *The Messenger*.
Juliet Stuart Poyntz, formerly of Barnard College.
Dr. George M.Price, authority on industrial hygiene, of the Joint Board of Sanitary Control in the Garment Industry.
A.Philip Randolph, civil rights activist, co-editor of *The Messenger*.
Dr. I.M.Rubinow, statistician and authority on social insurance.
Joseph Schlossberg, General Secretary of the Amalgamated Clothing Workers of America.
A.I.Shiplacoff, New York State Assemblyman.
John Spargo, writer and lecturer on scientific socialism.
Dr. N.L.Stone, statistician and authority on tariffs.
Helen L.Sumner, of the U.S. Children's Bureau.
Norman Thomas, member of the national committee of the American Civil Liberties Union.
Oswald Garrison Villard, publisher of *The Nation*.
Bernard C.Vladeck, New York City Alderman.
Dr. James P.Warbasse, President of the Co-opertaive League of America.
Prof. Lester F.Ward, sociologist, Brown University.
William Butler Yeats, Irish litterateur.
Prof. Charles Zueblin, lecturer on municipal affairs, formerly of Chicago University.

Appendix 4
Course Listing, Rand School of Social Science, 1919–1920*

ART & DRAMA

Social Aspects of the Modern Drama—"A number of plays by living authors, Continental, British, and American, will be read and discussed, with attention both to their quality as art-works and to their significance as presenting social types or dealing with social problems."

Talks on Art—"discuss types of Egyptian, Greek, Medieval, and Modern Art, considering them as expressions of the people's life in their respective periods."

ECONOMICS

**Fundamentals of Socialism*—"recommended to young party members and persons who are interested in Socialism, but have not yet made any systematic study of the subject."

Advanced Studies in Socialism I—"devoted to a careful reading and analysis of Marx' *Capital*"

Advanced Studies in Socialism II—"a more intensive study of certain leading points in Marxian theory—the Materialistic Conception of History, Classes and the Class Struggle, the Theory of Surplus Value, etc."

---

*Rand School of Social Science, *Bulletin for 1919±1920*, found in *LCF*, L0028, Reel 1, Box 1, Folder 1. Students could enroll in single courses through the Local Department on a "pay-as-you-go" basis for an average of $4 per course, or enroll as a full-time student for a total cost of $75. Those courses marked with an asterisk indicate the curriculum required of all full-time students. Most courses met one night per week for twelve weeks.

History of the Working-Class Movement—"Beginning with a brief summary of what distinguishes capitalism and the modern proletariat from earlier economic systems and older exploited classes, the instructors will trace the growth of organized proletarian activity from its beginnings in eighteenth-century England down to the present time, noting the differentiation of its co-ordinate forms—Trade Unionism, Socialism, Co-operation; the lessons learned from its successes and failures; and the theories which have corresponded to various phases of its experience. A due share of time will be reserved for the history of the working-class movement in the United States, and the record will be brought as nearly as possible to the present time."

Current Labor Problems—"At each session some live issue in the labor movement will be discussed by a man or woman active therein."

Wealth and Income—"a vivid and concrete exposition of leading economic facts of present-day society—the nature of wealth and of wealth production, the sources and distribution of various kinds of service-incomes and property-incomes, the effects of existing system of distribution upon institutions and upon the various classes concerned."

Elements of Economics I—"A study of basic ideas in economic science, aiming to develop a clear understanding of the significance of such terms as Commodity-Production, Price, Value, Wages, Surplus-Value, etc."

Elements of Economics II—"A continuation of Elements of Economics I, with a description of economic facts rather than an analysis of economic relations."

Elements of Statistics—"to acquaint students with the first principles of statistical method, so that they will be able to make correct deductions from statistical data and collect, arrange, and use such data themselves."

ENGLISH

English: Spelling, Grammar, and Composition—"These courses include not only instruction in the principles of grammar and composition, but also oral practice in class."

Secretarial English—"special instruction and training in such composition as is especially required of secretaries, organizers, and so forth—letters, minutes, press notices, resolutions, reports, etc."

Reporting and News Writing—"instruction in the art of getting news and presenting it in good journalistic form."

Composition and Literary Criticism—"It combines the writing of original themes with discussion of works read by the students; its aim is to develop both appreciation and mastery of literary style."

Philosophy of Literature—"a general survey of the main lines of development of European literature, with a psychological analysis of the subject from the point of view of social thought and the spirit of the time."

HISTORY

**American Social History I*—"covers the Colonial Period and the American Revolution, with special attention to the economic conditions which so largely determined the subsequent course of the political and social development of the United States."

**American Social History II*—"continues the record through the adoption of the Constitution, the early formative period of the Republic, and the so-called 'Era of Good Feeling."

**American Social History III*—"from shortly after the War of 1812 to the close of the Civil War; its two outstanding features are Westward Expansion and the Struggle over Slavery."

**American Social History IV*—"starting from the Reconstruction period and coming down to the recent years, attention is given both to the social and political institutions and traditions rooted in the earlier history of the country, and to the new forces, economic and other—Growth of Great Industry, Concentration of Capital, Immigration, the Labor Movement, etc.—which have come to the front in the last half-century, during which a comparatively isolated, sectionally divided, and mainly agricultural country has become a consolidated nation, a great exporter of goods and capital, and an active participant in world politics."

**Modern General History I*—"will cover the downfall of Feudalism, the Renaissance, and the Rise of the Great Nations, down to the Eve of the French Revolution."

**Modern General History II*—"centers in the French Revolution and the Napoleonic Dictatorship, with the transformation of European politics effected thereby, and looks forward to the revolutionary movements of 1830 and 1848."

**Modern General History III*—"The most striking features of the middle nineteenth century are the extensive, though not complete realization of national unity and independence (Germany, Italy, etc.), the powerful development of the British Empire under the regime of bourgeois Liberalism, the modernization of Russia, and the coming to the front of the dominant and conflicting tendencies of the new era— Imperialism and Militarism on the one hand, Internationalism and Social Democracy on the other."

Modern General History IV—"covers the last thirty or forty years, characterized above all by the maturing of the tendencies mentioned above— those representing the aspirations of a highly developed capitalist class and of a rapidly developing proletariat in all the principle countries of the world."

Russian Revolutionary History—"a thorough study of the economic, social, intellectual, and political development of Russian society, from the period of the consolidation of the monarchy, and with more detail from the time of Peter the Great, down to the present moment."

Current World History—"at each session some event which has figured largely in the news of the last few days will be taken up for discussion from the Socialist viewpoint."

LEGAL STUDIES

Elements of Criminology—"Beginning with a general statement of the nature and scope of the science of Criminology, the lecturer will summarize the ideas of the several leading schools—Classical, Humanitarian, Eclectic, Positive—and will then take up Criminal Anthropology, the Biological Causes of Crime, and Criminal Sociology, the Social Causes of Crime; Punishment and Prevention; Classification of Criminals; Treatment of Criminals; Bearings of Criminology on Criminal Law; Political Crime."

First Principles of Law—"to give such a treatment of the subject as will be useful to laymen, and particularly to working people who are actively engaged in political and individual movements."

ORAL TRAINING

Use of the Voice—"instruction in the physiology of the voice-producing parts of mouth, throat, and chest, and training in the art of producing various sounds and tones, controlling their quality, and volume, and so forth, with especial reference to the use of the voice in public speaking."

Public Speaking—"instruction and training in the art of gathering and arranging material for speeches, and of testing statements of fact and weighing arguments. Students have an abundant opportunity for speaking in class, and must be prepared to stand frank criticism."

Correction of Foreign Accent—"of great importance in so cosmopolitan a city as New York, for those who hope to become public speakers, or even to speak effectively in their party branches, local unions, or toher organizations."

Oral Reading—"Not only is the art of reading well aloud a source of pleasure to oneself and others, but the practice of oral reading is of great help in cultivating the voice, acquiring a correct pronunciation, extending one's vocabulary, and cultivating one's appreciation of literature."

POLITICAL SCIENCE

Elements of Political Science—"a study of the nature, origin, and development of governmental institutions, with reference to the economic and other conditions which determine them."

American Civics and Politics—"particularly recommended to persons of foreign birth, whether naturalized or not, who ought to have correct knowledge of the main features of American government, in order to take an intelligent part in the political life of the country."

Outlines of Comparative Government—"the various types of government, especially those now existing in the civilized world, are examined and compared, the newest type—that now prevailing in Russia—being given the especial attention which its historic importance warrants."

SCIENCE

Principles of Natural Science—"to introduce students to the scientific way of thinking, which is applicable to all the affairs of life."

Introduction to Biology—"will deal with the following topics: Scope of Biology and Brief History of Biological Thought; Plant Life and Animal Life; Man's Place Among the Animals; the Lower Animals; Plant Classification and Physiology; the Lower Plants—Bacteria and Disease; Theories of Evolution—Lamarack, Darwin, Haeckel, Weissman; The Theory of Heredity and Its Applications; Present Status of Biological Thought; Problems of Sex and Sex-Determination; the Life Cycle, and Applications of Biology to Individual Life."

Physiology and Hygiene—"aiming to give the students a sufficient knowledge of the structure and functions of the human body to guide them in promoting health and vigor."

Teaching of Nature-Study and Sex-Hygiene—"intended for parents, teachers, and others who have the duty of instructing children and youth in the facts of life and sex."

SOCIOLOGY

Ancient Society—"It covers the following topics: Animal Societies and Human Societies; Ancient Forms of Social Organization—Village, Family, Gens and Phratry, Tribe, Confederacy, State; Order of Development; Relation of Social Organization to Industry, to Religion, to Art, to Thought; Primitive Societies and Modern Societies compared."

Evolution of Civilization—"a dynamic treatment of certain aspects of social development, especially in the early stages, under the following heads: Heredity and Traditional Factors in Civilization; Leading Characteristics of Australian, American Indian, African Negro, Chinese, Ancient Greek, and Modern Western Societies; What It is that Evolves, in Material Culture, in Art, in Religion, in Ethics, in Social and Political Organization; Law and Accident in History; the Concept of Progress; Ways of Achieving Social progress."

Outlines of Dynamic Sociology—"the main outlines of sociology according to the school of Lester F. Ward. The main lecture topics are: Sociology as a Dynamic Science; Man, the Brute; Man, the Angel; Building Society; the Cake of Custom; Making a Living; Individual Morality; Social Morality; Evolution of Society; Human Inequality; Opportunity; Social Achievement."

Economics and Sociology of the Negro Problem—"to present in a scientific manner the fundamental facts covering the relations between the white and colored peoples in the United States, with especial reference to the economic and political struggles of the working class, so as to substitute knowledge and mutual understanding for prejudice and vague sentiment. The course will be of equal value to Negro and Caucasian students."

Interpretation of Social Facts—"of especial value to speakers, writers, and teacher. Among the topics considered are: Where to Look for Facts, and How; Classification of Data; Analysis; Deduction; Hypothesis; Presentation; Diagramming; Getting it Across; the

Scientific Spirit. Various bodies of fact concerning wage scales, cost of living, national debts, profiteering, etc., will be analyzed."

MISCELLANEOUS

Industrial Engineering—no description available.
Organization Methods—no description available.

Notes

NOTES TO THE INTRODUCTION

1. New York *Times,* January 19, 1919; New York *Tribune,* April 5, May 3, 1919. The dialogue is recreated from testimony originally provided by the students and Glassberg at a school board hearing concerning the teacher's dismissal, as reported by the New York *Times.*
2. New York *Tribune,* April 5, 1919.
3. *Ibid.*
4. *Ibid.,* April 6, 1919.
5. *Ibid.,* March 2, 1919.
6. Student Essays, November-December 1919, in the *Archibald Ewing Stevenson Papers* (hereafter referred to as AESP), in author's personal possession. This collection includes fourteen essays obtained by Stevenson during his examination of steps taken by various school districts throughout the country to combat radicalism.
7. John McCarthy, Student Essay, December 1,1919, *AESP.* .
8. The origins of the Red Scare are more fully examined in chapters 1 & 2 of this study. Robert Murray provided the seminal, and sole book-length, examination of the episode in his path-breaking work *Red Scare: A Study in National Hysteria, 1919±1920,* (Minneapolis, 1955). Subsequent studies by historians and political scientists support Murray's conclusions. Among such contributions are: Murray B. Levin, *Political Hysteria in America: The Democratic Capacity for Repression,* (New York, 1971); Robert J.Goldstein, *Political Repression in Modern America from 1870 to the Present,* (New York, 1978); Michael J.Heale, *American Anticommunism: Combatting the Enemy Within, 1830±1970,* (Baltimore, 1990); Margaret Blanchard, *Revolutionary Sparks: Freedom of Expression in Modern America,* (Oxford, 1992); and Joel Kovel, *Red Hunting in the Promised Land: Anticommunism and the Making of America,* (New York, 1994).

NOTES TO CHAPTER 1

1 Among recent scholarship detailing America's preparation for, and conduct of, the First World War, the most comprehensive is Byron Farwell, *Over There: The United States and the Great War, 1917±1918*, (New York, 1999). Also see Frank Freidel, *Over There: The Story of America's First Great Overseas Crusade*, (Philadelphia, 1990).
2 The Liberty Loan Act, which encouraged Americans to invest in the war effort by purchasing liberty bonds, raised over $5 billion, more than enough to pay for the country's war expenses, as well as loan the remainder to Allied nations. The Selective Service Act required all men aged 21 to 30 to register for the draft. The government eventually drafted 3 million men from the pool of 24 million registrants. The federal government later expanded the age range to 18 to 45; however, the vast majority of those men drafted were in their twenties, unmarried, and had no children.
3 Farwell, 56. Baruch had extensive control over the nation's manufacturing enterprises, including the power to allocate resources and set factory output levels. According to Farwell, the War Industries Board exercised power over 35,000 individual firms.
4 *Ibid.*, 56, 130. Literature produced by the Food Administration constantly reminded Americans that "Food Will Win the War." Over fourteen million citizens signed and mailed pledge cards to Washington, D.C., promising to observe Meatless Mondays, Wheatless Tuesdays, Fruitless Wednesdays, and so on.
5 Frank Cobb, "The Press and Public Opinion," *New Republic*, 21 (December 31, 1919): 144.
6 National Civil Liberties Bureau, *Wartime Persecutions and Mob Violence*, (New York, 1919), 5–11.
7 Farwell, 127–128.
8 *Ibid.*
9 Among the best overviews of the Bolshevik Revolution are Marc Ferro, *The Russian Revolution of 1917* (London, 1972; the "Problems in European Civilization Series" anthology compiled by Ronald Suny and Arthur Adams, *The Russian Revolution and Bolshevik Victory*, 3d ed., (Lexington, 1990); Sheila Fitzpatrick, *The Russian Revolution, 1917± 1932*, 2nd ed., (New York, 2001); and Rex Wade, *The Bolshevik Revolution and Russian Civil War* (Westport, 2001)..
10 George Soule, *Prosperity Decade: From War to Depression, 1917±1929*, (New York, 1947), 82–84. Statistics indicate that industrial production in America decreased by 10% between November 1918 and June 1919; however, by January 1920, factories had recovered that loss, and were producing at a level higher than any attained during the war.

11 For more details on military demobilization see Farwell, 285–294; Frederick L. Paxson, "The Great Demobilization," *American Historical Review,* 44 (January 1939): 243–247; and James R. Mock and Evangeline Thurber, *Report on Demobilization,* (Norman, 1944). At a time when returning soldiers most needed jobs and housing, the U.S. government down-sized the Housing Authority and terminated the Military Employment Service.

12 United States, Department of Labor, *Bulletin of the United States Bureau of Labor Statistics,* 357 (May 1924): 465–466.

13 Soule, *Prosperity Decade,* 188–189; John Milton Cooper, Jr., *Pivotal Decades: The United States, 1900±1920,* (New York, 1990), 322. Early efforts at associationalism, particularly in the coal, construction, and textile industries, largely failed. Limited success would not be achieved until the mid-1920s, due in large part to Herbert Hoover's extension of the Department of Commerce. A brief overview of the association movement can be found in Ellis Hawley, *The Great War and the Search for Modern Order: A History of the American People and Their Institutions, 1917±1933,* 2nd ed., (New York, 1992), 93–94, 101–104.

14 For further information on the link between the Committee on Public Information and the expansion of post-war intolerance in America, see Zechariah Chafee, Jr., *Free Speech in the United States* (Cambridge, 1941); William E. Leuchtenburg, *Perils of Prosperity, 1914±1932* (Chicago, 1958); and Donald Johnson, *The Challenge to American Freedom: World War I and the Rise of the American Civil Liberties Union* (Lexington, 1963).

15 The early stages of the socialist movement in America are best examined by Morris Hillquit in his contemporary work, *History of Socialism in the United States,* (New York, 1903). Founded in 1901, the Socialist Party represented a combination of the old Socialist Labor Party and the Social Democratic Party. Operating as a legitimate third party, the socialists emphasized power through the ballot box, rather than violence, in order to attain their goals. By 1912, the Socialist Party included over 100,000 members, and secured nearly a million votes for party founder Eugene V.Debs as their presidential candidate. The best account of Eugene Debs' life remains Nick Salvatore, *Eugene V.Debs: Citizen and Socialist,* (Urbana, 1982).

16 "War Proclamation and Program Adopted at the National Convention of the Socialist Party, St., Louis, Mo., April 1917," cited in Report of the Joint Legislative Committee Investigating Seditious Activities in New York State, *Revolutionary Radicalism: Its History, Purpose and Tactics,* I (Albany, 1920), 613–618 [hereafter referred to as *Lusk Committee Report*].

17 United States, House of Representatives, *Victor L.Berger,* Hearings before a Special Committee of the House, I (Washington, D.C., 1919),

53. Specifically, Berger charged businessmen with exchanging "the blood of American boys" for "swollen profits." America's war against Germany, he concluded "cannot be justified."

18 "Canton Speech," reprinted in Eugene V.Debs, *Writings and Speeches of Eugene V.Debs,* (New York, 1948), 417–433; David F.Karsner, *Debs, His Authorized Life and Letters* (New York, 1919), 23–55; Salvatore, 291–296. A fiery speaker by trade, Debs spent much of May traveling across the country and publicly decrying the government's persecution of his party. Anticipating his imminent arrest, he delivered one of his most notable speeches on June 16, 1918, in Canton, Ohio, before the state convention of the Socialist Party. As a crowd of 1,000 supporters cheered wildly, Debs urged all socialists to stand strong in the face of government repression. That America could fight a war to make the world safe for democracy, and yet deny free speech to a minority of its own citizens, seemed laughable to him. "But it is not the subject for levity," he said in all seriousness, for important democratic principles were at stake. Despite the apparent effectiveness of the campaign to crush socialism in America, Debs took solace in its result. "Every time they strike at us," he declared, "they hit themselves; they help us in spite of themselves. Socialism is a growing idea; it's coming, coming, coming all along the line." Debs urged his listeners to continue the fight against repression and war. "Do not worry over the charge of treason to your masters," he concluded. "This year we are going to sweep into power and in this nation we are going to destroy capitalistic institutions." Four days later, the U.S.Attorney for northern Ohio indicted Debs on ten counts of violating the Espionage Act. Within three months he was convicted and sentenced to serve ten years in a federal penitentiary.

19 Among the best examinations of the Industrial Workers of the World are Melvyn Dubofsky, *We Shall Be All: A History of the Industrial Workers of the World,* (Urbana, 1988), and William Preston, Jr., *Aliens and Dissenters: Federal Suppression of Radicals, 1903±1933,* (Cambridge, 1963). For information on William Haywood, consult his autobiography *Bill Haywood's Book,* (New York, 1929). In the preamble to their constitution, the I.W.W. explained how starving workers and affluent employers have nothing in common. The path labor must take was clear. "A struggle must go on until the workers of the world organize as a class, take possession of the earth and the machinery of production, and abolish the wage system; it is the historic mission of the working class to do away with capitalism." Paul F.Brissenden, *The I.W.W.: A Study of American Syndicalism,* (New York, 1920), 351–352.

20 Sec.19, Immigration Act of February 5, 1917, *United States Statutes at Large,* 39, (Washington, D.C., 1917), 889. For more information of I.W.W. success see Preston, *Aliens and Dissenters,* 35–62.

21 *Industrial Worker,* February 10, 24, 1917; *L'Era Nuova,* n.d., cited in Robert E.Park, *The Immigrant Press and Its Control,* (New York, 1922), 215. Commenting on the concept of patriotism, Haywood said, "Of all the idiotic and perverted ideas accepted by the workers from that class who live upon their misery, patriotism is the worst. Love of country? We have no country. Love of flag? None floats for us."

22 Carleton H.Parker, *The Casual Laborer and Other Essays,* (New York, 1920), 102.

23 San Diego *Tribune,* March 4, 1917, cited in Preston, *Aliens and Dissenters,* 275–276; David Mitchell, 1919 *Red Mirage,* (New York, 1970), 300.

24 "Manifesto of the Communist Labor Party, Adopted August 30, 1919," cited in *Lusk Committee Report,* I, 801. The best examination of the formative years of the Communist Labor Party remains Theodore Draper, *The Roots of American Communism,* (New York, 1957). For a first-hand account of its formation, see Benjamin Gitlow, *I Confess: The Truth About American Communism,* (New York, 1939). Gitlow was the Communist Party candidate for vice-president in 1924 and 1928, as well as served on the Executive Committee and Presidium of the Communist International.

25 "Manifesto of the Communist Party of America, Adopted September 7, 1919," cited in *Lusk Committee Report,* I, 755–756. Much of the animosity between the two new communist organizations stemmed from native-born radicals' beliefs that the Russian Language Federation controlled the Left Wing, a belief based upon the fact that Russian aliens comprised 35,000 of the 70,000 communists in the U.S.

26 United States, Department of Justice, *Annual Report of the Attorney General of the United States,* 1920, (Washington, D.C., 1920), 178–179; Gitlow, *The Whole of Their Lives,* (New York, 1948), 53.

27 Alfred G.Gardiner, *Portraits and Portents,* (New York, 1926), 13.

28 "Bolshevik Mutterings Here," *Literary Digest,* 59 (December 7, 1918): 17.

29 New York *Times,* January 1, 3, 4, 1919.

30 *Ibid.,* January 8, 1919; Franklin H.Giddings, "The Bolsheviki Must Go," *Independent,* 92 (January 18, 1919): 88, 97.

31 United States, Senate, *Brewing and Liquor Interests and German and Bolshevik Propaganda,* Hearings before a Subcommittee of the Committee on the Judiciary, 3 (1919): 2782–2785; New York *Times,* January 19, February 6, 1919.

32 *Brewing and Liquor Interests,* 2690–2694, 2701–2709.

33 *Ibid.,* 2709–2716.

34 *Ibid.,* 2716, 2778–2785.

35 *Ibid.,* 2782–2785; "The New Sherlock Holmes," *The Nation,* 108 (February 1, 1919): 155.

36 "By Stevenson Out of Lusk," *The New Republic,* 27 (June 15, 1921): 66.
37 Major Fred W.More to Colonel John Duff, Intelligence Report, January 11, 1919, found in *Directorate of Military Intelligence, Records: Surveillance of Radicals in the United States, 1917±1941,* (Washington, National Archives and Records Administration), Series 10110–1086:2, Reel 13, Frame 438 [hereafter referred to as *MID Records*]; New York *Times,* January 15, 16, 20, 1919.
38 New York *Call,* March 23, 1919; "Bolshevist School Teachers," *Literary Digest,* 61 (April 5, 1919): 31–32; "Bolshevism in New York and Russian Schools," *Literary Digest,* 61 (July 5, 1919): 40; New York *Times,* May 29, 1919.
39 New York *Times,* March 13, 14, 23, 1919.
40 John Bruce Mitchell, "'Reds' in New York's Slums—How Insidious Doctrines Are Propagated in New York's 'East Side,'" *The Forum,* 61 (April 1919): 442–445.
41 Julian Jaffe, *Crusade Against Radicalism: New York During the Red Scare, 1914±1924,* (New York, 1972), 81–85.

NOTES TO CHAPTER 2

1 New York *Tribune,* March 14, 1919.
2 New York *Times,* January 10, 1919; New York *Tribune,* March 14, 1919.
3 New York *Times,* March 14, 1919.
4 New York *Tribune,* March 21, 1919.
5 New York *Times,* March 21, 1919.
6 "ConcurrentResolution Authorizing the Investigation of Seditious Activities," reprinted in Lusk Committee Report, I, 1 (italics added); New York *Times,* March 21, 1919.
7 New York *Tribune,* March 21, 1919.
8 New York *Times,* March 21, 1919; New York *Tribune,* March 21, 1919.
9 New York *Times,* March 21, 1919; New York Tribune, March 21, 1919.
10 New York *Times,* March 27, 1919.
11 New York *Tribune,* March 27, 1919.
12 New York *Times,* March 27, 1919.
13 The eight Democrats who cast dissenting votes were: Martin McCue of Manhattan; Robert T.Mullen and J.Fairfax McLaughlin of the Bronx; C.C. Johnson and Daniel J.Lyons of Kings; and P.A.Leminger, William H.O'Hare, and Bernard Schwab of Queens. The two Socialists who cast dissenting votes were August Claessens of New York and Charles Solomon of Kings. New York *Times,* March 27, 1919; New York *Tribune,* March 27, 1919.
14 *Ibid.,* March 22, 27, April 1, 1919.
15 New York *Tribune,* April 1, 1919.
16 *Ibid.,* April 3, 1919.

17 *Ibid.,* March 22, 1919.
18 Clayton R.Lusk, "Radicalism Under Inquiry: Conclusions Reached After a Year's Study of Alien Anarchy in America," *American Review of Reviews,* 61 (1920): 168–171.
19 Despite maintaining a staff and overseeing a considerable budget, Lusk never made a full accounting of the committee's budget. He later admitted in January 1920 that its total expenditures had been $80,000, a sum far in excess of the original appropriation. The committee obtained additional funds in the form of a private loan from an Albany bank. The state controller distributed the proceeds of the loan in $10,000 installments, a significant portion of which paid for the printing of the four volume, 4,000 page final report. No record of loan repayment exists.
20 Walter Nelles, quoted in Paul L.Murphy, *The Meaning of Freedom of Speech: First Amendment Freedoms from Wilson to FDR,* (Westport, CT, 1972), 39–40.
21 People's Freedom Union, *The Truth About the Lusk Committee: A Report,* (New York, 1920), 4–6.
22 Brooklyn *Eagle,* April 30, 1919; New York *Tribune,* April 30, 1919.
23 New York *Call,* June 28, 1919.
24 New York *Times,* April 29, 1919. For an excellent account of the bomb scares of 1919, see Murray, *Red Scare,* 67–81.
25 New York *Tribune,* April 29, 1919; "Dreadful Bombs," *The Liberator,* 2 (June 1919): 7–8.
26 New York *Times,* May 1, 1919; New York *Tribune,* May 1, 1919. Accounts of the exact number of bomb packages vary. Newspapers reported a total of 36; but the Justice Department officially identified only 29.
27 New York *Tribune,* May 1, 2, 1919; United States, House of Representatives, *Attorney General A. Mitchell Palmer on Charges Made Against Department of Justice by Louis R Post and Others,* Hearings before the Committee on Rules, (Washington, D.C, 1920), 157–158.
28 Several newspaper editorials can be found in the New York *Times,* the New York *Tribune,* and the Chicago *Tribune,* May 1–3, 1919. Also see "Human Vermin," *American Law Review,* 53 (May 1919): 432; Philadelphia *Inquirer,* May 3, 1919; "Current Event and Commentary," *United Presbyterian,* 77 (May 8, 1919): 7.
29 United States, Senate, *Bolshevik Propaganda,* Hearings before a Subcommittee of the Committee on the Judiciary, (Washington, D.C., 1919), 1076; Murray, *Red Scare,* 69.
30 Pittsburgh *Post,* May 3, 1919; Seattle *Post-Intelligencer,* May 2, 1919; "More Bombs," *The Liberator,* 2 (July 1919): 6.
31 New York *Times,* May 4–13, 1919; Salt Lake *Tribune,* May 2, 1919.
32 New York *Tribune,* May 1, 1919.

33 *The Massachusetts Reports,* 235 (Boston, 1921): 449–453; Boston *Evening Transcript,* May 2, 1919.
34 New York *Times,* May 2, 3,1919; New York *Call,* May 2,1919; "May Day Rioting," *The Nation,* 108 (10 May 1919): 726.
35 Cleveland *Plain Dealer,* May 2, 1919.
36 Seattle *Post-Intelligencer,* May 3, 1919; Salt Lake *Tribune,* May 3, 1919; Washington *Post,* May 3, 1919.
37 New York *Times,* May 3, 7, 1919; New York *Tribune* May 7, 8, 1919.
38 "What Is Back of the Bombs?", *Literary Digest,* 61 (June 14, 1919): 9; Washington *Post,* June 3, 1919; New York *Times,* June 3, 1919.
39 New York *Times,* June 3, 1919; Washington *Evening Star,* June 3, 1919; *Palmer on Charges,* 165; Blair Coan, *The Red Web,* (Chicago, 1925), 48; Murray, 79.
40 New York *Tribune,* June 3, 1919; Washington *Evening Star,* June 3, 1919; Murray, *Red Scare,* 80.
41 Heale, *American Anticommunism,* 70; A. Mitchell Palmer, "The Case Against the Reds," *Forum,* 63 (February 1920): 179; New York *Times,* June 5, 1919.
42 Lusk, "Radicalism Under Inquiry," 171.

NOTES TO CHAPTER 3

1 Ludwig C.A.K.Martens, Official credentials, March 19, 1919, *Records of the Joint Legislative Committee Investigating Seditious Activities in New York State, 1919±1920,* L0032, Box 1, D165/4, Folder A14, (New York State Archives and Records Administration, Albany, NY) [hereafter referred to as LCF]. In addition, see "Soviet Envoy in America," *Current History,* 10 (April-June 1919): 267–8. Two recent works that offer detailed insight into the economic trade aspects of the bureau, as well as the subsequent efforts by the Bolsheviks to improve trade and diplomatic relations with the U.S. include Katherine A.S.Siegel, *Loans and Legitimacy: The Evolution of Soviet-American Relations, 1919±1933,* (Lexington, 1996), and David W. McFadden, *Alternative Paths: Soviets and Americans, 1917±1920,* (New York, 1993).
2 Russian Socialist Federal Soviet Republic, *A Memorandum to the State Department of the United States from the Representative of the Russian Socialist Federal Soviet Republic,* (New York, NY, 1919), 12–15, LCF, L0036, Box 2, D166/4, Folder 13. In addition, see "A Memorandum from the Soviet Representative," *Weekly Bulletin of the Bureau of Information of Soviet Russia* [hereafter referred to as *Weekly Bulletin*], 1 (March 31, 1919), 1. Although some doubt existed regarding Russia's ability to pay for such orders, Commercial Director A.A. Heller later reiterated Martens' claim: "Russia has all the means required to pay for these purchases. It is there in actual gold, it is there in the soil, and the air, and

the mountains; it is there in the mines and mills and forests, in the energy and skill of its unbounded million." See Abraham A. Heller, Handwritten notes, n.d., LCF, L0032, Box 1, D165/4, Folder A7.
3. Lansing to David Francis, February 14, 1919, in United States, *Records of the Department of State Relating to the Internal Affairs of Russia and the Soviet Union, 1910±1929,* (Washington, D.C.: National Archives and Records Administration), 861.00/1064 [hereafter referred to as *State Department Decimal File];* New York *Times,* March 21, 1919. In addition, see Leonid I. Strakhovsky, *American Opinion About Russia, 1917±1920,* Series of lectures delivered at the Lowell Institute in Boston, MA, in Spring 1946 (Toronto, 1961), 85; Committee on Russian-American Relations, *The United States and the Soviet Union: A Report on the Controlling Factors in the Relation Between the United States and the Soviet Union,* (New York, 1933), 27.
4. New York *Times,* March 22, 29, 1919.
5. William B.Phillips to American Mission in Paris, March 29, 1919, *State Department Decimal File,* 861.00/4214a. For an overview of the Bullitt Mission, see United States, Senate, *The Bullitt Mission to Russia,* Testimony before the Senate Foreign Relations Committee, (Washington, D.C.: Government Printing Office, 1919); Committee on Russian-American Relations, *The United States and the Soviet Union,* 27. The Bolsheviks demanded what amounted to official recognition: the withdrawal of foreign troops, cessation of aid to anti-Soviet forces, an exchange of representatives, and full rights of entry for Soviet citizens wishing to travel to foreign countries. Further difficulties arose when France balked at the U.S. and British efforts to negotiate with Lenin without French knowledge.
6. New York *Times,* May 7, 1919; Committee on Russian-American Relations, *The United States and the Soviet Union,* 27.
7. Gregory Weinstein, Rough Diagram of the Proposed Organization of the Bureau of Soviet Russia, n.d., LCF, L0032, Box 1, D165/4, Folder A14.
8. Heinrich E.Schulz et al., eds., *Who Was Who in the U.S.S.R.: A Biographic Directory Containing 5,015 Biographies of Prominent Soviet Historical Personalities,* (Metuchen, NJ, 1972), 372; Antony C.Sutton, *Wall Street and the Bolshevik Revolution,* (New Rochelle, NY, 1974), 114; Frederick L.Schuman, *American Policy Toward Russia Since 1917: A Study of Diplomatic History, International Law and Public Opinion,* (New York, 1928), 186; "Soviet Government Now Has Representative in the United States," *Weekly Bulletin,* 1 (March 24, 1919): 1; Gitlow, *I Confess,* 28; Strakhovsky, *American Opinion,* 85.
9. Santeri Nuorteva to Martens, Personal records submitted upon appointment, n.d., LCF, L0038, Box 2, D165/5, Folder 16.
10. New York *Tribune,* June 22, 1919; "New Appointments by Soviet Russia's Representative," *Weekly Bulletin,* 1 (April 7, 1919): 1.

11 Evans Clark to Martens, Biographical information, n.d., LCF, L0032, Box 1, D165/4, Folder A3. The investigation by the Lusk Committee also revealed that Clark was the son-in-law of the Federal Director of the U.S. Employment Service, Dr. George W.Kirchwey. R.W.Finch, Notes, n.d., LCF, L0040, Box 1, D166/6, Folder 6.
12 George V.Lomonossoff to Martens, Letter relinquishing assets, LCF, L0032, Box 1, D165/4, Folder A14; "New Appointments By Soviet Russia's Representative," *Weekly Bulletin,* 1 (April 7, 1919): 1.
13 New York *Tribune,* June 22, 1919; Directorate of Intelligence, Scotland House, "The Russian Soviet Bureau in the United States," *Special Report No. 5,* (July 14, 1919), 1–8 passim, cited in John W.Harris to Lansing, Consul Report from American embassy in London to the U.S. Department of State, July 18, 1919, *State Department Decimal File,* 861. 00/5065.
14 New York *Tribune,* June 22, 1919; Gitlow, *I Confess,* 28.
15 Armand Hammer with Neil Lyndon, *Hammer,* (New York, 1987), 71.
16 The Soviet Bureau payrolls from April 14–May 31, 1919, inclusive, can be found in LCF, L0032, Box 1, D165/4, Folder A1. The total weekly salaries ranged from $788.41 to $1,315.73, with most employees receiving between $15 and $75. The highest paid employees included the directors of the individual departments: Nuorteva, Heller, and Hourwich. Hammer received no salary, lending credence to the theory that he partially financed the bureau's operations. The records list no salary for Martens; although the weekly disbursement ledgers frequently indicated petty cash withdrawals in his name.
17 J.Edgar Hoover, *Masters of Deceit: The Story of Communism in America and How to Fight It,* (New York, 1958), 292. Other sources corroborate Hoover's assertion regarding bureau financing. Scotland Yard investigators concluded: "About four weeks before the raid on the Bureau, he [Martens] received a large sum which was brought to him by a person who left Petrograd in early April, and he [Martens] had in his possession about the middle of June the equivalent of almost five million roubles in cash." See Directorate of Intelligence, Scotland House, "The Russian Soviet Bureau in the United States," 3; James K.Libbey, *Alexander Gumberg and Soviet-American Relations, 1917±1933,* (Lexington, KY, 1977), 56–7.
18 Gitlow, *I Confess,* 60.
19 United States, Senate, *Russian Propaganda,* Hearings before a Subcommittee of the Committee on Foreign Relations, (1920), 76.
20 Thomas L.Chadbourne to Polk, January 7, 1919; Polk to Ira N.Morris, January 12, 1919; Polk to Chadbourne, January 12, 1919; Phillips to Chadbourne, April 3, 1919; Chadbourne to Phillips, April 5, 1919, cited in Sutton, *Wall Street and the Bolshevik Revolution,* 147–153. Chadbourne also served as the counselor for the War Trade Board, one of

the many federal government agencies which imposed restrictions on commercial trade between the U.S. and Bolshevik Russia.

21 Emerson P.Jennings, *Report to the Association* [American Commercial Association to Promote Trade with Russia], (New York, 1921). For an overview of the Association, see Libbey, *Alexander Gumberg,* 56–7, 142; Joan Hoff Wilson, *Ideology and Economics: U.S. Relations With the Soviet Union, 1918±1933,* (Columbia, MO, 1974), 52–7; Sutton, *Western Technology and Soviet Economic Development, 1917 to 1920,* (Stanford, 1968), 287–8; Jennings to Lansing, May 11, 1920, *State Department Decimal File,* 661.1115/11, 20–1, 68. While Sutton and Libbey agree that the association financed the Soviet Bureau, Wilson expresses doubt.

22 Gitlow, *I Confess,* 28; Perley Morse and Company to Lusk Committee, Accountant's report regarding the Soviet Bureau, June 16, 1919, LCF, L0038, Box 2, D165/5, Folder 14. The accountant's report included two entries listing cash receipts totaling $1,139.58 from "Dr. J.Hammer" on April 28 and May 2. For additional information on the issue of Hammer financing the Bureau, see Christine A.White, *British and American Commercial Relations With Soviet Russia, 1918±1924,* (Chapel Hill, 1992), 140. There has also been some suggestion that Guaranty Trust Company financed the bureau; although the charge was vehemently denied by Guaranty Trust. The only evidence supporting this charge is found in the previously cited Scotland Yard Report.

23 New York *Evening Journal,* February 21, 1920; Alexander Gak, "Lenin and the Americans," *New World Review,* 35 (1967): 37; New York *World,* February 21, 1920.

24 R.Poliakoff, "Trade with Russia After the War," Address delivered before the Foreign Trade Association of the Cincinnati Chamber of Commerce, April 17, 1917, LCF, L0036, Box 2, D166/4, Folder 11.

25 Karl Radek, *Radek and Ransome on Russia,* (Brooklyn, 1918), 3.

26 Martens to Boris Bakhmeteff, Letter regarding relinquishment of assets, April 10, 1919, LCF, L0032, Box 1, D165/4, Folder A14; "Soviet Envoy in America," *Current History* 10 (April-June 1919), 267; Schuman, 186. Three points deserve additional comment. First, it is clear that the Bolsheviks did not have $200,000,000 in gold with which to purchase American products, as Martens had announced in January upon his appointment as director of the bureau. In fact, a report from the Russian Economic League—a group in support of the Omsk government—concluded "There is no such sum as $200,000,000 in gold in the hands of the Bolsheviki. By far the greatest part of the gold reserve of the Russian Imperial Bank is in the possession of the Omsk Government, while the Bolsheviki have only a few score millions of rubles." See Russian Economic League, "To the Business Men of America," May 3, 1919, LCF, L0032, Box 1, D165/4, Folder B3. However, while acknowledging that enemies of Soviet Russia have managed to confiscate small amounts

of Russian gold, Heller continued to stress the Bolsheviks' ability to offer payment in precious metals. In his statement, the Commercial Director concluded "...this amount [lost to enemies] has been more than made up by new production, and by the nationalization of the royal and hierarchical properties. The proof of the pudding is in the eating. Russia is fully able to pay as she goes." See Heller, Statement, n.d., LCF, L0032, Box 1, D165/4, Folder A4; "Proposed Commercial Relations with Soviet Russia," *Weekly Bulletin* 1 (April 14, 1919): 1. In reality, the Bolshevik statement regarding $200,000,000 set aside for purchases rested solely upon their claim to the assets the Provisional Government held in America. Second, there is some support for the contention that Bakhmeteff exercised a measure of financial mismanagement while serving as ambassador, evidenced by the $60,000 "bonus" he received from the Russian Purchasing Commission in 1917. See Russian Purchasing Commission, Ledger of disbursements, n.d., LCF, L0032, Box 1, D165/4, Folder B3. Finally, although the State Department continued officially to recognize Bakhmeteff, private reports indicated a different sentiment among many department personnel. As early as April 1919, Polk felt that "the jig is up for the Bakhmeteff crowd, ...a lot of incapables whom it would serve right to have their hopes crushed as long as they themselves have shown such absolute lack of energy and ability to do anything." See Nuorteva to Morris Hillquit, Report on meeting with Frank Polk, April 20, 1919, LCF, L0032, Box 1, D165/4, Folder B6.

27 Martens to National City Bank, Guaranty Trust Co., Irving National Bank, MacCann Warehouse, Van Dam Warehouse, New York Dock Com., Marden Orth and Hastings Co., Coudort Bros., William Bradley and Son, U.S. Leather Co., Armor Leather Co., Howes Bros., Proctor Ellison Co., and Erie Railroad Co., Letters laying claim to Provisional government assets, April 14, 1919, LCF, L0032, Box 1, D165/4, Folders A11, B6.

28 Heller, *Statement of the Commercial Department, Bureau of the Representative in the U.S., Russian Socialist Federal Soviet Republic,* n.d., LCF, L0032, Box 1, D165/4, Folder A4. For additional information regarding Germany's inability to fulfill Russia's economic needs, see "Soviet Government Now Has Representative in the United States," *Weekly Bulletin,* 1 (March 24, 1919): 1.

29 New York *Times,* March 28, 1919.

30 Martens, Notes for article in New York *Tribune,* April 21, 1919, LCF, L0032, Box 1, D165/4, Folder A14.

31 New York *Tribune,* May 20, 1919. In an isolated attempt to circumvent the State Department's prohibition on export licenses to Bolshevik Russia, the Soviet Bureau arranged for an American meat packing firm to transport $15,000,000 of canned meats and condensed milk to Petrograd via Norway. The packing firm was to charter an American vessel to

Stockholm, from which it would sail to Christiania, Norway, to load the cargo. Eventually the ship would sail to Petrograd with Norwegian clearance papers, flying the American flag. According to Nuorteva, it was hoped that the Allied naval authorities enforcing the blockade would not attempt to intercept the vessel. Such a test of will never transpired, however, as the subsequent closing of the Soviet Bureau led to a cancellation of all existing contracts; New York *Tribune,* October 29, 1919.

32 Heller, Quoting Martens at the Conference for Technically Skilled Workers, July 4, 1919, LCF, L0032, Box 1, D165/4. Folder A4. The bureau's plan to utilize comrade technical advisors can be traced as far back as April 1919, when Heller first suggested a conference to Martens. By early May, a number of Russian-Americans—including lawyers, chemical engineers, clothing agents, and railway representatives—had offered their services to the bureau. Likewise, Ford Motor Company suggested training a corps of men to supervise the construction and operation of tractor factories in Russia. See Heller to Martens, Memorandum regarding technical advisors, April 19, 1919; Heller, Memorandum regarding personal conferences, April 16, 1919, LCF, L0032, Box 1, D165/4, Folders A7, B3.

33 Martens, Call for a Conference of Technically Skilled Workers, May 10, 1919, LCF, L0032, Box 1, D165/4, Folder A4.

34 Heller, Address before the Conference of Technically Skilled Workers, July 4, 1919, LCF, L0032, Box 1, D165/4, Folder A4.

35 Martens to E.E.Brown, Letter regarding educational programs, July 9, 1919, LCF, L0032, Box 1, D165/4, Folder A17.

36 *Commercial and Financial Chronicle,* 108 (March 1, 1919): 24.

37 New York *Times,* April 19, 1919; "Proposed Commercial Relations With Soviet Russia," *Weekly Bulletin,* 1 (April 14, 1919): 1.

38 New York *Times,* November 18, 1919; Apex Company to Heller, Letter regarding trade recognition, Excerpt included in memorandum from Heller to Nuorteva, June 11, 1919, LCF, L0032, Box 1, D165/4, Folder A5; Resolution introduced by Senator Joseph I.France—Maryland, *Congressional Record,* Senate, 66th Congress, 2nd session, 59:4 (February 27, 1920): 3554.

39 New York *Times,* May 7,1919; "Release of Tredwell," *Current History,* 10 (April-June 1919): 483; Strakhovsky, *American Opinion About Russia,* 86; Schuman, *American Policy Toward Russia,* 186–7. The State Department's control over commercial transactions and export licenses stemmed from powers granted by the War Trade Board. However, there was anything but unanimity regarding the policy of economic isolation and blockade. In December 1918, the War Trade Board recommended to the State Department that such a policy "is one calculated to prolong the control of the Bolshevik authorities," and therefore should be abandoned;

Minutes of the War Trade Board, 5 (December 5, 1918), 7, cited in Sutton, *Western Technology,* 296.
40 Heller, Reply to the State Department order regarding trade with the Bolsheviks, April 27, 1919, LCF, L0032, Box 1, D165/4, Folder A9.
41 *Ibid.*
42 Isaac Hourwich, Memorandum regarding American trade relations with unrecognized governments, n.d., LCF, L0032, Box 1, D165/4, Folder B3.
43 Heller to James P.Mulvihill, Letter regarding Soviet Bureau activities, May 19, 1919, LCF, L0032, Box 1, D165/4, Folder B3.
44 Heller, Report on trip to Washington, D.C., May 19, 1919, LCF, L0032, Box 1, D165/4, Folder A28. One such case to the contrary mentioned by Heller was Serbia where, following the assassination of King Alexander and the subsequent withdrawal of all American diplomatic representatives, trade relations continued without interruption.
45 *Ibid.* Heller, at a previous meeting, provided Mulvihill with the file. Aside from Ford Motor Company, the file included letters from the following firms: Advance-Rumely Thresher Co., Alexander Bros., American Screw Co., Avery Co., Buffalo Pitts Co., Curtis and Jones Co., Dennison Manufacturing Co., Duplex Truck Co., Fist and Co., Four Wheel Drive Auto Co., Hart-Parr Co., Howes Bros., International High Speed Steel Co., Interstate Pulp and Paper Co., J.E.Bates and Co., J.I.Case Plow Works, Maurice O'Meara Co., Paige-Detroit Motor Car Co., and Seller Distributing Co.
46 Nuorteva to Hillquit, Letter regarding meeting with Polk, April 20, 1919, LCF, L0032, Box 1, D165/4, Folder B6.
47 *Ibid.*
48 Clark to Heller, Memorandum regarding publicity campaign, May 20, 1919, LCF, L0032, Box 1, D165/4, Folder B2.

NOTES TO CHAPTER 4

1 Pierce to Richard Olney, Letter regarding prospects in Russia, June 30, 1896, cited in George S.Queen, *The United States and the Material Advance in Russia, 1881±1906,* (New York, 1976), 177; New York *Tribune,* November 19, 1899.
2 S.M.Williams, *Munsey's Magazine,* 26 (1902): 753; Sidney Brooks, "Russia as a Great Power," *World's Work,* 2 (1901): 1281.
3 Ebenezer J.Hill, "A Trip Through Siberia," *National Geographic,* 13 (1902): 53.
4 *Bradstreet's,* 28 (1900): 166; New York *Tribune,* April 19, 1900.
5 President John A.McCall, *Testimony: Legislative Insurance Investigating Committee of New York,* (1905), 1503, cited in Queen, *The United States and the Material Advance in Russia,* 198.

174 NOTES TO THE CHAPTER 1

6 National Association of Manufacturers, *American Trade Index,* 7th Annual Issue, (New York, 1905), 165, 231, 234.
7 Frank J.Taylor to Lansing, Cable regarding economic prospects in Russia, May 27, 1919, *State Department Decimal File,* 861.00/4707.
8 Francis to Lansing, Cable regarding German interest in Russia, February 15, 1918, *State Department Decimal File,* 861.00/1117.
9 William Mullins to Lansing, Cable regarding Allied commercial assistance to Bolsheviks, February 19, 1918, *State Department Decimal File,* 861.00/1125.
10 S.H.Ball, Henry H.Knox, H.V.Winchell, John B.Furnish, J.P.Hutchins, and J.W.Colt to Lansing, Letter regarding material assistance to Bolshevik Russia, June 4, 1918, *State Department Decimal File,* 861.00/282.
11 Benson Stoufer of Cooper and Cooper Chemical Co. to Martens, Letter offering services, March 21, 1919; Robert Grant of Grant Iron and Steel Co. to Nuorteva, Letter requesting conference, March 28, 1919, LCF, L0032, Box 1, D165/4, Folder A5.
12 Heller, Report of the Commercial Department, April 23–30, 1919, LCF, L0032, Box 1, D165/4, Folder A7.
13 Frederick Trumpett of Arnold, Hoffman and Co. to Heller, Letter regarding trade restrictions, April 26, 1919; Paul Noble of American Aniline Products to Heller, Letter regarding trade restrictions, April 29, 1919; C.E.Sholes of the Graselli Chemical Co. to Heller, Letter regarding trade restrictions, May 1, 1919, LCF, L0032, Box 1, D165/4, Folder A5.
14 W.S.Rupp of Baugh Chemical Co. to Heller, Letter regarding acquisition of export licenses, May 15, 1919; Charles Steiner of Marathon Tire and Rubber Co. to Heller, Letter regarding acquisition of export licenses, May 23, 1919, LCF, L0032, Box 1, D165/4, Folder A5.
15 Sylvester M.Weimer of the Old Reliable Motor Truck Corp. to Heller, Letter regarding recognition of the Soviet Bureau, April 14, 1919; Benjamin Smith of the Carolina Junk and Hide Co. to Jacob Hartman, Letter expressing sympathy with the Bolsheviks, June 4, 1919, LCF, L0032, Box 1, D165/4, Folder A5.
16 Heller, Memorandum of interviews, April 16, 1919; Heller, Memorandum of interview with Frazer of Swift and Co., April 14, 1919, LCF, L0032, Box 1, D165/4, Folders A7, B3.
17 Ella Tuch to Heller, Memorandum concerning interview with J.W.Abbott representing Lewis Walther Manufacturing Co. and Charlottesville Woolen Mills, April 23, 1919; Tuch to Heller, Memorandum concerning interview with George E. Barrows of Bridgeport Rolling Mills, April 24, 1919, LCF, L0032, Box 1, D165/4, Folder A7.
18 Heller to Martens, Report on trip to the Sixth National Foreign Trade Convention, April 29, 1919, *LCF,* L0032, Box 1, D165/4, Folder B3. No record or news accounts of the subsequent banker/manufacturer

conference could be found in the Soviet Bureau papers. Due to the brevity of Heller and Nuorteva's trip, it is unlikely that such a meeting took place.

19 Nuorteva to Martens, Report on trip to Sixth National Foreign Trade Convention, April 29, 1919; Heller to Martens, Report on trip to Sixth National Foreign Trade Convention, April 29, 1919, LCF, L0032, Box 1, D165/4, Folders A7, B3. For an example of the negative propaganda being circulated about the Soviet Bureau, see New York *Times,* May 9, 1919.

20 Heller, Form letter to chambers and associations, June 4, 1919, LCF, L0032, Box 1, D165/4, Folder A4. Other groups confirmed to have invited a speaker included the chambers in Ashtabula, OH; Patterson, NJ; Stamford, CT; Elmira, NY; Battlecreek, MI; Cass County, IN; and Kalamazoo, MI; the boards of trade in Gloucester, MA and Fitchburg, MA; and the Asociation of Commerce in Grand Rapids, MI. Only two groups were documented to have refused the offer: the chambers in Adrian, MI, and Middletown, CT. See M.M.Fischman of Fischman and Co. to Nuorteva, May 17, 1919; Clark to Max Geiger of National Merchandise Co., May 24, 1919; Heller to John Rahn of Rahn-Lerman Co., June 11, 1919; all found in LCF, L0032, Box 1, D165/4, Folder A5.

21 Item No. 1291, *National Archives Records Group* 165, Box 305, File 10110–137, cited in White, *British and American Commercial Relations,* 138; Directorate of Intelligence, Scotland House, "The Russian Soviet Bureau in the United States;" Directorate of Intelligence, Scotland House, "A Monthly Review of the Progress of Revolutionary Movements Abroad," *Secret Report No. 8,* (June 18, 1919), 14; Georgi Arbatov and Willem Oltmans, *The Soviet Viewpoint,* (New York, 1981), 49.

22 Clark to Heller, Memorandum regarding press release on the survey of manufacturers, May 20, 1919; Clark to Tuch, Memorandum regarding the results of the survey of manufacturers, May 29, 1919, LCF, L0032, Box 1, D165/4, Folders B2, B3.

23 New York *Tribune,* May 8, 1919; New York *Times,* November 17, 18, 1919.

24 New York *Times,* November 17, 18, 1919.

25 *Ibid.,* November 17, 18, 19, 1919; United States, Senate, *Russian Propaganda,* 140–1. Morris's denial came in spite of the fact that three months earlier, on August 7, his assistant, H.E. Boyer, wrote to Heller: "Should you be so kind as to place a contract with us, you have our assurance that it will not only be a pleasure to give you all the assistance possible in obtaining permits, shipping, &c., or in any other way we can expedite the shipment." Gary's statement was half-correct: although U.S. Steel never officially conducted business with the bureau, a subsidiary, U.S. Steel Products Co., did.

176 NOTES TO THE CHAPTER 1

26 New York *World,* June 21, 1919. For more information on Polk's previous meeting with Heller and Clark, see chapter two. To some extent, Polk's denial was true, in that he did hold a terse meeting with Nuorteva in January 1919; Polk, notes, January 29, 1919, *State Department Decimal File,* 861.00/3875. Regarding his comment on the sanctity of diplomatic and consular offices, Polk was referring to the Bolsheviks' efforts to detain American Consul to Russia, Roger C. Tredwell. Tredwell, one of the final consuls to escape Bolshevik Russia, was imprisoned in Tashkent, Turkestan, for five months—his imminent execution feared—until he was released in April 1919. He finally passed the frontier into Finland on April 28, 1919. For further information on this episode, see "Declining Power of the Russian Reds: Release of Tredwell," *Current History,* 10 (April-June 1919): 482–483.
27 See Appendix I for a list of firms that offered to do business with Bolshevik Russia via the Soviet Bureau.
28 Gaston Plaintiff to E.G. Liebold, Letter regarding conditions in Russia, July 26, 1916, *Ford Motor Company Archives,* Acc. 572, Box 16, cited in White, *British and American Commercial Relations,* 29–30.
29 Nuorteva to Martens, Memorandum regarding trip to Sixth National Foreign Trade Convention, April 29, 1919, LCF, L0032, Box 1, D165/4, Folder A7.
30 Heller to Martens, Memorandum of conference with Ernest Kanseler of Ford Motor Co., April 12, 1919; Martens to Ford, Personal letter, April 21, 1919; Frank Campsall to Martens, Western Union Telegram, April 26, 1919; Martens, Memorandum regarding reimbursement for Heller and Nuorteva's trip to Chicago and Detroit, April 30, 1919, Translated by Barbara Hillman, May 28, 1989; Heller to Martens, Report on Trip to Sixth National Foreign Trade Convention, April 29, 1919; Nuorteva to Martens, Report on trip to Sixth National Foreign Trade Convention, April 29, 1919, LCF, L0032, Box 1, D165/4, Folders Al, A5, A7, B3.
31 Contract with Ivan Stacheeff and Company, March 14, 1919; W.A. Ryan to R.I. Roberge, Results of the contract, March 17, 1921; Allied American Corporation with R.I. Roberge, March 30, 1923; Copy of Agreement between Ford Motor Company, the Supreme Council of National Economy, and Amtorg Trading Corporation, May 31, 1929, *Ford Motor Company Archives,* Acc. 49, Box 1, Acc. 199, Box 1A, cited in Mira Wilkins and Frank Ernest Hill, *American Business Abroad: Ford on Six Continents,* (Detroit, 1964), 208–212.
32 New York *Times,* November 16, 1919. Other estimates place the total value near $30,000,000. See Schuman, *American Policy Toward Russia,* 187; United States, Senate, *Russian Propaganda,* 60–63.
33 See Appendix II for a listing of all contracts between U.S. firms and Bolshevik Russia via the Soviet Bureau.
34 United States, Senate, *Russian Propaganda,* 72.

35 War Department, Office of the Chief of Staff, MI2, to Department of Commerce, "On the Resumption of Trade with Soviet Russia by the Allied Nations," May 10, 1920, *National Archives Records Group* 151, File 861, cited in White, *British and American Commercial Relations*, 139.
36 Directorate of Intelligence, Scotland House, "The Russian Soviet Bureau in the United States," 2.
37 Captain John B.Trevor to the Director of Military Intelligence, Report on financial meetings of Soviet Bureau, May 14, 1919, LCF, L0038, Box 2, D165/5, Folder 15.
38 Account maximum balances and duration: Corn Exchange Bank, unknown balance, August 27–October 3, 1918; Guaranty Trust Company, $6,800, April 15–29, 1919; Public National Bank, $6,352, May 3-June 12,1919; Irving National Bank, unknown balance, May 5–June 12, 1919; State Bank of New York, $2,000, May 22-June 12, 1919. See Perley, Morse and Company, Accountant's Report to the Lusk Committee, June 16, 1919, LCF, L0038, Box 2, D165/5, Folder 14. For individual records on the bank accounts, see Canceled Checks, Account with Corn Exchange Bank; Passbook and Balance Sheet, Account with Public National Bank; Passbook, Account with State Bank of New York; and Balance Sheet, Account with Guaranty Trust Company; Matthew T.Murray to Martens, Letter regarding Closing of Guaranty Trust account, April 29, 1919, LCF, L0032, Box 1, D165/4, Folders A11, B5.
39 Clark to Heller, Memorandum regarding banking interests, May 20, 1919, LCF, L0032, Box 1, D165/4, Folder B3. Clark did succeed in arranging a meeting with Frank Vanderlip of National City Bank. See Clark to Lomonossoff, Memorandum regarding meeting with Vanderlip, May 20, 1919, LCF, L0032, Box 1, D165/4, Folder B2.
40 Nothing of substantial interest was revealed in the Information Affidavit with the exception that the Soviet Bureau acknowledged its previous account with Guaranty Trust Company. Bodman to Martens, Letter requesting a meeting, April 21, 1919; Clark to Heller, Memorandum regarding April 25 meeting with Bodman, April 28, 1919; Hillquit to Clark, Letter regarding answers to Information Affidavit, April 26, 1919, LCF, L0032, Box 1, D165/4, Folders B2, B3, B6; War Trade Board Information Affidavit, April 30, 1919, LCF, L0038, Box 2, D165/5, Folder 14.
41 Little information exists regarding this interview. It is mentioned to indicate Palmer's interest in the activities of the Soviet Bureau. Finch, presenting himself as an investigator with the Department of Justice, was actually a former employee of the department, now serving as chief investigator for the Lusk Committee. Heller to Martens, Report of the Commercial Department, April 23–30, 1919, LCF, L0032, Box 1, D165/ 4, Folder A7.

178 NOTES TO THE CHAPTER 1

42 Clarence L.Converse to Alexander Brough, Petition for a warrant to search the Soviet Bureau, June 12, 1919, LCF, L0037, Box 1, D166/6, Folder 15.
43 Alexander Brough, Warrant to search the offices of the Soviet Bureau, June 12, 1919, LCF, L0037, Box 1, D166/6, Folder 15. For greater analysis on the question of search warrants versus subpoenas, see Lawrence H. Chamberlain, *Loyalty and Legislative Action: A Survey of Activity by the New York State Legislature, 1919±1949,* (Ithaca, 1951), 17–18, and Julian Jaffe, *Crusade Against Radicalism: New York During the Red Scare, 1914±1924,* (Port Washington, 1972), 120–121.
44 Although Lusk denied the participation of a British Secret Service Agent during the raid on the bureau, a significant amount of evidence supports the charge. R.N.Nathan, the British Secret Service representative in America, not only participated in the raid, but was allowed to possess original copies and photostats of bureau papers relating to commercial relations between Bolshevik Russia and U.S. firms. Five months later, Nathan reappeared in Copenhagen during the trade negotiations between Russia and Great Britain, apparently utilizing the information he garnered in New York to secure a British advantage in the Bolshevik market. See Norman Hapgood to Lansing, December 2, 1919; Robert Beale Davis to Lansing, December 6, 1919, *State Department Decimal File,* 861.00/5800, 5823; United States, Senate, *Russian Propaganda,* 71; *Times (London),* November 18, 1919; New York *Times,* January 9, 11, 1920; New York *Call,* June 23, 25, 1919, March 8, 1920; New York *World,* March 8, 1920; "By Stevenson Out of Lusk," 66; "Deportation of Alien Anarchists: Shipload Sent to Soviet Russia," *Current History,* 11 (October-December 1919): 233.
45 New York *Tribune,* June 14, 1919.
46 Martens to E.H.McColloch, Sworn affidavit, November 29, 1919, Included in Martens' application for cancellation of subpoena, Argued by Dudley Field Malone before New York State Supreme Court Justice Robert F. Wagner, November 30, 1919, LCF, L0037, Box 1, D166/6, Folder 15.
47 For detailed comments on the raid see: Inventory List, Raid on the Soviet Bureau, June 16, 1919; Sgt. W.R. Brey to C.O. Troop K of the New York State Troopers, Notes regarding the execution of the search warrant, June 18, 1919; Sgt. W.R. Brey, Inventory List, June 18, 1919; Alexander Brough, Receipt of seized material, June 20, 1919, LCF, L0037, Box 1, D166/6, Folder 15. For an overview of the raid see Chamberlain, *Loyalty and Legislative Action,* 18–20; Jaffe, *Crusade Against Radicalism,* 123–4; Committee on Russian-American Relations, *The United States and the Soviet Union,* 28; and "Russia in the Balance: Raid on Soviet Embassy," *Current History,* 10 (July-September 1919): 264.
48 New York *Times,* June 13, 1919.

49 Newton to Martens, Heller, Nuorteva, Weinstein, and Hourwich, Subpoena to appear before the Lusk Committee, June 12, 1919, LCF, L0037, Box 1, D166/6, (handwritten) Folder 18, (formal) Folder 15. Initially, Clark secured the services of the law firm of O'Gorman, Battle, and Vandiver to represent the Soviet Bureau. Stanton, a member of the firm, was the son-in-law of State Senator O'Gorman. On June 13, 1919, the bureau settled upon a counsel consisting of three lawyers: Gilbert E. Roe, former law partner of Senator Robert M.LaFollette; Dudley Field Malone, former Collector of the Port of New York; and George Gordon Battle. Martens retained the services of Recht as his personal attorney, apparently to appease left-wing socialists who felt the bureau was reluctant to employ "real Bolsheviki." Hillquit, long-time legal adviser and unofficial director of the Soviet Bureau's Legal Department, continued to offer his input, but never formally took part in the ensuing legal battles. See New York *Tribune,* June 14, 1919; Jaffe, 124. For information specific to the employment of Recht, see Nuorteva to Hillquit, Letter regarding Recht's employment, April 20, 1919, LCF, L0032, Box 1, D165/4, Folder B6; Walter Nelles to Hillquit, Letter regarding representation for bureau, May 9, 1919, *Microfilm Edition of the Morris Hillquit Papers, 1895±1944,* Reel 2, Document 841, (State Historical Society of Wisconsin, Madison, WI) [hereafter referred to as *Hillquit Papers*].

50 New York *Times,* June 13, 1919.

51 *Ibid.,* June 13, 18, 1919; Jaffe, *Crusade Against Radicalism,* 126; United States, Senate, *Russian Propaganda,* 231; Strakhovsky, *American Opinion About Russia,* 87–88.

52 New York *Times,* June 15, 1919.

53 New York *Tribune,* June 14, 1919.

54 Martens to Lansing, Cable protesting raid, June 12, 1919, cited in Strakhovsky, *American Opinion About Russia,* 87; Tchitcherin, Announcement protesting raid; Phillips, Reply to Tchitcherin, July 1, 1919, "Russia in the Balance: Raid on Soviet Embassy," 264–5.

55 *Lusk Committee Report,* I, 642; New York *Tribune,* June 14, 1919. Martens defended his failure to register as a German subject on technical grounds. He was born of German parents in Russia, educated there, and deported to Germany in 1899. German officials claimed him as a citizen due to his parentage and conscripted him into the national army. Living in England when the war began, Martens registered with the British authorities as an enemy alien. Upon immigrating to the U.S., Martens signed a customs declaration stating his German nationality, but later refused to register as an enemy alien in America due to his claim to Russian citizenship under the new Bolshevik government. See New York *Times,* November 18, 1919.

56 *Lusk Committee Report,* I, 645. Italics added.

57 Committee hearings, June 19, 26, 1919, LCF, L0026, Box 1, D165/6, Folders 5–7. For descriptions of the various individuals see T. Evertt Harre, "Plot to Overthrow the Government," *The National Civic Federation Review,* 4 (July 25, 1919): 2–3.

58 Heller to Syracuse Chilled Plow Co., Form letter announcing resumption of business, June 18, 1919, LCF, L0038, Box 2, D165/5, Folder 14; Martens to McColloch, Sworn affidavit, November 29, 1919, LCF, L0037, Box 1, D166/6, Folder 15.

59 Martens to Lusk, Letter regarding refusal to submit Soviet Bureau papers, November 15, 1919; L.A.Giegerich, Attachment against Martens, November 15, 1919, LCF, L0037, Box 1, D166/6, Folders 15, 18; Hourwich to Hillquit, Letter regarding subpoena on Martens and his papers, November 19, 1919; Hillquit to Hourwich, Letter offering advice regarding Martens and the subpoena, November 22, 1919; *Hillquit Papers,* Reel 2, Documents 910, 911.

60 Martens, Testimony before the Lusk Committee, November 25, 26, 1919, LCF, L0026, Box 1, D165/6, Folders 17–18; Martens to McColloch, Sworn affidavit, November 29, 1919; Robert F.Wagner, Application for cancellation of subpoena, November 30, 1919, LCF, L0037, Box 1, D166/6, Folder 15.

61 The hearings were held December 3–5, 1919, at which time Greenbaum spent a considerable amount of time listening to the testimony of Berger and Stevenson, as well as reading Marten's prior testimony before the committee. Samuel Greenbaum, Denial of Martens' Application, December 10, 1919, LCF, L0037, Box 1, D166/6, Folder 15.

62 "Deportation of Alien Anarchists," *Current History,* 11 (October-December 1919): 234; Louis F.Post, *The Deportation Deleriums of the NineteenTwenties,* (Chicago, 1923), 285–8.

63 United States, Senate, *Russian Propaganda,* 5–6, 55.

64 *Ibid.,* 233–235; New York *Times,* May 24, June 14, October 11, November 8, 1919, April 15, 1920; Strakhovsky, *American Opinion About Russia,* 85–89; Schuman, *American Policy Toward Russia,* 190–191; "Russia's Warfare on Many Fronts: Soviet Envoy in America," *Current History,* 10 (April-June 1919): 267.

65 Post, *The Deportation Deleriums,* 287–290; Committee on Russian-American Relations, *The United States and the Soviet Union,* 28.

66 Warrant served on L.C.A.K.Martens by the U.S. Department of Labor, January 2, 1920, in Charles Recht, *In the Matter of L.C.A.K. Martens,* cited in Schuman, *American Policy Toward Russia, 192.*

67 *Soviet Russia,* December 25, 1920; Schuman, *American Policy Toward Russia,* 193. For details on Wilson's decision, see Committee on Russian-American Relations, *The United States and the Soviet Union,* 28.

68 Tchitcherin to Martens, Cable regarding cancellation of business orders, December 27, 1920, in *Soviet Russia,* January 1, 1921; Post, 290–1. For

additional information, see New York *Times,* January 23, 1921; *Soviet Russia,* March 5, 1921; Schuman, *American Policy Toward Russia,* 293; Strakhovsky, *American Opinion About Russia,* 90; and Committee on Russian-American Relations, *The United States and the Soviet Union,* 28–29. Wilson's decision to cancel the deportation warrant was due largely to the diplomatic rule regarding recognition: that is, recognition dates back to the inception of the government. Once the U.S. government recognized the Soviet regime in 1933, it legally acknowledged that the Bolshevik authorities became a sovereign government in 1917. Therefore, Martens was eventually recognized as the first Bolshevik ambassador to the U.S., sixteen years after the fact. The official arrest and deportation of an ambassador would have been a difficult matter to reconcile; thus, Wilson vacated the warrant.

69 New York *Times,* March 22, 1919.
70 Heller to Mulvihill, May 19, 1919, LCF, L0032, Box 1, D165/4, Folder B3.
71 New York *Times,* March 22, 1919.
72 *Ibid.,* November 18, 1919.
73 New York *Tribune,* June 22, 1919; Heller's handwritten notes, n.d., LCF, L0032, Box 1, D165/4, Folder A4; New York *Times,* March 22, 1919.
74 *LuskCommittee Report,* I: 645–646.
75 United States, Senate, *Russian Propaganda,* 74–75.
76 Director of Intelligence, Scotland House, "The Russian Soviet Bureau in the United States," 7.
77 New York *Tribune,* June 22, 1919.

NOTES TO CHAPTER 5

1 Algernon Lee, "Story of the Rand School," *The Case of the Rand School,* (New York, 1919), 12, located in *Rand School of Social Science, Records, 1905±1962,* (New York: Tamiment Institute), R2678, F:2:9 [hereafter referred to as *RSR*]. For a detailed list of individual salaries, see LCF, L0038, Reel 5, Box 2, Folder 11.
2 For a detailed list of instructors and speakers at the Rand School of Social Science, see Appendix III.
3 For a detailed list of course offerings at the Rand School of Social Science, see Appendix IV.
4 *Rand School Bulletin for 1919±1920,* (New York, 1919), 2–3, found in *LCF,* L0028, Reel 1, Box 1, Folder 1; "Statement of Facts re: Relation to Socialist Party," (1919), 3, found in *RSR,* R2658, XIII:A:11:A.
5 *Ibid.,* 20–21.
6 *Ibid.,* 22–23; For a detailed list of the books available at the Rand School Book Store, see *Catalogue of the Rand School Book Store,* (New York, n.d.), found in LCF, L0028, Reel 1, Box 1, Folder 2. For specific figures

on book store profits, see Algernon Lee to Morris Hillquit, Personal letter, 9 February 1919, found in *Hillquit Papers,* Reel 2, Document 821.
7   Algernon Lee, Affidavit regarding investigation of Rand School, n.d., *RSR,* 2658, XIII:A:11:A.
8   New York *Tribune,* November 26, 1918, 7, 9, April 1919.
9   *Ibid.,* May 2, 1919.
10 *Ibid.,* May 2, June 8, 1919.
11 Details on Stevenson's testimony before the Overman Committee, as well as Lusk Committee views on education, can be found in chapters one and two, respectively. Archibald Stevenson, *Report of Radical Movement and Propaganda,* (December 30, 1918), 50, found in *MID Records,* Series 10110–1086, Reel 13, Frame 495; Anonymous Operative Report, n.d., found in LCF, L0038, Reel 5, Box 2, Folder 11.
12 Six hand-drawn maps of the People's House, "Program for the Raid," and "Instructions to Captains," all found in LCF, L0038, Reel 5, Box 2, Folder 11.
13 Clarence L.Converse, Affidavit for Search Warrant, June 21,1919; William McAdoo, Search Warrant for Rand School Raid, June 21, 1919, both found in RSR, R2658, XIII:A:11:A.
14 William McAdoo's interrogation of Clarence Converse re: application for search warrant, June 21, 1919, *RSR,* R2658, XIII:A:11:A.
15 New York *Times,* June 22, 1919.
16 *Ibid.;* New York Tribune, June 22, 23, 1919.
17 New York *Tribune,* June 23, 1919. A complete list of the documents seized during the raid can be found in RSR, R2658, XIII:A:11:A. The list was ten pages long, single-spaced, typed.
18 Clarence L.Converse, Affidavit for 2nd Search Warrant, June 22, 1919; William McAdoo, Search Warrant for Safe Located in the Society of the Commonwealth Center, June 22, 1919, both found in RSR, R2658, XIII:A:11:A.
19 New York *Times,* June 24, 1919; New York *Tribune,* June 24, 1919.
20 New York *Times,* June 23, 25, 1919. Ray Newton to Governor Alfred E. Smith, Letter, July 2, 1919; Resolution Adopted at the Conference of the Young Democracy, July 21, 1919, both found in *Alfred E.Smith Papers,* (Albany: New York State Archives and Records Administration), Reel 152, Series 260, Folder 126 [hereafter referred to as *Smith Papers*]. Waldman's comments included in Confidential Informant's Report, Socialist Meeting in the Bronx, June 23, 1919, found in *LCF,* L0027, Reel 1, Box 1, Folder 9.
21 New York *Tribune,* June 26, 1919. Allegedly the Soviet Bureau ordered a large amount of literature from the Rand School Book Store. At the same time, the bureau provided the school with a mailing list of supporters to whom the school should mail the literature. In an apparent rift, the school sent the Soviet Bureau a bill that the latter refused to pay. Martens

claimed that the mailing list provided the school with a slew of potential financial backers, and this was payment enough. Later, a person on the list bequeathed $10,000 to the school; but heirs challenged the bequeath in the courts. Thus, the Soviet Bureau intervened and offered to provide the school with legal representation as payment for sending the earlier literature.

22 New York *Times,* June 27, 1919; New York *Tribune,* June 27, 1919. Eventually, only the school's executive secretary, Bertha Mailly, appeared before a committee hearing. When she refused to answer Stevenson and Newton's questions, on the grounds that her legal counsel was barred from the room, Lusk expelled her from the chamber as well. As a result, Mailly faced possible contempt charges; but Attorney General Newton refused to prosecute her, announcing that "this witness being a woman, I am not going to ask that she be punished." See Transcript, Lusk Committee Hearing, (July 8,1919), 489–497, 529–530, found in *LCF,* L0026, Reel 1, Box 1, Folder 9.

23 New York *Tribune,* June 28, 1919; "Documents Produced Before the Lusk Committee," June 27, 1919, found in RSR, R2658, XIII:A:11:A. A copy of the original 1918 indictment against the American Socialist Society for publishing Nearing's pamphlet can be found in Appendix D to the original complaint, *The People of the State of New York v. American Socialist Society,* July 8, 1919, found in *LCF,* L0037, Reel 1, Box 1, Folder 2.

24 New York *Tribune,* June 28, 1919; W.A.Domingo to David Berenberg, Letter re: article for publication, June 6, 1919; W.A.Domingo, "Socialism Imperiled, or the Negro—a Potential Menace to American Radicalism," both found in LCF, L0028, Reel 1, Box 1, Folder 14.

25 New York *Tribune,* June 28, 1919; New York *Times,* June 30, 1919; David Berenberg to M.E.Raab, Letter, October 3, 1916, read into Transcript of Committee Hearing, (June 27, 1919), 308–309, found in *LCF,* L0026, Reel 1, Box 1, Folder 8.

26 New York *Times,* June 29, 1919.

27 *Ibid.*

28 *Ibid.,* July 8, 9, 1919. For an account of the July 7th exchange between S. John Block and Chief City Magistrate William McAdoo, see I.M.Sackin, Deposition before the State Supreme Court of New York, July 14, 1919, found in *RSR,* R2658, XIII:A:11:A.

29 Benjamin Levy, Operative Reports on Rand School Activities, July 5–August 4, 1919, found in *LCF,* L0038, Reel 4, Box 2, Folder 2.

30 New York *Times,* June 28, 29, July 8, 1919; New York *Tribune,* June 29, 1919. The 1901 charter of incorporation for the American Socialist Society can be found in Appendix A of the original complaint, *The People of the State of New York* v. *American Socialist Society,* July 8, 1919, found in LCF, L0037, Reel 1, Box 1, Folder 2.

31 *In the Matter of the Application of Charles D. Newton, as the Attorney General of the State of New York, for leave to commence an action against American Socialist Society,* July 8, 1919, found in LCF, L0037, Reel 1, Box 1, Folder 2. *The People of the State of New York v. American Socialist Society,* Formal complaint to vacate incorporation charter, July 8, 1919; *The People of the State of New York v. American Socialist Society,* Request for a permanent injunction, July 8, 1919; *The People of the State of New York v. American Socialist Society,* Summons to appear and show cause, July 8, 1919, all found in RSR, R2658, XIII:A:11:A. *The People of the State of New York v. American Socialist Society,* Defense Response to Complaint, July 12, 1919, found in *LCF,* L0037, Reel 1, Box 1, Folder 2. That the Rand School sold copies of Nearing's pamphlet was undeniable, as was the fact that the school raised nearly $3,000 to assist in the appeal of the American Socialist Society's conviction in 1918. At question was whether the State of New York could legally revoke the society's charter for violating a federal law.

32 New York *Times,* July 9, 1919.

33 Samuel Untermyer to Clayton Lusk, Letter, July 9, 1919, found in *RSR,* R2658, XIII: A: 11: A.

34 New York *Times,* July 10, 11, 1919.

35 *Ibid,* July11, 1919.

36 *Ibid.* The risky nature of Untermyer's bluff in calling for an immediate hearing was questioned by Gilbert Roe, an attorney who represented many socialist clients, and who was a close friend of Morris Hillquit. In numerous letters to Hillquit, Roe noted that "the risk of answering 'ready' was too great." However, he acknowledged, it was a "good bluff" which, if called by the prosecutor, "would have been unfortunate for the school." See Gilbert Roe to Morris Hillquit, Letter, July 10, 1919, found in *Hillquit Papers,* Reel 2, Document 854.

37 New York *Times,* July 11, 1919; "Brief for Relator," *American Socialist Society v.William McAdoo, et al.,* July 25, 1919, found in *LCF,* L0037, Reel 1, Box 1, Folder 3.

38 New York *Times,* July 11, 1919; "Respondent's Brief," *American Socialist Society v.William McAdoo, et al,* July 25, 1919, found in *LCF,* L0037, Reel 1, Box 1, Folder 3.

39 New York *Times,* July 11, 1919; John McAvoy to Alfred E.Smith, Letter, May 14, 1920, found in *Smith Papers,* Reel 152, Series 260, Folder 129.

40 New York *Times,* July 12, 19, 1919. At the request of both parties, McAvoy eventually postponed the date of the trial by two days, until July 30th. Subsequent efforts by S.John Block for the Rand School, and I.M.Sackin for the Commonwealth Center, to obtain a formal writ of prohibition to prevent the Lusk Committee or the Attorney General from using the papers also failed; throughout the remainder of the summer, the

committee and state prosecutors continued to make great use of the information, although they remained in the possession of Judge McAvoy. For more details on the struggle for a writ of prohibition, see depositions by Max Schonberg, I.M.Sackin, Bertha Mailly, and Samuel Rohman, July 14, 1919; *American Socialist Society v.William McAdoo*, et al., Temporary writ of prohibition, July 15, 1919; American Socialist Society to William McAdoo, et al., Notice of hearing re: temporary writ of prohibition, July 15, 1919, all found in *RSR,* R2658, XIII: A: 11: A.

41 New York *Times,* July 12, 1919. Special Agent W.A.Carothers to Chief Special Agent R.W.Finch, Report on Socialist Party meeting in Brownsville, July 4, 1919; Special Agent John G. Purdie to Finch, Report on Mass Meeting at Rand School, July 11, 1919, all found in *LCF,* L0027, Reel 1, Box 1, Folder 10.

42 New York State Trooper E.A. Kruse to Clarence Converse, Reports on Mass Meetings in the Bronx, July 13, 14, 1919, both found in *LCF,* L0027, Reel 1, Box 1, Folder 10.

43 Advertisement and all letters excerpted from *Rand School News,* 3:1 (September 1919): 1, 4, found in *RSR,* R2683, XIII: F: 5:7.

44 *Ibid.*

45 Excerpts from *The Nation,* July 19, 1919; *The Public,* July 19, 1919; New York *World,* July 10, 1919, all found in *RSR,* R2658, XIII: A: 11: A.

46 New York *Times,* July 30, 1919; "Classified List of Witnesses," found in *RSR,* R2658, XIII: A: 11: A. While some prominent individuals agreed to appear on behalf of the Rand School, including Charles Beard and Scott Nearing, others remained reluctant to fall victim to negative publicity, including the editor of *The Nation,* Oswald Garrison Willard, who refused the request, and Robert H.Lowie of the American Ethnological Society and the Rev. John Haynes Holmes of the Community Church of New York, both of whom offered their help a day *after* the trial ended. See Oswald Willard to Bertha Mailly, Letter, July 9, 1919; Robert Lowie to S.John Block, Letter, July 31, 1919; and John Haynes Holmes to Bertha Mailly, Letter, August 1, 1919, all found in *RSR,* R2658, XIII: A: 11: A.

47 New York *Times,* July 31, 1919.

48 *Ibid.;* S.John Block and Samuel Berger, Transcript of telephone conversation, July 24, 1919, found in *LCF,* L0037, Reel 2, Box 1, Folder 7; S.John Block to Samuel Berger, Letter, July 26, 1919, found in *LCF,* L0037, Reel 1, Box 1, Folder 4.

49 New York *Times,* July 31, 1919; *People of the State of New York v. American Socialist Society,* Dismissal of charges, July 31, 1919, found in *LCF,* L0037, Reel 1, Box 1, Folder 5.

50 New York *Times,* July 31, 1919.

51 S.John Block, Statement Regarding Rand School Proceeding, July 30, 1919, found in *American Socialist Society, Records, 1905±1955,* (New York: Tamiment Institute), R2659, XIII: B [hereafter referred to *AmSS*].
52 *Ibid.;* "Statement by the Attorney General," July 30, 1919, found in LCF, L0037, Reel 2, Box 1, Folder 7.

NOTES TO CHAPTER 6

1 New York *Times,* September 3, 1919. As the weeks and months passed, legal proceedings against the Rand School and the American Socialist Society grew increasingly unlikeiy, despite Newton's best efforts. In October, Newton opened the state's previous default against the society; however, since the state lacked any new, substantial evidence, and was also unable to meet Untermyer's demand for an immediate trial, Justice Gavegan once again dismissed the charges. See New York *Tribune,* October 7, 1919; New York *Call,* November 27, 1919; Transcript, *People of the State of New York v. American Socialist Society,* October 6, 1919; Samuel Berger to Charles Newton, Letter, October 10, 1919, both found in *LCF,* L0037, Reel 1, Box 1, Folders 4–5.
2 New York *Times,* November 10, December 29, 1919.
3 *Ibid.,* February 29, 1920.
4 For the best brief account on the Socialist expulsion, see Melvin I.Urofsky, "A Note on the Expulsion of Five Socialists," *New York History,* 47 (January 1966): 41–49. Eventually, all five men returned to the assembly in September, 1920, as the result of a special election; however, Sweet again orchestrated the expulsion of three of them (Waldman, Claessens, and Solomon). The other two (DeWitt and Orr) refused to take their seats as a result. During the regular election in November, 1920, Orr and Solomon again regained their seats, along with a newcomer, Henry Jager. Sweet tried to expel the men a third time; however, he was stopped by Republican colleagues who felt their party received too much negative publicity for the previous actions.
5 Frank Dickinson Blodgett, Testimony before the Lusk Committee, (January 16, 1920), 2037, 2047 found in *LCF,* L0026, Reel 2, Box 1, Folders 25–26.
6 John Jacob Coss, Testimony before the Lusk Committee, (January 16, 1920), 2057; Elmer Ellsworth Brown, Testimony before the Lusk Committee, (January 17, 1920), 2137–2138; both found in *LCF,* L0026, Reel 2, Box 1, Folders 25–26.
7 William L.Ettinger, Testimony before the Lusk Committee, (January 19, 1920), 2222–2223, found in *LCF,* L0026, Reel 2, Box 1, Folder 27; New York Call, January 21, 1920.
8 Anning S.Prawl, Testimony before the Lusk Committee, (January 19, 1920), 2241; John L.Tildsley, Testimony before the Lusk Committee,

(January 19, 1920), 2250, 2254, 2261; both found in *LCF,* L0026, Reel 2, Box 1, Folder 27; New York Call, January 21, 1920.
9 "Preliminary Report and Recommendations of the Joint Legislative Committee Investigating Seditious Activities," *Legislative Documents of the State of New York,* 143rd Session, 23 (Albany, 1920), No. 52.
10 *Ibid.*
11 *Ibid.*
12 New York *Tribune,* March 19, 1920; New York *Times,* March 18, 19, 1920.
13 New York *Call,* April 1, 1920; New York *Times,* April 1, 1920.
14 New York *Times,* April 14, 1920. Other strong critics of the Lusk measures included Democratic Senators J.Samuel Fowler of Chautauqua and Salvatore R. Cotillo of New York City.
15 *Ibid.; Journal of the Senate of the State of New York,* 143rd Session, 2 (Albany, 1920), 1212–1214.
16 New York *Times,* April 16, 1920; *Journal of the Assembly of the State of New York,* 143rd Session, 3 (Albany, 1920), 2280–2283, 2682–2683. Other strong opponents of the measures included Minority Leader Charles Donohue, and Assemblymen Theodore Roosevelt, Jr. and Sol Ullman. Evans' comments regarding the political ambitions of the governor of Massachusetts referred to the national prominence Calvin Coolidge gained when he crushed the Boston police strike in November, 1919, a move which propelled him to the Republican vice-presidential nomination in 1920.
17 NewYork *Times,* May 2, 1920. Ironically, while serving as a member of the New York City Board of Education during the First World War, Giddings voted to expel three high school teachers on the grounds of disloyalty. At the time, he believed the charges were true. However, in 1920, he feared that the Lusk bills would be counterproductive, and serve only to reinforce the cause of radicalism by forcing the movement into secrecy.
18 *Ibid.*
19 *Ibid.,* May 12, 1920.
20 Wood read a variety of obscene passages from Married Love, including detailed accounts of sexual intercourse. According to many reports, women left the hearing from embarrassment and disgust. Algernon Lee to Alfred E.Smith, Letter and Memorandum re: *Married Love,* May 14, 1920; Alfred E.Smith to Algernon Lee, Letter, May 18, 1920; Alfred E.Smith to Edward Swann (District Attorney, New York County), May 18, 1920; Henry A.wise Wood to Alfred E.Smith, May 19, 1920; Mabel T.R.Washburn to Alfred E.Smith, Letter, May 15, 1920, all found in *Smith Papers,* Reel 152, Folder 260–126; New York *Times,* May 15, 1920.

21 Alfred E.Smith to Ogden L.Mills, Letter, May 28, 1920, found in *Smith Papers,* Reel 152, Folder 260–126; New York *Times,* May 15, 1920.
22 Algernon Lee to Alfred Smith, Memorandum re: Lusk Bills, May 3, 1920, found in *RSR,* R2658, XIII: A: 6; New York *Times,* May 15, 1920. Even before Smith issued a final decision on the bills, Lee hinted that the Rand School would purposely violate the law in order to test its constitutionality in court, should it come to that; see Memorandum of conversation between Algernon Lee and Morris Hillquit, April 8, 1920, found in *RSR,* R2658, XIII: A: 6.
23 Both of Smith's veto messages are reprinted in Alfred E.Smith, *Up to Now: An Autobiography,* (New York, 1929), 204–205; New York *Times,* May 20, 1920.
24 *Ibid.*
25 *Smith, Up to Now,* 219–221.
26 New York *Times,* January 4, February 8, March 23, 1921.
27 *Ibid.,* April 7, 1921; State of New York, Senate, Bills No. 1648 and 1649, April 6,1921, found in *New York State Bill Jacket,* Chapters 666 and 667, (Albany, 1921).
28 New York *Times,* April 10, 1921.
29 *Ibid.,* April 14, 1921; New York *Tribune,* April 15, 1921.
30 *Journal of the Senate of the State of New York,* 144th Session, 2 (Albany, 1921), 1423–1424; *Journal of the Assembly of the State of New York,* 144th Session, 3 (Albany, 1921), 2747–2749; New York *Times,* April 17, 19, 1921.
31 New York *Times,* April 25, 1921.
32 *Ibid.,* April 27, 1921.
33 Gilbert Raynor to Nathan Miller, Letter, April 29, 1921; Harry A.Davies to Nathan Miller, Letter, April 23, 1921; Aaron I.Dotey to Nathan Miller, April 23, 1921, all found in *New York State Bill Jacket,* Chapters 666 and 667; New York *Times,* May 2, 1921.
34 S.John Block to Nathan Miller, Letter, May 2, 1921; Harold Riegelman to Nathan Miller, Letter, April 23, 1921; Edward Devine to Nathan Miller, Letter, April 30, 1921; William H.Allen (Institute for Public Safety) to Nathan Miller, April 28, 1921; all found in *New York State Bill Jacket,* Chapter 667.
35 Nathan Miller, Memoranda accompanying approval of Senate Bills No. 1648 (teacher certification) and 1649 (school licensing), May 9, 1921, *New York State Bill Jacket Collection,* Chapters 666 and 667; Chapt. 666, "An Act to Amend the Education Law in Relation to the Qualification of Teachers" and Chapt. 667, "An Act to Amend the Education Law in Relation to Licensing and Supervision of Schools and School Courses," *Laws of the State of New York,* 144th Session, 3 (Albany, 1921), 2047–2051; New York *Times,* May 10, 1921.

36 Rand School Board of Directors, Resolution Opposing Lusk Laws, September 1, 1921, found in *RSR,* R2658, XIII: A: 11: A; New York *Times,* September 4, 1921.
37 *Rand School News and Book Review,* 2 (September 1921): 1; New York *Times,* September 25, 1921.
38 American Socialist Society Board of Directors Meeting, Minutes, September 25, 1921, found in *AmSS,* R2659, XIII: A: 15; New York *Times,* September 26, 1921.
39 New York *Times,* September 27, 1921.
40 *Ibid.,* September 28, 1921.
41 *Ibid.,* September 28, October 25, 1921; *Rand School News and Book Review,* 2 (October-November, 1921): 2.
42 New York *Times,* January 1, 1922.
43 *Ibid.,* May 5, 1922.
44 Plaintiff's Complaint, *People of the State of New York v. American Socialist Society,* May 4, 1922, found in *RSR,* R2658, XIII: A: 11: C; New York *Times,* May 5, 1922.
45 *Ibid.*
46 *Ibid.*
47 New York *Times,* July 15, 1922. Concurring with Justice Merrell were Presiding Justice John Proctor Clarke, and Justices Walter Lloyd Smith and Alfred R.Page. The lone dissenting vote came from Justice Samuel Greenbaum.
48 *Rand School News and Book Review,* 2 (October 1, 1922): 2; New York *Times,* July 16, October 7, 1922. Hillquit later announced his intention to appeal the ruling all the way to the U.S. Supreme Court, if necessary; see Annual Meeting of the American Socialist Society, Minutes, February 5, 1923, found in AmSS, R2659, XIII: A: 16.
49 New York *Times,* April 25, 1922.
50 *Ibid.,* May 17, 19, 22, 1922.
51 *Ibid.,* November 23, 1921, May 15, 17, 25, 1922.
52 *Ibid.,* May 17, 22, 1922.
53 *Ibid.,* June 2, 4, 7, 8, 9, 13, 14, 1922.
54 *Ibid.,* October 18, 19, 23, November 6, 1922.
55 Smith, *Up to Now,* 235–252; New York *Times,* November 3, 1922.
56 Orlo J.Price (Federation of Churches of Rochester and Monroe County) to Alfred E.Smith, Letter, November 27, 1922; William J.Dwyer (Meat Cutters & Butchers No.l) to Alfred E.Smith, Letter, January 4, 1923, both found in *Smith Papers,* Series 13682, Folder 200–5; "One College President Speaks Out for Freedom," *Rand School News and Book Review,* 2 (December 1922): 4; New York *Times,* December 17, 30, 1922.
57 Governor's Annual Message, January 3, 1923, found in *Journal of the Senate of the State of New York, 146th Session,* (Albany, 1923), Appendix, 12–13; New York *Times,* January 4, 5, 1923.

58 New York *Times,* January 9, 12, 1923.
59 *Ibid.,* January 19, 1923.
60 Edward G.Riggs to Alfred E.Smith, Letter, February 23, 1923, found in *Smith Papers,* Series 13682, Folder 200–5; New York *Times,* January 21, 1923.
61 A.V.Brandon (Socialist Party, Bronx County Organization) to Alfred E. Smith, Resolution, January 18, 1923; Raymond Ingersoll (Executive Committee for the Repeal of the Lusk Laws) to Alfred E.Smith, Letter, February 3, 1923, found in *Smith Papers,* Series 13682, Folder 200–5; New York *Times,* January 29, February 27, 1923. For more information on the Citizen's Committee, see American Socialist Society Board of Directors, Minutes, June 22, 1921, found in *AmSS,* R2659, XIII: A: 16; Rand School Board of Directors, Minutes, December 11, 1922, found in *RSR,* R2658, XIII: A: 8.
62 *Journal of the Senate of the State of New York,* 146th Session, 1 (Albany, 1923), 257–259; New York *Times,* February 28, 1923.
63 New York *Times,* March 19, 28, 1923.
64 Oswald Garrison Villard to Alfred E.Smith, Letter, March 31, 1923; H.H. MacCracken to Alfred E. Smith, Letter March 31, 1923; both found in *Smith Papers,* Series 13682, Folder 200–5; New York *Times,* March 31, 1923.
65 *Journal of the Assembly of the State of New York,* 146th Session, 2 (Albany, 1923), 1516–1519, 1984–1987; New York *Times,* April 11, 25, 1923.
66 New York *Times,* May 23, 1923.
67 Chapter 798, "An Act to Repeal Section 555a of the Education Law Relating to the Qualifications of Teachers" and Chapter 799, "An Act to Repeal Section 79 of the Education Law Relating to Licensing and Supervision of Schools and School Courses," *Laws of the State of New York,* 146th Session (Albany, 1923), 1441; New York *Times,* May 26, 1923.
68 Stevenson, Handwritten notes for Lusk Committee final report, n.d., found in *AESP.*

NOTES TO THE CONCLUSION

1 Clayton Lusk to A.Mitchell Palmer, Letter, July 7, 1919, *LCF,* L0040, Box 2, Folder 15. This letter, along with a small amount of other official correspondence (also located in *LCF,* Series L0040) between committee officials and the Department of Justice, indicates that Lusk kept Palmer apprised of his investigation into radicalism. Specifically, Lusk forwarded information from the raid on the Soviet Bureau, as well as names of individuals for possible deportation proceedings.
2 For details on the Palmer raids, see Murray, *Red Scare,* 210–222.

3 National Popular Government League, *Report Upon the Illegal Practices of the United States Department of Justice,* (Washington, D.C., 1920).
4 Louis F.Post, *The Deportations Delirium of Nineteen-Twenty,* (Chicago, 1923).
5 Palmer's presidential aspirations are fully explored by Stanley Coben in his biography of Palmer, *A.Mitchell Palmer: Politician,* (New York, 1963). Lusk Committee members John Boylan became a U.S. Congressman from New York from 1922 to 1938, and Louis Martin was a State Supreme Court Justice from 1921 to 1926. Thaddeus Sweet, the key person in the expulsion of the five socialists from the State Assembly served as a U.S. Congressman from 1923 to 1928. Deputy Attorney General Samuel Berger became the chief of counterintelligence for the Army Air Force during World War Two, and later served on a special committee investigating communist lawyers on behalf of the Association of the Bar of New York. Even Clarence Converse, the investigator who swore out the search warrant that led to the raid on the Rand School became an agent for the Internal Revenue Service, where he gained fame for his investigation of Al Capone in the 1920s.
6 Clayton Lusk to Archibald Stevenson, Memorandum, June 23, 1919, *LCF,* L0038, Reel 5, Box 2, Folder 11; Clayton Lusk to Alfred Smith, Letter, June 30, 1919, *Smith Papers,* Reel 152, Series 260, Folder 129.
7 Louis A.Levine to R.W.Finch, Confidential Informant Reports, August 5, 10, 14, 1919; Louis Levine to Archibald Stevenson, Confidential Informant Report, August 13, 1919; all found in *LCF,* L0038, Reels 4–5, Box 2, Folders 2, 3, 11.
8 *Rand School News and Book Review,* 3 (January 1920): 1.
9 Charles A.Brent to Alfred E.Smith, Letter, January 2, 1923; A.V.Brandon to Alfred E.Smith, Letter, January 18, 1923; Alfred E.Smith to Edward G.Riggs, Letter, March 1, 1923; all found in *Smith Papers,* Series 13682, Folder 200–5.
10 Robert E.Cushman, cited in Paul Murphy, *The Meaning of Freedom of Speech: First Amendment Freedoms from Wilson to FDR,* (Westport, 1972), 273; Henry R.Linville, "Teachers Loyalty Oaths and Freedom in Education," in Julia E. Johnson, comp., *Freedom of Speech,* (New York, 1936), 217.
11 Heale, *American Anticommunism,* 85; Levin, *Political Hysteria,* 81–84.
12 NewYork *Times,* September 18, 2001; New York *Newsday,* September 18, 2001.
13 *Ibid.*
14 New York *Times,* February 12, 2003.
15 *Ibid.*
16 For additional information on the subsequent efforts by state legislatures to combat radicalism in public schools see Chamberlain, *Loyalty and Legislative Action,* and Howard K.Beale, *Are American Teachers Free?*

An Analysis of Restraints Upon the Freedom of Teaching in American Schools, (New York, 1972). In many ways, the Lusk Committee's decision to focus on education paralleled a later effort by the N.A.A.C.R to attack Jim Crow segregation. When devising a strategy, the association's lawyers chose to begin their legal challenges in the realm of education, in the hope that most Americans, white and black, could not deny the importance of quality education. As a result, Thurgood Marshall appeared before the U.S. Supreme Court and won an important victory for civil rights in the famous *Brown v. Board of Education* decision in 1954. Other legal victories for desegregation quickly followed.

17 In his brief examination of the nature of U.S.-Soviet trade, James Libbey explains how "concessions" (essentially short-term leases to commercial investors) failed to lead to extensive trade between the two countries during the 1920s. Having lost money in previous commercial ventures, fewer than 200 firms were willing to invest in concession agreements. Among the most notable were Armand Hammer, the son of Julius Hammer who served as Financial Director for the Soviet Bureau, and W.Averell Harriman, whose manganese concession became one of the most significant commercial ventures in Soviet Russia. See Libbey, *Russian-American Economic Relations, 1763±1999,* (Breeze, FL: Academic International Press, 1999).

18 New Canaan (CT) *Advertiser,* February 16, 1961.
19 New York *Times,* July 26, 1921; July 15, 1924.
20 *Ibid.,* August 13, 1925.

Bibliography

ARCHIVAL SOURCES

American Socialist Society. Records, 1905–1955. New York, NY: Tamiment Library, New York University.

Claessens, August. Papers, 1919–1955. New York, NY: Tamiment Library, New York University.

Clark, Evans. Papers, 1921–1969. Amherst, MA: Amherst College Library.

Debs, Eugene V.Papers, 1884–1955. New York, NY: Tamiment Library, New York University.

Hillquit, Morris. Papers, 1886–1944. Madison, WI: State Historical Society of Wisconsin.

Hillquit, Morris. Papers, 1906–1959. New York, NY: Tamiment Library, New York University.

Hylan, John F.Papers. Albany, NY: New York State Archives and Records Administration.

Intercollegiate Socialist Society. Records, 1904–1921. New York, NY: Tamiment Library, New York University.

Lee, Algernon. Papers, 1896–1952. New York, NY: Tamiment Library, New York University.

New York State. Bill Jacket Collection. Albany, NY: New York State Archives and Records Administration.

New York State. Records of the Joint Legislative Committee Investigating Seditious Activities in New York State, 1919–1920. Albany, NY: New York State Archives and Records Administration.

New York State. Veto Jacket Collection. Albany, NY: New York State Archives and Records Administration.

National Civic Federation. Records, 1918–1921. New York, NY: New York Public Library.

Palmer, A.Mitchell. Papers. Washington, D.C.: Library of Congress.

Rand School of Social Science. Records, 1906–1956. New York, NY: Tamiment Library, New York University.

Smith, Alfred E.Official Papers, 1919–1929. Albany, NY: New York State Archives and Records Administration.

Socialist Party, New York. Records, 1872–1946. New York, NY: Tamiment Library, New York University.

194 BIBLIOGRAPHY

Socialist Party of the United States. Records, 1900–1961. Durham, NC: Perkins Library, Duke University.
Solomon, Charles. Papers, 1916–1962. New York, NY: Tamiment Library, New York University.
Stevenson, Archibald E.Papers, 1917–1923. In personal possession of author.
United States. Records of the Department of Justice. Washington, D.C.: National Archives and Records Administration.
United States. Records of the Department of State Relating to the Internal Affairs of Russia and the Soviet Union, 1910–1929. Washington, D.C.: National Archives and Records Administration.
United States. Records of the Directorate of Military Intelligence, Surveillance of Radicals in the United States, 1917–1941. Washington, D.C.: National Archives and Records Administration.

DOCUMENTS AND GOVERNMENT PUBLICATIONS

Congressional Record. Volumes 58–60. Washington, D.C.: Government Printing Office, 1919–1921.
Cumming, C.K. and Walter W.Pettit. *Russian-American Relations, Documents and Papers.* New York, NY: Harcourt, Brace and Howe, 1920.
Katkov, George. "German Foreign Office Documents on Financial Support to the Bolsheviks in 1917." *International Affairs* 32 (1956).
Massachusetts (Commonwealth of). *Massachusetts Reports.* Vol. 235. Boston, MA: Little, Brown and Co., 1921.
New York State. *Annual Reports of the Attorney General.* Albany, NY: J.B. Lyons Co., 1919–1921.
——. *Journal of the Assembly of the State of New York.* Sessions 142–146. Albany, NY: J.B. Lyons Co., 1919–1923.
——. *Journal of the Senate of the State of New York.* Sessions 142–146. Albany, NY: J.B.Lyons Co., 1919–1923.
——. *Laws of the State of New York.* Sessions 144, 146. Albany, NY: J.B.Lyons Co., 1921.
——. *Legislative Documents of the State of New York.* Session 143. Albany: J.B.Lyons Co., 1920.
——. *Proceedings of the Judiciary Committee of the Assembly in the Matter of the Qualifications of Its Socialist Members.* Legislative Document No. 135. 3 Volumes. Albany, NY: J.B.Lyons Co., 1920.
——. *Revolutionary Radicalism: Its History, Purpose and Tactics.* Final Report of the Joint Legislative Committee Investigating Seditious Activities in New York State. 4 Volumes. Albany, NY: J.B.Lyons Co., 1920.
United States. Committee on Public Information. *The German-Bolshevik Conspiracy.* War Information Series, 20 (1918).

——. Department of Commerce. Bureau of Foreign and Domestic Commerce. *Statistical Abstract of the United States, 1919±1923.* Washington, D.C.: Government Printing Office, 1920–1924.
——. Department of Justice. *Annual Reports of the Attorney General.* Washington, D.C.: Government Printing Office, 1919–1921.
——. Department of Labor. *Bulletin of the United States Bureau of Labor Statistics.* 357 (May 1924).
——. Department of Labor. *Reports of the Secretary of Labor and Reports of the Bureaus.* Washington, D.C.: Government Printing Office, 1919–1921.
——. House of Representatives. *Attorney General A.Mitchell Palmer on Charges Made Against the Department of Justice by Louis F.Post and Others.* Hearings before the Committee on Rules. Washington, D.C.: Government Printing Office, 1920–1921.
——. House of Representatives. *Communist and Anarchist Deportation Cases.* Hearings before the Committee on Immigration and Naturalization. Washington, D.C.: Government Printing Office, 1920.
——. House of Representatives. *Communist Labor Party Deportation Cases.* Hearings before a Subcommittee of the Committee on Immigration and Naturalization. Washington, D.C.: Government Printing Office, 1920.
——. House of Representatives. *Exclusion and Expulsion of Aliens of Anarchistic and Similar Classes.* Report of the Committee on Immigration and Naturalization. Washington, D.C.: Government Printing Office, 1919.
——. House of Representatives. *Investigation of Administration of Louis F.Post, Assistant Secretary of Labor, in the Matter of Deportation of Aliens.* Hearings before the Committee on Rules. Washington, D.C.: Government Printing Office, 1920.
——. House of Representatives. *I.W.W. Deportation Cases.* Hearings before a Subcommittee of the Committee on Immigration and Naturalization. Washington, D.C.: Government Printing Office, 1920.
——. House of Representatives. *Sedition.* Hearings before the Committee on the Judiciary. Washington, D.C.: Government Printing Office, 1920.
——. House of Representatives. *Sedition, Syndicalism, Sabotage, and Anarchy.* Hearings before the Committee on the Judiciary. Washington, D.C.: Government Printing Office, 1919.
——. House of Representatives. *Victor L.Berger.* Hearings before a Special Committee of the House. Washington, D.C.: Government Printing Office, 1919.
——. Senate. *Bolshevik Propaganda.* Hearings before a Subcommittee of the Committee on the Judiciary. Washington, D.C.: Government Printing Office, 1919.
——. Senate. *Brewing and Liquor Interests and German and Bolshevik Propaganda.* Report of the Subcommittee of the Committee on the Judiciary. Washington, D.C.: Government Printing Office, 1919.

——. Senate. *The Bullitt Mission to Russia.* William Christian Bullitt's testimony before the Committee on Foreign Relations. Washington, D.C.: Government Printing Office, 1919.

——. Senate. *Relations with Russia.* Hearings before the Committee on Foreign Relations. Washington, D.C.: Government Printing Office, 1921.

——. Senate. *Russian Propaganda.* Hearings before a Subcommittee of the Committee on Foreign Relations regarding the status and activities of Ludwig C.A.K. Martens. Washington, D.C.: Government Printing Office, 1920.

——. *Statutes at Large.* Vol. 39. Washington, D.C.: Government Printing Office, 1917.

AUTOBIOGRAPHIES AND MEMOIRS

Debs, Eugene V. *Writings and Speeches of Eugene V.Debs.* New York, NY: Charles Scribner's Sons, 1948.

Gitlow, Benjamin. *I Confess: The Truth About American Communism.* New York, NY: E.P.Dutton and Co., 1940.

Hammer, Armand with Neil Lyndon. *Hammer.* New York, NY: G. Putnam's Sons, 1987.

Haywood, William D. *Bill Haywood's Book.* New York, NY: Scribner's, 1929.

Hillquit, Morris. *Loose Leaves From a Busy Life.* New York, NY: Macmillan, 1934.

Howe, Frederic C. *The Confessions of a Monopolist.* New Jersey: The Gregg Press, 1968.

Hylan, John F. *Mayor of New York: An Autobiography.* New York, NY: Rotary Press, 1922.

Kerensky, Alexander F. with Robert P.Browder. *The Russian Provisional Government, 1917.* Stanford, CA: Stanford University Press, 1961.

Lamont, Thomas. *Across World Frontiers.* New York, NY: Harcourt, Brace, 1951.

Lenin, Vladimir I. *Lenin on the United States.* New York, NY: International Publishers, 1970.

Lockhart, Robert H.Bruce. *British Agent.* New York, NY: Putnam's, 1933.

——. *The Diaries of Robert Hamilton Bruce Lockhart.* New York, NY: St. Martin's Press, 1974.

Smith, Alfred E. *Let's Look at the Record.* New York, NY: Thistle Press, n.d.

——. *Up to Now: An Autobiography.* New York, NY: Viking Press, 1929.

Trotsky, Leon. *My Life.* New York, NY: Scribner's, 1930.

Vanderlip, Frank A. *From Farm Boy to Financier.* New York, NY: A. Appleton Century, 1935.

Waldman, Louis. *Labor Lawyer.* New York, NY: E.P.Dutton and Co., 1944.

PAMPHLETS, REPORTS AND SPEECHES

American-Russian Chamber of Commerce. *Handbook of the Soviet Union.* New York, NY: American-Russian Chamber of Commerce, 1936.

American Trade Union. *Russia After Ten Years: Report of the American Trade Union Delegation to the Soviet Union.* New York, NY: International Publishers, 1927.

Association of the Bar of the City of New York. *Brief of the Special Committee Appointed by the Bar of the City of New York in the Matter of L.Waldman, A.Claessens, A.DeWitt, S.Orr, C.Solomon.* Reports, XXI, Leg. Doc. 219. New York, NY: The Association, 1920.

——— *Resolution Adopted January 13, 1920, Respecting the Suspended Socialists.* Reports, XXI, Leg. Doc. 217. New York, NY: The Association, 1920.

———. *Statement by the Special Committee Appointed by the Association of the Bar of the City of New York.* Reports, XXI. New York, NY: The Association, 1920.

Catalogue of the Rand School Book Store. New York, NY: Rand School, n.d.

Claessens, August. *Didn't We Have Fun.* New York, NY: The Rand School, 1953.

———. *The Socialists in the New York Assembly: Work of the Ten Socialist Members During the Legislative Session of 1918.* New York, NY: The Rand School, 1918.

Clark, Evans. *Facts and Fabrications About Soviet Russia.* New York, NY: The Rand School, 1920.

Committee on Russian-American Relations. *The United States and the Soviet Union: A Report on the Controlling Factors in the Relation Between the United States and the Soviet Union.* New York, NY: The American Foundation, 1933.

Heller, A.A. *Russian Socialist Federal Soviet Republic: Bureau of the Representative in the U.S.A.: Commercial Department.* New York, NY: Russian Soviet Bureau, 1919.

Jennings, Emerson P. *Report to the Association.* New York, NY: American Commercial Association to Promote Trade with Russia, 1921.

Kellock, Harold. *Points on American-Soviet Relations.* Washington, D.C.: Russian Information Bureau, 1926.

Lee, Algernon. *The Case of the Rand School.* New York, NY: Rand School, 1919.

National Association of Manufacturers. *American Trade Index.* 7th Annual Issue. New York, NY: 1905.

National Civil Liberties Bureau. *Wartime Persecutions and Mob Violence.* New York, NY: n.p., 1919.

National Popular Government League. *Report Upon the Illegal Practices of the United States Department of Justice.* Washington, D.C.: n.p., 1920.

National Republican Club. *The Spread of Socialist Doctrine in New York City.* Report of a Special Committee Appointed by the Honorable Charles D.Hilles, September 16, 1919. n.p., n.d.
Nelles, Walter. *Seeing Red: Civil Liberties and Law in the Period Following the War.* New York, NY: American Civil Liberties Union, 1920.
People's Freedom Union. *The Truth About the Lusk Committee: A Report.* New York, NY: The Nation Press, 1920.
Poliakoff, R. *Trade with Russia After the War.* An Address before the Foreign Trade Association of the Cincinnati Chamber of Commerce, April 17, 1919.
Radek, Karl and Arthur Ransome. *Radek and Ransome on Russia.* Brooklyn, NY: The Socialist Publication Society, 1918.

NEWSPAPERS

Albany *Journal.*
Baltimore *News.*
Boston *Evening Transcript.*
Brooklyn (New York) *Eagle.*
Catholic News.
Chicago *Tribune.*
Cleveland *Plain Dealer.*
Commercial and Financial Chronicle.
The Communist.
Industrial Worker.
The Liberator.
New Canaan (CT) *Advertiser.*
New York *American.*
New York *Call.*
New York *Communist.*
New York *Evening World.*
New York *Globe.*
New York *Herald.*
New York *Newsday.*
New York *Post.*
New York *Sun.*
New York *Telegram.*
New York *Times.*
New York *Tribune.*
New York *World.*
Philadelphia *Inquirer.*
Pittsburgh *Post.*
Rand School News and Book Review.

Russian Soviet Bureau Weekly Bulletin.
Salt Lake *Tribune.*
Seattle *Post-Intelligencer.*
Times (London).
Washington *Evening Star.*
Washington *Post.*

SECONDARY BOOKS

Abernathy, M.Glenn. *Civil Liberties Under the Constitution.* 2nd Edition. New York, NY: Dodd, Mead and Co., 1972.

Allen, Frederick L. *Only Yesterday: An Informal History of the Nineteen-Twenties.* New York, NY: Blue Ribbon Books, Inc., 1931.

Anderson Paul H. *The Attitude of American Leftist Leaders Towards the Russian Revolution, 1917±1923.* South Bend, IN: University of Notre Dame Press, 1942.

Arbatov, Georgi and Willem Oltmans. *The Soviet Viewpoint.* New York, NY: Dodd, Mead and Co., 1981.

Beale, Howard K. *Are American Teachers Free? An Analysis of Restraints Upon the Freedom of Teaching in American Schools.* New York, NY: Octagon Books, 1972.

Bennett, David H. *The Party of Fear: From Nativist Movements to the New Right in American History.* Chapel Hill, NC: University of North Carolina Press, 1988.

Blanchard, Margaret. *Revolutionary Sparks: Freedom of Expression in Modern America.* Oxford, England: Oxford University Press, 1992.

Brissenden, Paul. *The I.W.W.: A Study in American Syndicalism.* New York, NY: Russell and Russell, 1957.

Chafee, Zechariah, Jr. *Free Speech in the United States.* Cambridge, MA: Harvard University Press, 1942.

———. *Freedom of Speech.* New York, NY: Harcourt, Brace and Howe, 1920.

———. *The Inquiring Mind.* New York, NY: Harcourt, Brace and Company, 1928.

Chamberlain, Lawrence H. *Loyalty and Legislative Action: A Survey of Activity by the New York State Legislature, 1919±1949.* Ithaca, NY: Cornell University Press, 1951.

Coan, Blair. *The Red Web: An Underground Political History of the United States from 1918 to the Present Time.* Chicago, IL: Northwest Publishing Co., 1925.

Coben, Stanley. *A.Mitchell Palmer: Politician.* New York, NY: Columbia University Press, 1963.

Cooper, John Milton, Jr. *Pivotal Decades: The United States, 1900±1920.* New York, NY: W.W. Norton, 1990.

Corey, Lewis. *House of Morgan: A Social Biography of the Masters of Money.* New York, NY: G.H.Watt, 1930.

Curti, Merle. *The Roots of American Loyalty.* New York, NY: Columbia University Press, 1946.

Dmytryshyn, Basil. *U.S.S.R.: A Concise History.* Fourth edition. New York, NY: Charles Scribner's Sons, 1984.

Donner, Frank. *The Age of Surveillance.* New York, NY: Alfred Knopf, 1980.

Draper, Theodore. *American Communism and Soviet Russia: The Formative Period.* New York, NY: Viking, 1960.

——. *The Roots of American Communism.* New York, NY: Viking Press, 1957.

Dubofsky, Melvyn. *We Shall Be All: A History of the I.W.W.* Chicago, IL: Quadrangle Books, 1969.

Eldot, Paula. *Governor Alfred E. Smith: The Politician as Reformer.* New York, NY: Garland Publishing Co., 1983.

Farwell, Byron. *Over There: The United States in the Great War, 1917±1918.* New York, NY: W.W.Norton and Co., 1999.

Ferro, Marc. *The Russian Revolution of 1917.* London, England: Rutledge Press, 1972.

Fitzpatrick, Sheila. *The Russian Revolution, 1917±1932.* 2nd ed. New York: Oxford University Press, 2001.

Foner, Philip S. *The Bolshevik Revolution: Its Impact on American Radicals, Liberals, and Labor.* New York, NY: International Publishers, 1967.

Foster, William Z. *The History of the Communist Party in the United States.* New York, NY: International Publishers, 1952.

Freidel, Frank. *Over There: The Story of America's First Great Overseas Crusade.* Philadelphia, PA: Temple University Press, 1990.

Gambs, John. *The Decline of the I.W.W.* New York, NY: Columbia University Press, 1932.

Gardiner, Alfred G. *Portraits and Portents.* New York, NY: Harper and Brothers, 1926.

Gellhorn, Walter, ed. *The States and Subversion.* Westport, CT: Greenwood Press, 1976.

Gengarelly, W.Anthony. *Distinguished Dissenters and Opposition to the 1919± 1920 Red Scare.* Lewiston, NY: E.Mellen Press, 1996.

Gitlow, Benjamin. *The Whole of Their Lives.* New York, NY: Charles Scribner's Sons, 1948.

Goldman, Eric F. *Rendezvous with Destiny: A History of Modern American Reform.* New York, NY: Vintage Books, 1952.

Goldstein, Robert J. *Political Repression in Modern America from 1870 to the Present.* Cambridge, MA: Schenkman Publishing Co., 1978.

Hagedorn, Hermann. *The Magnate: William Boyce Thompson and His Time (1869- 1930).* New York, NY: Reynal and Hitchcock, 1935.

Hawley, Ellis W. *The Great War and the Search for a Modern Order: A History of the American People and Their Institutions, 1917–1933*. 2nd ed. New York, NY: St. Martin's Press, 1992.

Heale, Michael J. *American Anticommunism: Combatting the Enemy Within, 1830–1970*. Baltimore: Johns Hopkins University Press, 1990.

Hicks, Granville. *John Reed, 1887–1920*. New York, NY: Macmillan, 1934.

Higham, John. *Strangers in the Land: Patterns of American Nativism, 1860–1925*. New Brunswick, NJ: Rutgers University Press, 1955.

Hillquit, Morris. *History of Socialism in the United States*. New York, NY: Funk and Wagnalls, 1903.

Hillquit, Morris and John Ryan. *Socialism: Promise or Menace*. New York, NY: Macmillan, 1920.

Hoover, J.Edgar. *Masters of Deceit: The Story of Communism in America and How to Fight It*. New York, NY: Henry Holt and Co., 1958.

Howe, Irving and Lewis Coser. *The American Communist Party*. New York, NY: Frederick A.Praeger, 1962.

Hoyt, Edwin P. *The Palmer Raids, 1919–1920: An Attempt to Suppress Dissent*. New York, NY: Seabury Press, 1969.

Jaffe, Julian F. *Crusade Against Radicalism: New York During the Red Scare, 1914–1924*. Port Washington, NY: Kennikat Press, 1972.

Johnson, Donald O. *The Challenge to American Freedoms: World War I and the Rise of the American Civil Liberties Union*. Lexington, KY: University of Kentucky Press, 1963.

Johnson, Julia E., comp. *Freedom of Speech*. New York, NY: Scribner's, 1936.

Karsner, David F. *Debs, His Authorized Life and Letters*. New York, NY: Funk and Wagnalls, 1919.

Kennan, George F. *Decision to Intervene: Soviet-American Relations, 1917–1920*. Princeton, NJ: Princeton University Press, 1958.

———. *Russia Leaves the War: Soviet-American Relations, 1917–1920*. Princeton, NJ: Princeton University Press, 1958.

Killen, Linda. *The Russian Bureau: A Case Study in Wilsonian Diplomacy*. Lexington, KY: University Press of Kentucky, 1983.

Klingaman, William. *1919: The Year Our World Began*. New York, NY: St. Martin's Press, 1987.

Kovel, Joel. *Red Hunting in the Promised Land: Anticommunism and the Making of America*. New York: Basic Books, 1994.

Larkin, Emmet. *James Larkin: Irish Labour Leader, 1876–1947*. Cambridge, MA: M.I.T. Press, 1965.

Lenin, Vladimir. *Imperialism: The Highest Stage of Capitalism*. Peking, China: Foreign Language Press, 1975.

Lens, Sidney. *Radicalism in America*. New York, NY: Crowell Publishing, 1969.

Leuchtenburg, William E. *The Perils of Prosperity, 1914–1932*. Chicago, IL: University of Chicago Press, 1958.

Levin, Murray B. *Political Hysteria in America: The Democratic Capacity for Repression.* New York, NY: Basic Books, 1971.
Libbey, James K. *Alexander Gumberg and Soviet-American Relations, 1917±1933.* Lexington, KY: University Press of Kentucky, 1977.
——. *Russian-American Economic Relations, 1763±1999.* Gulf Breeze, FL: Academic International Press, 1999.
McFadden, David W. *Alternative Paths: Soviets and Americans, 1917±1920.* New York, NY: Oxford University Press, 1993.
Mereto, Josph J. *The Red Conspiracy.* New York, NY: National Historical Society, 1920.
Mitchell, David. *1919, Red Mirage.* New York, NY: Macmillan, 1970.
Mock, James R. and Evangeline Thurber. *Report on Demobilization.* Norman, OK: University of Oklahoma Press, 1944.
Murphy, Paul L. *The Meaning of Freedom of Speech: First Amendment Freedoms from Wilson to F.D.R.* Westport, CT: Greenwood Publishing Co., 1972.
——. *World War I and the Origin of Civil Liberties in the United States.* New York, NY: W.W.Norton and Co., 1979.
Murray, Robert K. *Red Scare: A Study in National Hysteria, 1919±1920.* Minneapolis, MN: University of Minnesota Press, 1955.
Nielsen, Kim E. *Un-American Womanhood: Antiradicalism, Antifeminism, and the First Red Scare.* Columbus, OH: Ohio State University Press, 2001.
O'Neal, James. *American Communism.* New York, NY: The Rand School, 1927.
Panunzio, Constantine. *Deportation Cases of 1919±1920.* New York, NY: Federal Council of Churches of Christ in America, 1921.
Park, Robert E. *The Immigrant Press and Its Control.* New York, NY: Putnam's, 1922.
Parker, Carelton. *The Casual Laborer and Other Essays.* New York, NY: Scribner's, 1920.
Possony, Stefan. *Lenin: The Compulsive Revolutionary.* London, England: George Allen and Unwin, 1966.
Post, Louis E *The Deportation Deliriums of the Nineteen-Twenties.* Chicago, IL: Charles Kerr, 1923.
Preston, William Jr. *Aliens and Dissenters: Federal Suppression of Radicals, 1903±1933.* Cambridge, MA: Harvard University Press, 1963.
Queen, George S. *The United States and the Material Advance in Russia, 1881±1906.* New York, NY: Arno Press, 1976.
Rabinowitch, Alexander. *The Bolsheviks Come to Power.* New York, NY: W.W.Norton and Co., 1976.
Salvatore, Nick. *Eugene V.Debs: Citizen and Socialist.* Urbana, IL: University of Illinois Press, 1982.

Schmidt, Regin. *Red Scare: FBI and the Origins of Anticommunism in the United States, 1919±1943.* Copenhagen, Denmark: Museum Tusculanum Press, University of Copenhagen, 2000.

Schultz, Bud and Ruth. *It Did Happen Here: Recollections of Political Repression in America.* Berkeley, CA: University of California Press, 1989.

Schulz, Heinrich E., et al., eds. *Who Was Who in the U.S.S.R.: A Biographic Directory Containing 5,015 Biographies of Prominent Soviet Historical Personalities.* Metuchen, NJ: Scarecrow Press, 1972.

Schuman, Frederick Lewis. *American Policy Toward Russia Since 1917: A Study of Diplomatic History, International Law and Public Opinion.* New York, NY: International Publishers, 1928.

Shannon, David A. *Between the Wars: America, 1919±1941.* Boston, MA: Houghton Mifflin Co., 1965.

———. *The Socialist Party of America.* New York, NY: Macmillan Co., 1955.

Siegel, Katherine A.S. *Loans and Legitimacy: The Evolution of Soviet-American Relations, 1919±1933.* Lexington, KY: University Press of Kentucky, 1996.

Soule, George. *Prosperity Decade, From War to Depression: 1917±1929.* New York, NY: Harper and Row, 1947.

Strakhovsky, Leonid I. *American Opinion About Russia, 1917±1920.* Toronto, Canada: University of Toronto Press, 1961.

Suny, Ronald and Arthur Adams. *The Russian Revolution and Bolshevik Victory: Visions and Revisions,* 3rd edition. New York, NY: D.C. Heath and Co., 1990.

Sutton Antony C. *Wall Street and the Bolshevik Revolution.* New York, NY: Arlington House, 1974.

———. *Western Technology and Soviet Economic Development.* Volume One. Stanford, CA: Hoover Institution Press, 1968.

Wade, Rex. *The Bolshevik Revolution and Russian Civil War.* Westport, CT: Greenwood Press, 2001.

Waldman, Louis. *Albany: The Crisis in Government: The History of the Suspension, Trial and Expulsion from the New York State Legislature in 1920 of Five Socialist Assemblymen by Their Political Opponents.* New York, NY: Boni and Liveright, 1920.

Weinstein, James K. *The Decline of Socialism in America, 1912±1925.* New York, NY: Monthly Review Press, 1967.

White, Christine A. *British & American Commercial Relations with Soviet Russia, 1918±1924.* Chapel Hill, NC: University of North Carolina Press, 1992.

Whitney, Richard M. *Reds in America.* New York, NY: Berkwith Press, 1924.

Wilkins, Mira and Frank Ernest Hill. *American Business Abroad: Ford on Six Continents.* Detroit, MI: Wayne State University Press, 1964.

Williams, William Appleman. *American-Russian Relations, 1781±1947.* New York, NY: Rinehart and Co., 1952.

Wilson, Joan Hoff. *Ideology and Economics: U.S. Relations with the Soviet Union, 1918±1933*. Columbia, MO: University of Missouri Press, 1974.

Wise, Jennings C. *Woodrow Wilson: Disciple of Revolution*. New York, NY: Paisley Press, 1974.

SECONDARY ARTICLES

"Albany's Ousted Socialists."*Literary Digest.* 62 (January 24, 1920): 19–20.

"American Labor and Bolshevism."*Literary Digest.* 61 (June 21, 1919): 9–11.

"The Anarchist Deportations." *New Republic.* 21 (December 24, 1919): 96–98.

"Are American Liberties Worth Saving?" *Nation.* 110 (April 17, 1920): 506–508.

"Are Socialists Citizens?" *Survey.* 43 (January 17, 1920): 417.

Blum, John M. "Nativism, Anti-Radicalism, and the Foreign Scare, 1917–1920." *Midwest Journal.* 3 (Winter 1950–1951): 46–53.

"Bolshevik Mutterings Here." *Literary Digest.* 59 (December 7, 1918): 17–19.

"Bolsheviki in the United States." *Literary Digest.* 60 (February 22, 1919): 11–13.

"Bolshevism in New York and Russian Schools." *Literary Digest.* 61 (July 5, 1919): 40–41.

"Bolshevist School Teachers." *Literary Digest.* 61 (April 5, 1919): 31–32.

Brooks, Sidney. "Russia as a Great Power." *World's Work.* 2 (1901): 1280–1287.

Brown, Rome G. "The Disloyalty of Socialism." *American Law Review.* 53 (September 1919): 681.

"By Stevenson Out of Lusk." *New Republic.* 27 (June 1921): 64–66.

"Campaign to Repeal Lusk Loyalty Laws in New York." *School and Society.* 16 (December 9, 1922): 658–659.

Chafee, Zechariah, Jr. "Progress of the Law—Evidence." *Harvard Law Review.* 35 (1922): 694–704.

——."The Rand School Case." *New Republic.* 32 (September 1922): 118–121.

Claghorn, Kate. "Aliens and Sedition in the New Year." *Survey.* 43 (January 17, 1920): 422–423.

Cobb, Frank. "The Press and Public Opinion." *New Republic.* 21 (December 31, 1919): 142–145.

Coben, Stanley. "A Study in Nativism: The American Red Scare of 1919–1920." *Political Science Quarterly.* 79 (1964): 52–75.

Colburn, David R. "Governor Alfred E.Smith and the Red Scare, 1919–1920." *Political Science Quarterly.* 88 (1973): 423–444.

Collins, Peter W. "Bolshevism in America." *Current Opinion.* 68 (March 1920): 322–327.

"Current Event and Commentary." *United Presbyterian.* 77 (May 8, 1919): 7.

"Demoralized Schools." *New Republic.* 31 (May 31, 1922): 8–9.

"Declining Power of the Russian Reds: Release of Tredwell." *Current History.* 10 (1919): 482–483.

"Deportation of Alien Anarchists: Anti-Red Drive Continues." *Current History.* 11 (1919–1920): 231–234.

"The Deportations." *Survey.* 41 (February 22, 1919): 722.

"Deporting the Communist Party." *Literary Digest.* 62 (February 14, 1920): 18–19.

"Deporting a Political Party." *New Republic.* 21 (January 14, 1920): 186.

DeSilver, Albert. "The Lusk-Stevenson Report: A State Document." *Nation.* 113 (July 13, 1921): 38–40.

"The Dismissal of Communist Teachers in New York City." *School and Society.* 10 (November 22, 1919): 605–606.

"Education from Albany." *Nation.* (May 8, 1920): 613.

"Educators Demand Repeal of Lusk 'Loyalty' Law for New York Teachers." *School and Society.* 15 (June 3, 1922): 605–606.

"Extent of Bolshevism Here." *Literary Digest.* 62 (January 17, 1920): 13–15.

Frank, Glenn. "Al Smith Pardons Jim Larkin." *Century Magazine.* 105 (1923): 797–800.

"Freedom of Speech in the New York City Schools." *School and Society.* 9 (February 8, 1919): 178.

Gak, Alexander. "Lenin and the Americans." *New World Review.* 35 (1967): 37–43.

Gannett, Louis S. "The Socialist Trial at Albany: A Summary." *Nation.* 110 (March 20, 1920): 361–363.

Giddings, Franklin H. "The Bolsheviki Must Go." *Independent.* 92 (January 18, 1919): 87–97.

———."Three Vicious Bills." *Independent.* 102 (April 10, 1920): 53–55.

"Governor Smith of New York on Education." *School and Society.* 17 (February 3, 1923): 123–124.

Harre, T.Evertt. "Plot to Overthrow the Government." *The National Civic Federation Review.* 4 (July 25, 1919): 2–3.

Hart, Joseph K. "The Lusk Reports." *Survey.* 46 (May 28, 1921): 264–265.

Hill, Ebenezer J. "A Trip Through Siberia." *National Geographic.* 13 (1902): 49–57.

"How the Russian Bolshevist Agent Does Business in New York City." *Literary Digest.* 61 (May 17, 1919): 60–63.

Howard, Sidney. "Our Professional Patriots." *New Republic.* 40 (September 13, 1924): 12–16.

"Human Vermin." *American Law Review.* 53 (May 1919): 430–435.

"Is Bolshevism in America Becoming a Real Peril?" *Current Opinion.* 67 (July 1919): 4–6.

Josephson, Harold. "The Dynamics of Repression: New York During the Red Scare." *Mid-America.* 59 (1977): 131–146.

"Justice for Alien Reds: Policy of Louis F.Post." *Literary Digest.* 63 (May 22, 1920): 25.
Karsner, David. "The Passing of the Socialist Party." *Current History.* 20 (1924): 402–407.
Lusk, Clayton R. "Hatching Revolution in America." *Current Opinion.* 71 (September 1921): 290–294.
———. "Radicalism Under Inquiry: Conclusions Reached After a Year's Study of Alien Anarchy in America." *American Review of Reviews.* 61 (1920): 167–171.
"The Lusk Bills." *Outlook.* 133 (March 21, 1923): 523–524.
"The Lusk Committee." *Survey.* 42 (July 19, 1919): 602.
"The Lusk Laws and New York City Teachers." *School and Society.* 16 (October 28, 1922): 494–495.
"The Lusk Loyalty Laws."*School and Society.* 17 (January 13, 1923): 45.
"The Lusk School Laws." *School and Society.* 17 (February 10, 1923): 154–155.
"Making Teaching Efficient and Patriotic." *Outlook.* 122 (May 21, 1919): 100.
"May Day Rioting." *Nation.* 108 (May 10, 1919): 725–726.
Mitchell, John Bruce. "Reds' in New York's Slums—How Insidious Doctrines Are Propagated in New York's Lower 'East Side.'" *Forum.* 61 (April 1919): 442–445.
"The New Sherlock Holmes." *Nation.* 108 (February 1, 1919): 155–156.
O'Neal, James. "The Changing Fortunes of American Socialism." *Current History.* 20 (1924): 92–97.
Palmer, A.Mitchell. "The Case Against the Reds." *Forum.* 63 (February 1920): 173–185.
Paxson, Frederick L. "The Great Demobilization." *American Historical Review.* 44 (January 1939): 243–247.
"Promoters of Agitation and Unrest." *Industry.* (June 15, 1919): 3.
Robins, Col. Raymond. "U.S. Recognition of Soviet Russia Essential to World Peace and Stabilization." *Annals of the American Academy of Political and Social Science.* 126 (1926): 100–104.
"Rounding Up the Parlor Reds." *Literary Digest.* 62 (July 5, 1919): 27–28.
"Russian in the Balance: Raid on Soviet Embassy." *Current History.* 10 (1919): 264–265.
"Russia's Warfare on Many Fronts: Soviet Envoy in America." *Current History.* 10 (1919): 267–268.
Ryan, John. "The Lusk Report's Brazen Industrial Feudalism." *Nation.* 113 (July 27, 1921): 99–100.
"Schools a la Lusk." *Survey.* 43 (March 27, 1920): 799–800.
"Shipping Lenin's Friends to Him." *Literary Digest.* 62 (January 3, 1920): 14–15.
"Small and Lusk." *Outlook.* 128 (August 17, 1921): 596–597.
"Socialism on Trial at Albany." *Literary Digest.* 62 (February 7, 1920): 14–15.
"Soviet Envoy in America." *Current History.* 10 (April-June 1919): 267–268.

"The Subversion of Public Education." *New Republic.* 29 (February 1, 1922): 259–262.

"The *Times* and the Lusk Bills." *New Republic.* 26 (May 25, 1921): 369–370.

"The Truth About Soviet Russia and Bolshevism." *American Federationist.* 27 (March 1920): 254.

Urofsky, Melvin I. "A Note on the Expulsion of Five Socialists." *New York History.* 47 (1966): 41–49.

Vadney, Thomas E. "The Politics of Repression: A Case Study of the Red Scare in New York." *New York History.* 49 (1968): 56–75.

"Veto of the New York State Legislature Bills." *School and Society.* 11 (May 29, 1920): 645–646.

Warth, Robert D. "The Palmer Raids." *South Atlantic Quarterly.* 48 (1949): 1–23.

"What Is Back of the Bombs?" *Literary Digest.* 61 (June 14, 1919): 8–11.

"Where Do the Reds Come From?" *American Legion Weekly.* (January 30, 1920): 12–13.

Woll, Matthew. "The Thing Called Bolshevism." *American Federationist.* 26 (March 1919): 236.

UNPUBLISHED MANUSCRIPTS

Fithian, Floyd J. "Soviet-American Economic Relations, 1918–1933: American Business in Russia During the Period of Nonrecognition." Ph.D. Dissertation, University of Nebraska, 1964.

Graves, Thomas W. "The Lusk Committee and the People of New York State." M.A.Thesis, American University, 1959.

Kugel, Barbara. "The Export of American Technology to the Soviet Union, 1918–1933." Z M.A Thesis, Wayne State University, 1956.

Petix, Joseph R. "An Account of the Investigation of Radical Activities in New York Following World War I, Chiefly as Reported in the New York *Times*." M.A.Thesis, New York University, 1951.

Wingo, Patricia W. "Clayton R.Lusk: A Study of Patriotism in New York Politics, 1919- 1923." Ph.D. Dissertation, University of Georgia, 1966.

Index

A.Klipstein and Co. 145
A.Mecky Co. 146
A.Rosalsky and Brother 147
A.B.Farquhar Co. Ltd. 143
A.D.Baker Co. 139
A.E.Nettleton Co. 146
A&F Brown Co. 141
A.G.Hyde and Sons 144
A.J.Alsdorf Co. 138
A.J.Lindemann and Hoverson Co. 145
A.P.W.Paper Co. 139
A.S.Haight and Co. 144
Aaronson, I. 138
Abbott, J.W. 57, 138
Abbott Ball Co. 138
Abbott Laboratories 138
Abendroth Brothers 138
Acason Motor Trucks 138
Acme Knit Goods Novelty Co. 138
Acme Shear Co. 138
Acushnet Mill Corp. 138
Adams, B.F. 138
Adams Co. 138
Adams-Grunewald Private Detective Agency 65
Addams, Jane 11, 13
Adelphi College 102
Adler, Simon 124
Admiral Hay Press Co. 138
Adrian Knitting Co. 138
Advance Rumley Thresher Co. 138

Aermeter Co. 138
Aerothrust Engine Co. 138
African-Americans 5, 16, 77, 87–88, 91
Agrippa Manufacturing Co. 138
Ajax Rubber Co. 138
Akron-Selle Co. 138
Alaska Packers Association 138
Alexander Brothers 138
Alexander, Leo and Co. 138
All Souls Church (New York City) 22
Alliance Machine Co. 138
Allied American Corp. 61
Allied Drug and Chemical Co. 40
Allied Machinery Co. of America 138
Allied Manufacturers Export Co. 138
Allied Patriotic Societies 124
Alpine Knitting Mills 138
Alsberg, Carl 50
Aluminum Goods Manufacturing Co. 60, 138
Amalgamated Clothing Workers 111, 151
Amalgamated Textile Workers 111
Ambrosia Chocolate Co. 138
American Agricultural Chemical Co. 138
American Alcohol Co. 138
American Aniline Products 56, 138
American Asphalt Association 138
American Bleached Goods Co. 138
American Blower Co. 138

American Bosch Magneto Co. 138
American Brass Co. 138
American Car Co. 138
American Car and Foundry Export Co. 138
American Cast Iron Pipe Co. 138
American Chain Co. 138
American Civil Liberties Union 151
American Commercial Association to Promote Trade with Russia 40–42
American Defense Society 1, 22, 81, 113
American Distilling Co. 138
American-European Industries Inc. 138
American Envelope and Paper Co. 138
American Federation of Labor 17, 22
American Food Products Co. 139
American Fork and Hoe Co. 139
American Friends Service Committee 13
American Graphite Co. 139
American Guardian Society 22
American Hoist and Derrick Co. 139
American Horse Show Works 139
American Hosiery Co. 139
American Insulated Wire and Cable Co. 139
American International Corp. 139
The American Labor Year Book 80
American Lead Pencil Co. 139
American Legion 113, 123
American Linoleum Manufacturing Co. 139
American Manufacturing Co. 139
American Milling Co. 139
American Mining Tool Co. 139
American Motors Inc. 139
American Museum of Natural History 77, 151
American Pad and Textile Co. 139
American Paper Export Inc. 139
American Paper Exporters 139

American Potash Co. 139
American Protective Association 84
American Red Cross viii–x
American Sewer Pipe Co. 139
American Six Automobiles 139
American Socialist Society 76, 85, 87, 91–98, 115–116, 130
American Spinning Co. 139
American Steam Pump Co. 139
American Steel Export Co. 139
American Sterilizer Co. (NY) 139
American Sterilizer Co. (PA) 139
American Thermos Bottle Co. 139
American Tobacco Co. 139
American Tool Works Co. 139
American Transformer Co. 139
American Tube and Stamping Co. 139
American Tube Works 139
American Type Founders 139
American Universal Service 42
American Valve Co. 139
American Vanadium 139
American Wire Fabrics Co. 139
American Wood Working Machinery Co. 139
Americanism xi, 1–3, 8, 10, 24, 100–103, 124
Amherst College 38
Amitale Corp. 139
Amory, Browne and Co. 139
Amtorg Trading Corp. 61
Anderson Tool and Supply Co. 139
Ansco Co. 139
Anthaus Trading Co. 62, 139, 149
Antin, Benjamin 122
Anti-Terrorist Act I 133
Apex Spark Plug Co. 47, 139
Appleton Wire Works 139
Arabel Paper Co. 139
Arbatov, Georgi 58
Armour and Co. 56, 59, 60, 139
Armour Leather Co. 139
Armstrong Cork Co. 139

Armstrong Manufacturing Co. 139
Arner, G.B.L. 150
Arnold and Co. 139
Arnold, Hoffman and Co. 56, 139
Arnold Print Works 139
Atlantic Bag Co. 139
Atlas Co. 139
Atlas Tack Co. 139
Atwater Manufacturing Co. 139
Audiffren Refrigerating Machine Co. 139
Aultman and Taylor Machinery Co. 139
Austin Co., Inc. 139
Austin Manufacturing Co. (IL) 139
Austin Manufacturing Co. (NY) 139
Automatic Button Co. 139
Automatic Transportation Co. 139
Automobile Products Corp. 139
Automotive Products Corp. 139
Avery Co. 139
Ayre, Lincoln 42

B.Souto Co. 147
B.F.Avery and Sons 139
B.F.Drakenfeld and Co., Inc. 142
B.H.Howell and Son Co. 144
B.K.Elliott Co. 142
Babbitt, B.A. 139
Bachman and Co. 139
Baeder, Adamson and Co. 139
Baer Brothers 139
Bail Brothers Glass Manufacturing Co. 139
Bailey, William 65
Baker, Newton 13
Baker Chemical Co. 139
Baker Manufacturing Co. 139
Bakhmeteff, Boris 43
Balboni, Michael 134
Baldwin, Roger 11
Balfour, Guthrie and Co. 139
Balfour, Williamson and Co. 139
Ball, Charles J. 139

Baltimore Pearl Hominy Co. 139
Bankhead, John H. 47
Banting Manufacturing Co. 139
Barcale Manufacturing Co. 139
Barker, William C. 140
Barnard College 151
Barr Shipping Co. 140
Barrows, George E. 57
Barstow Stove Co. 140
Bartley Crucible Co. 140
Bateman Manufacturing Co. 140
Baruch, Bernard xiv
Batuibak Brass Co. 140
Baugh Chemical Co. 56, 140
Baum and Bender 140
Bausche and Lomb Optical Co. 140
Bay State Milling Co. 140
Bay State Threading Works 140
Beacon Falls Rubber Shoe Co. 140
Beard, Charles A. 11, 77, 150
Beardsley, Samuel 150
Beaver Companies 140
Beck, N. 140
Beckwith Co. 140
Beckwith-Chandler Co. 140
Beggs and Cobb, Inc. 140
Belais, David 140
Belcher and Loomis Hardware Co. 140
Belden Manufacturing Co. 140
Benedict Manufacturing Co. 140
Berenberg, David P. 77, 79, 88
Berg Brothers 140
Berg Co. 140
Berger, Samuel 23, 70, 84, 85, 91, 93–94, 96, 97, 107, 116
Berger, Victor L. 6, 27
Berger Manufacturing Co. 140
Berkman, Alexander 30
Berlin Construction Co., Inc. 140
Bernstein, C.A. 140
Bernstein, N. 140
Berry, A.Hall 140

INDEX   211

Bertelson and Peterson Engineering Co. 140
Bessemer Gas Engine Co. 140
Best-Clymer Manufacturing Co. 140
Bethlehem Motors Corp. 140
Bethlehem Steel Co. 140
Bettendorf Co. 140
Binney and Smith Co. 140
Birch, James H. 140
Bishop and Babcock Co. 140
Bishop Guta-Percha Co. 140
Bishop's Service 140
Blackstone Manufacturing Co. 140
Blake and Johnson Co. 140
Blake Pump and Condenser Co. 140
Block, S.John 84–85, 90–91, 97–98, 104, 109, 113, 115
Blodgett, Frank Dickinson 102
Bloom, Berle C. 140
Blumenthal, M. 140
Bobroff Foreign Trading and Engineering Co. 42, 140, 149
Bodman, G.M. 63
Boise, E.C. 140
Boker Cutlery and Hardware Co. 140
Bolshevism viii–xi, 3, 5, 8–11, 14, 15, 16, 17, 20–25, 30, 33, 34, 44, 48, 73, 74, 81, 84, 91, 99, 135
Bomack Paper Corp. 140
bomb scares xi, xii, 10, 25–29, 32, 33, 64, 126
Bonn, A. 140
Bonner and Barnewell 140
Boot and Shoe Recorder Publishing Co. 140
Borah, William E. 71
Borden's Condensed Milk Sales Co. 140
Bossert Corp. 140
Boston Corp. 140
Boston Molasses Co. 140
Boston Thread Co. 140
Boston Varnish Co. 140

Boston Woven Hose and Rubber Co. 140
Botany Worsted Mills 140
Bourne-Fuller Co. 140
Bovaird and Seyeang Manufacturing Co. 140
Bowen Products Corp. 140
Boylan, John J. 20, 23, 85, 105
Bradley Pulverizer Co. 140
Bradstreet's 54
Brand Breadhead Worsted Mills 140
Brandegee, Frank B. 71
Brandeis, Louis 49, 50
Braude-Goodman Shoe Co. 140
Brecht Co. 140
Brennan Packing Co. 140
Brent, Charles 122
Brey, W.R. 65
Bridgeport Chain Co. 140
Bridgeport Rolling Mills 57, 140
Brimberg, H. 140
Bristol Brass Corp. 140
British Woman's Trade Union League 151
Brockway Motor Truck Co. 140
Brooks, A.M. 140
Brooks, Sidney 52
Brooks Unifrom Co. 141
Broom and Newman 141
Brough, Alexander 64–67
Browder, Earl 136
Brown, Elmer E. 45, 102
Brown, Elon 107–108
Brown Hoisting Machine Co. 141
Brown Shoe Co. 141
Brown University 77, 151
Brown Whales Co. 141
Bruno, Joseph 133–134
Bryant Electric Co. 141
Bryn Mawr College 122
Buckeye Aluminum Co. 141
Bud, Reginald viii
Buffalo Pitts Co. 141
Bullard Machine Tool Co. 141

212 INDEX

Bullitt, William 36
Bureau of Labor Statistics 4
Burleson, Albert S. 27
Burnham and Merrill Co. 141
Burns and Bassick Co. 141
Burr, Frederick S. 23
Bush, Beach and Gent, Inc. 141
Butler, Nicholas Murray 3
Byblcki, Edward C. 104

C.B.Cottrell and Sons Co. 141
C.B.Hayward and Co. 144
C.D.Brown and Co. 141
C.D.Durkee and Co. 142
C.T.Silver, Inc. 147
Cairo Thread Works 141
Calder, William N. 47
California Fruit Growers Exchange 141
California Packing Corp. 141
Caminetti, Anthony J. 27
Cannon Mills 141
Cape Ann Fish Net Co. 141
Capewell Horse Rail Co. 141
Carborundum Co. 141
Carl Dernberg and Son 142
Carolina Junk and Hide Co. 56, 141
Carpenter Steel Co. 141
Carrol, Martin viii
Carroll, Daniel J. 23
Carter, C.L. 141
Carter, Cynthia x–xi
Carter, Macy and Co., Inc. 141
Carus Chemical Co. 141
Carver-Beaver Yarn Co., Inc. 141
Castle Tobacco Works 141
Catlin and Co. 141
Cattaraucus Cutlery Co. 141
Central Rope Manufacturing Co., Inc. 141
Central Scientific Co. 141
Certain-teed Products Corp. 141
Chadbourne, Thomas L. 41
Chaffee, Zechariah A. 100, 127–129

Chalmers Knitting Co. 141
chambers of commerce 42, 58
Chanutin, J.V. 141
Charles Leffler and Co. 145
Charles Maschwitz, Jr., Inc. 146
Charles Parker Co. 146
Charles Pfizer and Co., Inc. 146
Charles R.Flint and Co. 143
Charles T.Stork and Co. 147
Charlottesville Woolen Mills 141
Chatham Manufacturing Co. 141
Chatham Shirt Co. 141
Chicago *Daily Tribune* 57
Chicago Pneumatic Tool Co. 141
Chicago Spring Butt Co. 141
Christian Science Monitor 10
Church of the Messiah (New York City) 11, 150
Churchill, S. 141
Cincinnati (OH) Chamber of Commerce 42
Citizens' Committee for the Repeal of the Lusk Laws 123
City Club of Cleveland 121
City College of New York 77
Claessens, August 20–21, 102, 150
Clarence Whitman and Son, Inc. 148
Clark, Evans 38, 48, 49, 50–51, 56, 60, 63, 64, 67, 150
Cleveland Brass and Copper Mills 141
Cleveland Twist Drill Co. 141
Clift and Goodrich 141
Clifton Manufacturing Co. 141
Clyde Mills 141
Cobb, Frank 1
Cohen, Paula 95
Colcord, Lincoln 69
Colgate and Co. 141
Collegiate League for Morris Hillquit 38
Collins and Co. 141
Columbia University 3, 10, 11, 38, 39, 69, 77, 102, 106, 150

INDEX 213

Columbian Bronze Corp. 141
Columbian Chemical Co. 141
Columbian Enameling and Stamping Co. 141
Columbus McKinnon Chain Co. 141
Commercial Acceptance Trust Co. 141
Commercial High School (New York City) viii, 113, 138
Committee on Public Information 1, 5
The Communist 88
Communist Labor Party 6, 8–9, 37, 95, 126
Communist Party of America 6, 8–9, 40, 72, 126–127, 136
Coneybear, Robert W. 141
Conference of the Young Democracy 86

Conkling, Robert S. 65
Connecticut Brass and Mfg. Corp. 141
Connecticut Steel Corp. 141
Consolidated Rendering Co. 141
Consolidated Safety Pin Co. 141
Consolidated Steel Corp. 141
Consolidated Tea Co. 141
Contecook Mills 141
Continental Rubber Works 141
Converse, Clarence L. 24, 64, 83–85, 94, 96
Cooper, John Milton, Jr. 4
Cooper and Cooper Chemical Co. 55, 141
Cooperative League of America 151
Corbitt Motor Truck Co. 141
Corn Exchange Bank 63
Corn Products Refining Co. 141
Cornell University 23
Coss, John Jacob 102
Cotillo, Salvatore 112
Coulter and McKenzie Machine Co. 141
Cowan Trucking Co. 141

Cowen, Mark 141
Crane and Co. 141
Creel, George 1, 3, 5
Crescent Forge and Shovel Co. 141
Crescent Trading Co. 141
Cribben and Sexton Co. 141
Croft, Ralph 141
Crompton Co. 141
Crompton and Knowles Loom Works 141
Cronk and Carrier Mfg. Co. 141
Crown Optical Co. 141
Crystal Knitting Mills, Inc. 141
Cudahy Brothers, Inc. 141
Cudahy Packing Co. 57, 59, 141
Cumberland Steel Co. 141
Curtis and Curtis Co. 142
Cushman, Robert E. 132
Cushman-Hollis Co. 142
Cyclops Steel Co. 142

D.J.Faour and Brothers 143
Damascus Manufacturing Co. (NY)
Dangler Stove Co. (NY)
Daniel Saks, Inc. 147
Dartmouth College 77, 150
Davenport, Frederick S. 105, 112
David Bradley Manufacturing Works 140
David Maydale Hammer Co. 146
Davis Machine Tool Co., Inc. 142
Davis Manufacturing Co. 142
Debs, Eugene 6–7, 80, 116
Deere and Co. 142
Defiance Machine Works 142
Deforest Sheet and Tin Plate Co. 142
Delvin Sales Co. 142
Demidoff Iron and Steel Works 37
Dennison Manufacturing Co. 142
DeSilver, Albert 86
Detroit Electric Car Co. 142
Detroit Stove Works 142
Devine, Edward T. 113
DeWitt, Samuel 102

214 INDEX

DeWitt Clinton High School (New York City) 14
Dickinson and Co. 142
Dillon, John 150
Diswick, Elais 142
Dodge, W.Copeland 105
Doherry and Wadsworth Co. 142
Domingo, William A. 87, 88, 91
Dominion Brush Manufacturing Co. 142
Doninger and Co. 142
Donohue, Charles D. 21
Dotey, Aaron 113
Dougherty, A. 142
Douglas Co. 142
Downing, Bernard 122, 123
Draman, Dwight 124
Dress and Waist Manufacturers Association 14
Driver-Harris Co. 142
Drueding Brothers Co. 142
Dry Milk Co. 142
Duane, Thomas 134
DuBois, W.E.B. 77, 150
Duckwell Belting and Hose Co. 142
Duesenberg Motors Corp. 142
Duff Manufacturing Co. 142
Dunbar Molasses and Syrup Co. 142
Duncan, James 150
Dundee Textile Co. 142
Duplex Channel Pin Co. 142
Duplex Printing Press Co. 142
Duplex Truck Co. 142

E.Clemens Horst Co. 141
E.Ingram Co. 144
E.B.Hindley and Co. 144
E.I.duPont de Nemours Export Co. 142
E.N.Arnold Shoe Co. 139
E.W.Rosenthal and Co. 147
Eakle, Charles M. 142
Eastern Talc Co. 142
East Side Packing Co. 142

Eaton, Charles A. 16
Eberhard Faber 142
Economy Fuse and Mfg. Co. 142
education viii–xii, 14–15, 76–126
    Americanization courses 104
    Lusk Committee hearings on 102–103
    school licensing 103–118, 121–126, 131, 135
    teacher loyalty oaths 103–114, 118–126, 131, 135
Edward L.Ladew Co. 145
Eimer and Amend 142
Einstein-Wolff Co. 142
Elber Co. 142
Elder Manufacturing Co. 142
Electric Hose and Rubber Co. 142
Electric Wheel Co. 142
Electro Dental Manufacturing Co. 142
Eline Berlow Commercial Agency 62, 140, 149
Elliott Frog and Switch Co. 142
Ellis, Wade H. 71
Ellis Steel Cushion Tire Co. 142
Elwell-Parker Electric Co. 142
The Emancipator 87
Emergency Education Conference of the Central Federated Union 104, 111
Emergency Peace Federation 1
Emerson-Brantingham Implement Co. 142
Emerson International Inc. 142
Emery Candle Co. 142
Emil Kaufmann Co. 145
Emlenton Refining Co. 142
Empire Cream Separator Co. 142
Empire Manufacturing Co. (IL) 142
Empire Manufacturing Co. (NY) 142
Endicott Johnson Shoe Co. 145
Enright, Richard 16, 27
Enterprise Co. 142
Equitable Life Assurance Society 54

INDEX 215

Ervin, Charles 95
Erwin Cotton Mills Co. 142
Espionage Act 1, 6, 87
Estes Mills 142
Ettinger, William 14, 102–103
Eugene Ditzgen Co., Inc. 142
Evans, William S. 106
Ever Ready Specialty Co. 142
Executive Committee of Seventeen 111
Exporters Drygoods Exchange 142
Exporters Purchasing Association 142

F.Mayer Boot and Shoe Co. 146, 149
F.A.Brady, Inc. 140
F.D.Dirwick and Co., Inc. 142
F.E.Myers and Brothers 146
F.H.Lawson Co. 145
F.I.A.T. 143
F. & J.Meyer Co. 146
F.S.Webster Co. 148
Faber, A.W. 142
Fabyan Bliss and Co. 140
Fairbanks Co. 142
Falk Co. 143
Fashion Childrens Dress Co. 143
Federal Glass Co. 143
Federal Plate Glass Co. of Illinois 143
Federal Motor Truck Co. 143
Federal Reserve Board 41, 47
Federal Rope Co. 143
Feingolf, Nathaniel 143
Fellows Gear Shaper Co. 143
Felt and Tarrant Manufacturing Co. 143
Ferrari, Robert 150
Fertig, M.Maldwin 20
Finch, R.W. 64
Finch Manufacturing Co. 143
Findelsen and Kropf Manufacturing Co. 143
Finnish Labor Movement 38

First National Bank of New York 63
Fischmann and Co. 62, 143, 149
Fish Clearing House 143
Fisher, Willard C. 150
Fisk Rubber Co. 143
Fitch, John 150
Fitzgerald, M.D. 143
Fitzsimons Co. 143
Five-Year Plan 135
Flagg, James Montgomery 1
Flash Chemical Co. 143
Florence Manufacturing Co. 143
Flynn, Elizabeth Gurley 150
Food Administration xiv
Ford, Henry 61
Ford Corporation 143
Ford Motor Co. 49, 56, 60–61, 135, 143
Ford Roofing Products Co. 143
Foreign Products Co., Inc. 143
Forstmann and Huffmann Co. 143
The Forum 15
Foster, Walter 119
Foster Wheel Drive Auto Co. 143
France, Joseph 47, 48
Francis, David 55
Franco-American Food Co. 143
Frank B.Graves Co. 143
Frank S.Betz Co. 140
Frank W.Hunt and Co. 144
Frankfurter, Felix 127–129
Franklin Manufacturing Co. 143
Frayne, Hugh 22
Frazer, D.O. 56–57, 59
Fred Reed Corp. 147
Frederick Lausser and Son 145
Frederick Motor Truck Co. 143
Free Sewing Machine Co. 143
Frick Co., Inc. 143
Frye and Co. 143
Fuld and Match Knitting Co. 143
Futterman and Co. 143

G.W.Hume Co. 144

Galbraith, F.W. 113
Gardener Governor Co. 143
Garford Manufacturing Co. 143
Garford Motor Truck Co. 143
Garland Manufacturing Co. 143
Gary, Elbert H. 59
Gas Oil Stove Co. 143
Gash, Abraham 143
Gaston, Williams & Wigmore, Inc. 62, 143
Gavegan, Edward J. 91–92
Gaynor Glass Works 143
Gegan, James 15
Gehl Brothers Manufacturing Co. 143
Geisman, Nusliner and Brightman 143
General Asbestos and Rubber Co. (NC) 143
General Asbestos and Rubber Co. (NY) 143
General Electric Co. 60, 135, 143
General Fastener Co. 143
General Motors Corp. 60
General Motors Truck Co. 143
General Ordnance Co. 143
George W.Blabon Co. 140
Georgetown University 27
Gerber, Julius 22
Getz Brothers and Co. 143
Gibbs, Stephen 105
Giddings, Franklin 10–11
Giddings, William H. 106
Giegerich, Leonard A. 70
Gilbert, Charles K. 121
Gilbert, Frank G. 115, 138
Gilbert and Barker Manufacturing Co. 143
Gilbert Knitting Co. 143
Gill, Robert 143
Gill Brothers Co. 143
Gillette Safety Razor Co. 143
Gilman, Charlotte Perkins 150
Gimbel Brothers Co. 26

Gitlow, Benjamin 9, 37, 39, 40–41, 42
Glassberg, Benjamin viii–x, xii, 14, 136–138
Globe Soap Co. 143
Globe Stove and Range Co. 143
Glover Machine Works 143
Glunhanck and Hill Co. 143
Goldblatt, Leo 143
Goldman, Emma 30
Goldstein, Robert J. 132
Goldstein and Newburger Co. 143
Goodall Worsted Co. 143
Goodell-Pratt Co. 143
Goodman Manufacturing Co. 143
Goodyear Rubber Co. 60, 135, 143
Gordon Tire and Rubber Co. 143
Goshen Shirt Manufacturing Co. 143
Goss Printing Press Co. 143
Grace American International Co. 143
Grafton Johnson Co. 143
Grand Rapids Underwear Co. 143
Grant, Robert 55
Grant Iron and Steel Co. 55, 143
Grasselli Chemical Co. 56, 143
Graton and Knight Manufacturing Co. 143
Graves, Frank R 118–121
Great Depression 135, 136, 138
Great Republic Tire and Rubber Manufacturing Co. 143
Great Western Electric Chemical Co. 144
Green and Daniels Co., Inc. 144
Green Fuel Economiser Co. 144
Greenbaum, Samuel 70
Greenberg, Maurice 144
Greenfield Tap and Die Corp. 144
Greenlee Brothers and Co. 144
Griffen, Benjamin 144
Griffith, D.W. 1
Grimmel, Edgar viii–x
Grunewald, Henry 65

Gruzenberg, Michael 41
Guaranty Trust Co. 43, 54, 62, 63
Guggenheim and Co. 144
Guyot, Henrí 80

H.Leben Co. 145
H.D.Merblum Co. 146
H.W.Cotton, Inc. 141
H.W.Johns-Manville Co. 145
Hale, Hartwell and Co. 144
Hamilton College 105
Hamilton Manufacturing Co. 144
Hammer, Armand 40
Hammer, Julius 39–40, 42, 61
Hammer Brothers White Lead Co. 144
Hammond Multiplex Typewriter Co. 144
Hanet Hat Co. 144
Hansen and Dieckmann Co. 144
Hanson, Ole 25–26, 29, 82
Hapgood, Norman 100
Harding, Warren G. 109, 121
Harding, Tilton and Co. 144
Hardwick, Thomas 26, 71–72
Harris, Charles E. 90, 96
Harris Construction Co. 144
Harris and Stern Co. 144
Harrisburg Pipe & Pipe Bending Co. 144
Hart-Parr Co. 144
Hartford City Paper Co. 144
Hartford *Courant* 10
Hartley Silk Co., Inc. 144
Harvard Univeristy 38, 100
Hawkeys Tire and Rubber Co. 144
Hayes, Carleton J.H. 69
Haynes Automobile Co. 144
Haywood, William 7, 27, 85–86
Hazard Manufacturing Co. 144
Heald Machine Co. 144
Heale, Michael 132
Hearst, William Randolph 50

Heath and Milligan Manufacturing Co. 144
Heckanam Mills Co. 144
Helenholz Mitten Co. 144
Heller, Abraham A. 38, 43–44, 45, 47, 49, 50, 51, 56–61, 63, 65, 67, 72–74
Henry, Alice 150
Henry and Wright Manufacturing Co. 144
Henry Disston and Sons, Inc. 142
Henry N.Day and Co., Inc. 142
Henry Street Settlement 69
Herman Behr and Co. 140
Hershey Chocolate Co. 144
Hewitt Rubber Co. 144
High School Teachers' Association of New York 119
Hill, Ebenezer J. 52
Hillquit, Morris 11, 14, 38, 63, 80, 112–118, 130, 150
Hires Turner Glass Co. 144
Hodgman Rubber Co. 144
Hodkins, Walter 144
Hoefer Manufacturing Co. 144
Holbrook Brothers 144
Holbrook, Cabot and Rollins Corp. 144
Hollingsworth and Co. 144
Holmes, John Haynes 11, 150
Holmes, Oliver Wendell, Jr. 3, 27
Homes Brothers Co. 144
Hood Rubber Co. 144
Hoofnagle, W.T. 144
Hooper, C.N. 144
Hoopes and Townsend Co. 144
Hoover, Herbert xiv
Hoover, J.Edgar 27, 33, 40
Hope Webbing Co. 144
Horse Twist Drill and Machine Co. 144
Horst, E.Clemens 144
Horton and Diago S. en C. 144
Hospital Supply Co. 144

218 INDEX

Housman, Laurence 100
Hornaday, William T. 22
Hourwich, Isaac 39, 48, 65, 67, 150
Howard L.Curry Co. 142
Howe, Frederic 13, 27, 150
Hughes, Charles Evans 16, 19
Hull House 11
Hunt-Rankin Leather Co. 144
Hunter, Charles N. 144
Hunter Manufacturing and Commission Co. 144
Hunter Pressed Steel Co. 144
Hunter Saw and Machine Co. 144
Hurd, Richard M. 21
Huson, M.B. 144
Hyams, Sarah 119
Hylan, John 10, 14, 16, 27

I.Gumport and Sons, Inc. 144
Illinois State Federation of Labor 151
Illinois Tool Works 144
Immigration Acts (1917 & 1918) 72
Imperial Glass Co. 144
Incandescent Supply Co. 144
Indian Refining Co. 144
Indiana Truck Corp. 144
Industrial Workers of the World 6, 7–8, 11, 17, 27, 29, 80, 84, 86, 99, 150
Industrial Works 144
Industrial World 7
Innis, Speidon and Co., Inc. 144
Institute of United States and Canadian Studies 58
Intercollegiate Socialist Society 38
International Association of Machinists 150
International Bell Telephone Co. 54
International Cotton Mills 144
International Harvester Co. 54, 57, 59, 60, 144
International High Speed Steel Co. 144

International Jewelry Workers' Union 150
International Ladies Garment Workers Union 95
International Machine Tools Co. 144
International Manufacturers Sales Co. of America, Inc. 144
International Oxygen Co. 38, 44, 145
International Packing Corp. 145
International Paper Co. 145
International Silver Co. 145
Interstate Pulp and Paper Co. 145
Intertype Corp. 145
Interwoven Stocking Co. 145
Irving National Bank 63
Isaac Prouty Shoe Co. 147
Isaac Winkler Brothers and Co. 148
Ivan Stacheeff and Co. 61

J.Wolkind and Co., Inc. 148
J. & G.Lippmann Co. 145
J.A.Kirsch and Co. 145
J.E.Bates and Co. 140
J.E.Gilson Co. 143
J.H. and C.K.Eagle Co. 142
J.H.Decker and Son Co. 142
J.I.Case Plow Works 141
J.I.Case Threshing Machine Co. 141
J.L. and D.S.Riker 147
J.L.Sommer Manufacturing Co. 147
J.R.Bockendorff and Co., Inc. 140
J.S.Johnston Co. 145
J.S.Woodhouse Co. 148
J.T.Polk Co. 147
J.W. and A.Howard Co. 144
J.W.Polly 147
J.W.Salvage 145
Jacob Dold Packing Co. 142
Jacobs, S. 145
James Cunningham, Son and Co. 141
James Magee Webbing Co. 146
James R Mulvihill Shoe Co. 146
Jason H.Millikin and Sons 146
Jeffrey Manufacturing Co. 145

INDEX 219

Jenks, Edmund B. 23
Jennings, Emerson P. 42
Jewish Daily Forward 95
John and James Dobson, Inc. 142
John B.Ellison and Sons 142
John Hassall, Inc. 144
John J.Lattermann Sheet Manufacturing Co. 145
John Lauson Manufacturing Co. 145
John Lawrie and Sons 145
John Morrell and Co. 146
John O.Heinze Co. 144
Johnson, Albert 71
Johnson, F.H. 104
Johnson, Hiram W. 48
Johnson Brokerage Co. 145
Joint Board of Sanitary Control in the Garment Industry 151
Joint Legislative Committee of the State of New York Investigating Seditious Activities (Lusk Committee) xi–xiii, 40, 51, 55, 60, 61–63, 81, 91–96, 98, 99–100, 105, 107–109, 115, 118–119, 125–126, 126–127, 131–136
    final report 103–104, 114, 126
    formation of 17–34
    investigation of Rand School 82–91, 129–130
    investigation of Soviet Bureau 64–70, 72–75
    public hearings on education 102–103
    recommendations 103–104
Jones, H.S. 145
Jones and Laughlin Steel Co. 145
Jordan, David Starr 77, 151
Joseph Branner and Co. 140
Joseph Dixon Crucible Co. 142
Jospeh Meisel Co. 146
Joseph N.Herman Shoe Co. 144
Joseph Wild and Co. 148
Joshua L.Bailey and Co. 139
Julian School Co. 145

K—G Welding and Cutting Co., Inc. 145
Kalamazoo Stove Co. 145
Kanseler, Ernest 56, 61
Kantor, Louis 58, 75
Kaplan, Charles 26
Katzenbach and Bullock Co. 145
Keller and Tamm Manufacturing Co. 145
Kelley, Florence 77, 151
Kellogg, Paul V. 69
Kelloggs and Miller 145
Kelly-Sprigfield Motor Truck Co. 145
Kemble, Calvin viii–x
Kempsmith Manufacturing Co. 145, 149
Kent, William 49
Kentucky Wagon Manufacturing Co. 145
Kerensky, Alexander 3
Keystone Type Foundry Supply House 145
Keystone Watch Case Co. 145
Kidder Peabody Bank 63
King, William H. 27, 71
Kimble Glass Co. 145
Knickerbocker Knitting Works 145
Knox Motors Associates 145
Knox Woolen Co. 145
Kohler Co. 145
Koken Barbers' Supply Co. 145
Kokomo Rubber Co. 145
Korein Brothers 145
Kousnetzoff, N.C. 145
Kresty Jail 37
Kuane, James B. 145
Kunhardt, George E. 145

L.Agoos and Co. 138
labor xiv, 4–6, 16–17, 22–23, 45
LaFollette, Robert 3, 106
La Golondrina Co. 145
Lakeside Forge Co. 145

220 INDEX

Lakshmi International Merchandising Co. 145
Lamborn and Co. 145
Lancaster Glass Co. 145
Landeck Lumber Co. 145
Landis, Kenesaw 27
Lansing, Robert 36, 54, 55, 68
Larkin, James 95
Larkin, William, Jr. 134
Lautz Brothers and Co. 145
Lavene, P.A. 151
Lawrence Brothers 145
Lawrence Neebe, Inc. 146
League of Free Nations Association 100
Leary, Daniel 145
Leather Workers' Union 81
Lee, Algernon viii, 22–23, 77, 79, 81, 84, 87, 92, 95, 96, 108, 109, 114–115, 125, 130, 135
Lee Tire and Rubber Co. 145
Lehigh Machine Co. 42, 62, 145, 149
Lenin, Vladimir viii, 3, 5, 34, 36, 42, 44, 71, 73
Lenin's League for the Liberation of the Working Class 37
Lettish Workmen's Association 30, 41
Levin, Murray 132
Levine and Greenbaum 145
Levinson and Shapiro 145
Levy, Benjamin 91
Levy Overall Manufacturing Co. 145
Lewis Manufacturing Co. 145
Lewis Walther Manufacturing Co. 148
The Liberator 26, 29
Liberty Commerce Corp. 145
Liberty Loan Act xiv, 6
Liberty Tire and Rubber Co. 145
Lidgerwood Manufacturing Co. 145
Liebold, E.G. 61
Limoneira Co. 145
Lindsay J. Riggins Co. 147

Linen Thread Co. 145
Linograph Co. 145
Linville, Henry R. 118–121, 125, 132
Lippman, Walter 98Lloyd, William B. 9
Little Giant Co. 145
Litzenberger, B. 145
Lockwood Co. 145
Locomobile Company of America 145
Lodge and Shipley Co. 145
Lomonossoff, George V. 39, 40, 41, 42
London, Jack 77, 151
London, Meyer 77, 151
Long Wear Rubber Co. 145
Lord, Chester S. 115
Louis Meyer and Son 146
Louis Schlessinger and Co. 147
Lovejoy, Owen 77, 151
Lowry, Robert 77, 151
Ludlow-Saylor Wire Co. 145
Ludlow Valve Manufacturing Co. 145
Ludlum Steel Co. 146
Luhring, Oscar R. 47
Luitwieler Pumping Engine Co. 146
Lundham and Moore 146
Lusk, Clayton R. xi, 16, 23, 24, 25, 29–32, 33, 65–67, 69, 70, 74, 75, 82–84, 86–92, 95, 96, 99–103, 105–107, 109–114, 122, 123, 125, 129–136
Lusk Committee see Joint Legislative Committee of the State of New York Investigating Seditious Activities
Luster, Martin 133
Luther Grinder Manufacturing Co. 146
Lux Manufacturing Co. 146
Lynchburg Foundry Co. 146

M.Mishel and Co. 146

M.C.D.Borden and Sons 59, 140
M.S.Brooks and Sons 140
MacArthur, Mary 151
MacCracken, Henry N. 124
MacFarland, Grenville 50
Machen, J.Gresham 123
Machold, Thomas 124
Mack, George viii–x
Maclead Co. 146
Macomber and Whyte Rope Co. 146
Magee Carpet Co. 146
Mailly, Bertha 77, 88–90, 109, 125
Majestic Machine & Tool Co., Inc. 146
Majestic Mills Paper Co., Inc. 146
Malkiel, Theresa 22
Mallinckrodt Chemical Works 146
Malone, Dudley Field 69, 70
Mangus Co. 146
Manning, Maxwell and Morre, Inc. 146
Manufacturers Clearing House Association 146
Manufacturers Iron and Steel Co. 146
Marathon Tire and Rubber Co. 56, 146
Marietta Paint and Color Co. 146
Marion Steam Shovel Co. 146
Maris Brothers 146
Market Warehouse Co. 146
Markt and Hammacher 146
Marlboro Cotton Mills 146
Marlowe and Iwaya Co. 146
Marshall, Louis 108
Marshall Field and Co. 57, 143
Martens, Ludwig C.A.K. 34–48, 50, 51, 55, 56, 58–63, 65–75, 83, 90, 99, 126–127, 135
Martin, Louis M. 23, 93
Martin-Senour Co. 146
Marx, Karl 80
Martin-Senour Co. 146
Maryland Co. 146
Massey, Harris Harvester Co. 146

Mast, Foos and Co. 146
Mathieson Alkali Works, Inc. 56, 146
Maurer, James H. 151
Maurice O'Meara Co. 146
Max Ames Machine Co. 139
Max Elkind and Simon Fagan Co. 142
Max Grinding Wheel Corp. 146
May Day occurrences 25–26, 30–31, 33, 81–82, 129
Mayer, Edward x
McAdoo, William 83–86, 90, 94, 96
McAuliffe, William 119
McAvoy, John E. 93–95, 97–98
McCall Co. 146
McCarthy, John xi
McCarthy, Joseph 133
McCue, Martin G. 106
McDonald, Duncan 151
McEligott, Peter P. 23
McKeesport Tin Plate Co. 146
McKesson and Robbins 146
McKibben, Driscoll & Dorsey, Inc. 146
McNaboe Committee xii
Mechanical Appliance Co. 146
Mendelssohn Brothers 146
Mercer Pottery Co. 146
Mercury Chemical Co. 146
Merrell, Edgar S.K. 117
Merrick, H.H. 57
The Messenger 16, 87, 151
Messinger Manufacturing Co. 146
Mesta Machine Co. 146
Meyer, Eugene, Jr. 49
Meyer Brothers Sales Co. 146
Mianus Motor Works 146
Michaels, Stern and Co. 146
Michelin Tire Co. 146
Michigan Copper and Brass Co. 146
Michigan Refining and Preserving Co. 146
Michigan Wire Cloth Co. 146
Miles, Basil 49

Mill, John Stuart 80
Miller, Nathan 109, 121, 122, 136
Miller Supply Co. 146
Millers Falls Co. 146
Mills, J.C. 10
Milwaukee Shaper Co. 146, 149
Miner-Edgar Co. 146
Minford, Lueder and Co. 146
Mishawaka Woolen Manufacturing Co. 146
Mississippi Valley Association 57
Missouri Meerschaum Co. 146
Mitchell, David 8
Mitchell, John Bruce 15
Mittelberger, Henry 146
Modern Machinery Exchange 146
Mohawk Valley Cap Factory 146
Moline Malleable Iron Co. 146
Moline Plow Co. 60, 146
Molle Typrewriter Co. 146
Monarch Knitting Co., Ltd. 146
Monitor Stove Co. 146
Monroe Calculating Machine Co. 146
Moore, Fred W. 14
Moore Motor Vehicle Co. 146
Morgan, J.P. 26, 54, 62, 63
Morris, Ira N. 41
Morris, Edward 59
Morris, Robert C. 16
Morris and Company 146, 149
Morris Glass Co. 146
Morris Meatpacking Co. 42, 57, 59, 62
Morse Twist Drill and Machine Co. 146
Moses, George H. 41, 71
Moskowitz Brothers 146
Mullan, John B. 23
Mullins, William 55
Mulvihill, James P. 49, 72
Murphy, William D. 16
Murray Robert 33, 132
Myers, Henry L. 47

N.B.Thayer and Co. 147
N.K.Fairbank Co. 142
N.O.Nelson Manufacturing Co. 146
N.R.Allen's Sons Co. 138
Nairn Linoleum Co. 146
Napier Saw Works, Inc. 146
The Nation 11, 13, 96, 124, 151
National Acme Co. 146
National Association for the Promotion of Labor Unionism Among Negroes 16
National Association of Attorneys General 99
National Association of Hosiery and Underwear Manufacturers 58
National Blank Book Co. 146
National Brass Co. 146
National Carbon Co. 146
National Child Labor Committee 77, 151
National City Bank 41, 43, 54, 63
National Civic Federation 107
National Civil Liberties Bureau 11, 86, 95
National Consumers' League 77, 151
National Lead Co. 146
National Leather Belting Co. 146
National Manufacturing Export Co. 146
National Marine Lamp 146
National Merchandise Co. 146
National Oats Co. 146
National Republican Club of New York City 123
National Sanitary Co. 146
National Security League 1
National Sewing Machine Co. 146
National Shoe Co. 146
National Standard Co. 146
National Storage Co. 62, 146, 149
National War Labor Board xiv, 4, 22
National Wire Wheel Works, Inc. 146
National Woolen Co. 146
Natwill Co. 146

Nearing, Scott 77, 87, 88, 91, 95, 151
Nelles, Walter 24
Nemours Trading Corp. 146
New, Harry S. 47
New Deal 136
New Departure Manufacturing Co. 146
New Hide Manufacturing Co. 146
New Jersey Car Spring & Rubber Co., Inc. 146
New Republic 100
New York *Call* 25, 30–31, 82, 95
New York City Board of Education x, xii, 14–15, 103, 118–119, 138
New York City Detectives Association 114, 136
New York City Police Department 10, 15, 16, 24, 26, 29, 81–83
New York City Women's Club 122
New York *Daily News* 43
New York *Evening World* 26
New York Export Purchasing Co. 146
New York Leather Belting Co. 146
New York Life 54
New York Merchandise Co. 146
New York Rubber Co. 146
New York School of Philanthropy 150
New York State Advisory Council on the Qualification of Teachers 118–121
New York State Department of Education 118, 138
New York State Legislature 86, 98, 99, 109, 114
   consideration of Lusk education bills 104–106, 111–112, 121–124, 131
   expulsion of socialist members 100–102, 105, 108, 109
   formation of Lusk Committee 17–20
   post-9/11 legislation 133–134
   repeal of Lusk Laws 121–125, 131–134, 136
New York *Times* 15, 16, 21, 36, 59, 88, 99–100, 104, 105, 106, 112, 114, 119, 123, 124, 126, 131, 136
New York *Tribune* 16, 26, 44, 58–59, 75, 104, 123
New York University 45, 77, 102, 136, 150
New York *World* 1, 42, 96
Newton, Charles D. 23, 65, 67, 70, 87, 91–98, 99, 100, 115, 130
Niagara Alkalai Co. 146
Nicholson File Co. 146
Nilson Tractor Co. 146
Ninety Six Cotton Mills 146
Noble, Harry 146
Noble Electric Steel Co. 146
Nordberg Manufacturing Co. 146
Nordyke and Marmon Co. 146
normalcy 109, 121
North American Copper Co. 146
Northwestern Knitting Co. 146
Novy Mir 37, 39
Nunn, Bush and Weldon Shoe Co. 146
Nuorteva, Santeri 38, 44, 50, 57, 60, 61, 62, 65–68, 72, 75
Nyanza Mills 146

O. & J.Machine Co. 146
Oak Knitting Co. 146
Oelbaum Brothers and Bauer 146
Official Manufacturing Co. 146
Offley, Frederick E. 64
Ohio Valley Pulley Works 146
Ohio Wire Goods Manufacturing Co. 146
Old Reliable Motor Truck Corp. 56, 146
Oliver Ames and Sons Corp. 139
Oliver Typewriter Co. 146
Onondaga Pottery Co. 146
Openheimer Casing Co. 146

Oppenheimer and Berliner 146
Oriental Trading Co. of America 146
Orr, Samuel 102
Ostemoor Co. 146
Otto Engine Manufacturing Co. 146
Overman Committee, see U.S. Senate Committee on the Judiciary
Overman, Lee S. 27
Owen, Chandler 77, 151

P.M.Edwards Co., Inc. 142
P.S. 68 (Manhattan) 119
Pacific and Eastern Steamship Co. 60, 146
Packard Motor Co. 60, 146
Page-Storm Drop Forge Co. 146
Palmer, A.Mitchell 27, 32–33, 64, 71, 99, 127–129, 132–133
Palmer raids xi, 99, 127–129, 132
Palmolive Co. 146
Parke-Davis Pharmaceutical Co. 54
Parker, Carleton 8
Parker, Kevin 134
Parsons Paper Co. 146
Pataki, George 133–134
Patent Button Co. 146
Paterson Parchment Paper Co. 146
Patterson, Gottfried & Hunter, Inc. 146
Patterson-Sargent Co. 146
Pellett, William W. 23
Peninsular Stove Co. 146
Pennsylvania State Federation of Labor 151
People's Freedom Union 24
Peoria Cordage Co. 146
Pepperell Manufacturing Co. 146
Perley, Morse and Co. 63
Perlman and Co. 146
Peru Plow and Wheel Co. 146
Petersburg Technological Institute 37
Petigor Bramson Co. 146
Pettit, Marshall and Co. 146
Philadelphia *Inquirer* 27

Phillips, William B. 68
Phillips Wire Co. 146
Physicians & Hospital Equipment Co. 146
Pierce, J.F. 56
Pinchot, Amos 69
Pittsburgh Plate Glass Co. 147
Pittsburgh *Post* 29
Pittsburgh Steel Co. 147
Plaintiff, Gaston 60
Plant Brothers and Co. 147
Plottel Raincoat Co. 147
Polack Tire and Rubber Co. 147
Poliakoff, R. 43
Polk, Frank 41, 49, 50, 60
Pomerene, Atlee 71
Porter, Stephen G. 47, 48, 49
Post, Louis 71–72, 129
Power Equipment Co., Inc. 147
Poyntz, Juliet Stuart 151
Prawl, Anning S. 103
Precious Castings Co. 147
Prest-O-Lite Co., Inc. 147
Preston B.Keith Shoe Co. 145
Preston Shirt Co. 147
Price, George M. 151
Princeton Theological Seminary 123
Princeton University 38, 77, 150
Proctor & Gamble Distribution Co. 60, 147
The Public 96
Public National Bank 63
Puritan Fibre Co. 147
Pussey and Jones Co. 147

R.Hoe and Co. 144
R.B.Davis Co. 142
R.C.Williams and Co. 148
R.D.Nuttall Co. 146
R.G.Dunn and Co. 142
R.H.Beaumont Co. 140
R&J.Dick Co. 142
R&L.Baker, New York Corp. 139
R.P.Hazzard Co. 144

R.Z.Graves, Inc. 143
Radek, Karl 43
Rahn-Lerman Co. 147
Rand, Carrie 76
Rand School News 114
Rand School of Social Science x, xii,
    22, 30, 75, 99–109, 112, 125, 131,
    135–136
  book store 80, 83, 84, 87, 88, 91
  challenges to the Lusk Laws 114–
    121
  course offerings 77–79, 152–158
  court proceedings against 92 98
  Department of Labor Research
    79–80
  financing of 76–77
  formation of 76–77
  instructors 77, 150–151
  investigated by Lusk Committee
    82–91, 126–130
  physical raids of 81–82
  Workers' Training Course 79
Randolph, A.Philip 77, 151
Rapp-Coudert Committee xii
Rawlins Clenzene Co. 147
Raynor, Gilbert 113
Recht, Charles 64, 67, 68, 72
Reed, John 9,88
Regents of the University of the State
    of New York 104, 105, 107, 111,
    115
Reisman, Rothman and Beiber 147
Reliable Glove Co. 147
Reliance Yarn Co. 147
*Report Upon the Illegal Practices of
    the United States Department of
    Justice* 129
Republic Rubber Co. 147
Republic Varnish Co. 147
Revolutionary Labor Party 10
Rhodes Engineering Co. 147
Ricardo, David 80
Rich, E.E. 147
Rickitts and Shaw 147

Riegelman, Harold 104, 113
Riggs, Edward 123
Ringling Brothers and Barnum &
    Bailey's Circus 1, 16
Rippen, H. 147
Robbins, Raymond x
Rockefeller, John D. 26, 54
Rockefeller Institute 151
Rockwell, Mrs. William H. 108
Roe, Gilbert x, 69, 119
Roosevelt, Franklin D. 136
Rosenfeld-Kessam Co. 147
Rosen-Reichardt Brokerage Co. 147
Rosensweig, Pincus and Hollender
    147
Rower and Bearak 147
Rubinow, I.M. 151
Rupp, W.S. 56
Russ, John D. 147
Russell and Co. 147
Russian-American Chamber of
    Commerce 57
Russian Federative Socialist Soviet
    Republic 25, 30, 38, 39, 49, 72–73
  attempts to gain recognition 34–
    37, 47–48, 57, 68, 73, 127
  business opportunities 48, 55, 58–
    62, 73–74, 135
  Comintern 72
  revolution x, 3, 5, 8
Russian Government Purchasing
    Commission 42
Russian People's House 30
Russian Provisional Government 34,
    39, 40, 42–45
Russian Star Co. 147
Ruthenberg, Charles 31
Ryan, George J. 119

S.Fels and Sons 143
S.Fole and Sons 143
S.Liebovitz and Son, Inc. 145
S.Robert Schwartz and Brother 147
S.L.Hoffman and Co. 144

S.R.Dresser Manufacturing Co. 142
S.R. and I.C.McConnell Co. 146
S.S.Stockholm 40, 72
S.S.White Central Manufacturing Co. 54
Sabin, Henry 62
Sackin, I.M. 85, 115
Sage, Henry M. 104
Salant and Salant Co. 147
Salt Lake City *Tribune* 31
Sanders Dental Supply Co. 147
Saxny, Theodore F. 16
Schiff, Gustave H. 147
Schlossberg, Joseph 151
Scientific Utilities Co. 147
Scotland Yard Directorate of Intelligence 58, 62, 74
Scott, Thomas 64
Sears, Roebuck and Co. 57, 60, 147
Seattle General Strike 26, 33, 82
Seattle *Post-Intelligencer* 29
Sedition Act 1, 3, 6
Selective Service Act xiv, 6
Seller Distributing Co. 147
September 11 terrorist attacks xii, 133–134
Sheffield Farms-Slawson Decker Co. 60, 147
Sherman Brothers Co. 147
Shiplacoff, A.I. 151
Siff Brothers Co. 147
Sigmund Eisner Co. 142
Signal Accessories Co. 147
Silver Manufacturing Co. 147
Singer Sewing Co. 54
Silver, Sheldon 133
Sixth National Foreign Trade Convention 57–58, 59, 61
Smith, Alfred E. 19, 99, 106–109, 113–114, 121–126, 130–131, 135–136
Smith, Benjamin 56
Smith, Thomas 52
Smith, William M. 147

Smith and Co. 56
Smoot, Ellis 27
Social Service Commission of the Episcopal Diocese of New York 121
Socialist Aldermen's Bureau of Research 38
Socialist Party of America 1, 6–9, 14, 20–22, 30, 38, 76–80, 95, 102, 105, 108, 109, 112, 115, 116, 118
Socialist Sunday Schools 30
Society of the Commonwealth Center 76, 85, 90
Soldiers, Sailors, and Marines Protective Association 81
Solomon, Charles 20–21, 102, 109
Southseas Import and Export Co. 147
Soviet Bureau 33, 73–75, 82, 83, 84, 86, 87, 90, 99, 126–127, 130, 135
  contact with American businesses 55–63
  contracts with American businesses 149
  federal investigations of 63, 71–72
  formation of 34–51
  investigated by the Lusk Committee 64–70
Spargo, John 80, 151
Sproul, Harold 27
Standard Shoe Co. 147
Stanford University 151
Stanton, Edwin 67
State Bank of New York 63
Steel Sole Shoe Co. 147, 149
Stein, Herman 147
Steiner, Charles 56
Sterling, Geneen Corp. 147
Stevenson, Archibald E. 11–14, 16, 16–17, 24–25, 65–70, 75, 82, 84–88, 95–96, 107–109, 113, 118–119, 125–126, 130, 132, 136
Stillman, James A. 54
Stodel, Samuel A. 57

Stone, N.L. 151
Stoufer, Benson 55
Straus, Nathan, Jr. 111–112
Strohmeyer and Arpe Co. 147
Submarine Salvage Co. 147
Sullivan, William L. 22
Sumner, Helen L. 151
Supreme Council of National Economy (U.S.S.R.) 61
Surpless, Dunn and Co. 147
Survey 69, 113
Sutliff, Samuel M. 147
Sweet, Thaddeus 19, 23, 100–102, 104
Swift, G.H. 59
Swift, O.H. 59
Swift and Co. 56, 59, 60, 147

Taber, Wheeler Co. 147
Talcum Puff Co. 147
Tamiment Institute 135
Tammany Hall 106
Taylor, Clapp and Beall 147
Taylor, Frank J. 54
Tchitcherin, Gregory 34, 68, 72
Teachers' Council 113, 123
Teachers' Union 108, 118–121, 124, 132
Thayer, Everet, Terhune 147
Theodore Booth Rubber Co. 140
Third International 5, 9
Thomas, M.Carey 122
Thomas, Norman 69, 95, 151
Thomas, Vincent 85, 98, 126
Thompson, George F. 105
Thompson, W.B. 147
Tildsley, John L. 103
Tindel-Morris Co. 147
Tobacco Products Export Corp. 147
Trachtenberg, Alexander L. 77
Trans-Oceanic Commercial Corp. 147
Trevor, John B. 62, 63
Trotsky, Leon viii, 3, 37
Trott, Ralph 81
Twin Rock Drill Co., Inc. 147

U.S. Army General Staff 11, 123
U.S. Bureau of Immigration 13, 24, 150
U.S. Chain & Forging Co. 147
U.S. Children's Bureau 151
U.S. Department of Agriculture 50
U.S. Department of the Army 58
U.S. Department of Justice 11, 24, 27, 63, 64, 71, 127–129
U.S. Department of Labor 39, 70–72, 129
U.S. Department of State 34, 36–38, 41, 47–50, 55–59, 68, 70, 74
U.S. Department of the Treasury 58, 63
U.S. Department of War 13
U.S. Directorate of Military Intelligence 62, 63, 82
U.S. Distributing Co. 147
U.S. House of Representatives Committee on Immigration 10
U.S. House of Representatives Committee on Foreign Affairs, 47
U.S. Manufacturers' Export Corp. 148
U.S. Packing Co. 57, 148
U.S. Provision Export Corp. 148
U.S. Rubber Co. 148
U.S. Senate Committee on Foreign Relations 41, 74
U.S. Senate Committee on Immigration 26
U.S. Senate Committee on the Judiciary 71
Overman Subcommittee 11–14, 15, 16, 19, 24, 82, 84, 136
U.S. Steel Corp. 59, 60, 135
U.S. Steel Export Co. 148
U.S. Steel Products Co. 148
Ullman, Sol 124
Union Card and Paper Co. 147

228   INDEX

Union League Club 16–17, 19, 68, 100, 107
Union of Russian Peasant Workers 15
Union Smelting and Refining Co. 147
United Clothing Co. 147
United Methodist Church (New York City) 16
United Neighborhood Settlement Houses 104, 113
United Presbyterian 27
United Press of America 54
United Skirt Co. 147
University of Chicago 39, 151
University of Geneva 39
University of Helsingfors 38
University of Pennsylvania 77, 151
Untermyer, Samuel 92–98

Vanderlip, Frank A. 69
Vassar College 124
Veblin, Thorstein 80
Victor, Achelis and Frederick 148
Villard, Oswald Garrison 11, 124, 151
Virginia Wagon Co. 148
Vladeck, B.Charney 95, 151
von Wiegand, Karl H. 42

W.Smith Grubber Co. 147
W.D.Allen's Co. 138
W.H.Duval and Co. 142
W.H.McElwain Co. 146
W.J.Wollman and Co. 148
W. & L.E.Gurley Machinery 144
W.M.Pringle and Co. 147
W.R.Ostrader and Co. 146
W.W.Cross and Co., Inc. 141
Wachernin, Boris A. 148
Wagner, Robert F. 70
Wald, Lillian D. 69
Waldman, Louis 86, 102, 109
Walker, James J. 111, 112, 121, 124
Wall Street Journal 10
Walsh, Thomas 33

Walter Baker and Co., Ltd. 139
Walter J.Townsend and Co. 147
Walters, J.Henry 17–19, 20, 24–25, 104, 105
Ward, Lester 77
War Industries Board xiv
War Trade Board 41, 50, 63
Warbasse, James P. 151
Ward, Lester F. 151
Washburn, Mabel 107
Washburn-Crusby Co. 148
Washington *Post* 31, 82
Weber Engine Co. 148
Weimer, Sylvester M. 56
Weinberg and Posner Engineering Co. 37, 62, 148, 149
Weinstein, Gregory 37, 39, 65, 67
Wellington, Sears and Co. 148
Wentworth Hat Manufacturing Co. 148
Werner and Pfleiderer Machine Tools Co. 54
Western Electric Co. 148
Western Electric Export Co. 148
Western Knitting Mills 148
Westinghouse Co. 60
Weyenberg Shoe Manufacturing Co. 148, 149
White Co. 148
Whittaker, Benjamin 148
Wiebusch and Hilger, Ltd. 148
William Barrell and Co. 140
William Demuth and Co. 142
William E.Hooper and Sons Co. 144
William F.Mosser Co. 146
William Galdonay Co. 143
William H.Anderson and Co. 139
Williams, Clark and Co. 148
Wilmarth and Morman Co. 148
Wilson, William B. 27, 72
Wilson, Woodrow xiv, 4, 17, 24, 36, 47, 106, 109
Wilson and Co. 148
Wolverine Tractor Co. 148

Women's Trade Union League 150
Wood, Henry A. Wise 107, 123
Wood, William W. 27
Wooley, Clarence 50
Workman and Silver Import Co. 148
World War One xi, xiv–5, 7, 16, 30, 54, 74, 76, 95–96, 132
World's Work 52
Wright's Underwear Co. 148
Wyandotte Worsted Co. 148

Yale University 77
Yeats, William Butler 77, 151
Young, Corley and Dolan 148
Young Men's Christian Association 105
Young Women's Christian Association 105, 108
Youroveta Home and Foreign Trade 148
Yu Ess Manufacturing Corp. 148

Zueblin, Charles 151